7.99

HERE TO ETERNITY

D0505165

WITHDRAWN

Here to Eternity
An Anthology of Poetry

elected by
ANDREW MOTION

faber and faber

First published in 2001
by Faber and Faber Limited
3 Queen Square London WC1N 3AU

This paperback edition first published in 2002

Photoset by Wilmaset Ltd, Birkenhead, Wirral
Printed in England

Introduction and this selection © Andrew Motion, 2001

The right of Andrew Motion to be identified as editor of
this work has been asserted in accordance with Section 77
of the Copyright, Designs and Patents Act 1988

A CIP record for this book
is available from the British Library

ISBN 0–571–21565–3

10 9 8 7 6 5 4 3 2 1

For Jesse Motion, Sidonie Motion and Luke Motion

Contents

HOME

TOWN

WORK

LOVE

TRAVEL

BELIEF

Introduction

'Who am I?' Every child wants to know that. 'Where am I?' They want to know that too – which is partly why children love to spin out their addresses. My own version went like this: name first, then house, village, nearest town, county, region, country, hemisphere . . . and so on and so on, rippling towards the great closing trinity: the world, the universe, space. Everyone I knew did the same thing, and so did lots of people I didn't know (including, it later turned out, Stephen Daedalus in James Joyce's *A Portrait of the Artist as a Young Man*).

I thought I was just having fun. With hindsight, I can see that I was taking part in a kind of folk ritual. It all came back to me when I started thinking about this anthology. I liked the combination of things – of self and other, of description and revelation, of gathering in and reaching out – and I decided to take it as my model. There wasn't much to be said for sticking to its geographical scheme. But maybe if I adapted the idea of expanding rings? That way, I thought readers would be able to get their bearings, while at the same time feeling they were part of an adventure – a journey across boundaries and into new worlds.

In the end, I decided to make ten rings, each of which would deal with different kinds of experience – some physical, others social, emotional, political and philosophical. I settled on: Self, Home, Town, Land, Work, Love, Travel, War, Belief, and Space. Although each ring is distinct, there are plenty of overlaps. (Questions about the 'self', for instance, dominate the first section but also surface in several others.) This is as it should be, in view of life's odd links and coincidences. It also makes the book a unity, rather than a collection of mini-anthologies.

Each section tells its own story. The Home section, for

example, begins by celebrating safety, then moves on to explore threats of suffocation and decay. In the same sort of way, the Love section moves through courtship to fulfilment, then on to disappointment, before finally coming to poems of old age and reconciliation. Once again, the purpose is to create a sense of stretching and expanding. To reinforce this still further, I decided that no poet should have more than one poem in each section, and that no poet should be represented by more than five poems over all.

Only a very few kinds of poem have not been able to find a place in the anthology – entire long ones (for obvious reasons of space), and certain sorts of performance poem (because they suffer on the page, however well they work out loud). Nowhere, however, have I wanted to include poems which 'make a point' in any narrow spirit. What is here is here because it proves the unique power of poetry to enrich our lives as it diversifies them.

ANDREW MOTION

Self

Prayer before Birth

I am not yet born; O hear me.
Let not the bloodsucking bat or the rat or the stoat or the
    club-footed ghoul come near me.

I am not yet born, console me.
I fear that the human race may with tall walls wall me,
    with strong drugs dope me, with wise lies lure me,
        on black racks rack me, in blood-baths roll me.

I am not yet born; provide me
With water to dandle me, grass to grow for me, trees to talk
    to me, sky to sing to me, birds and a white light
        in the back of my mind to guide me.

I am not yet born; forgive me
For the sins that in me the world shall commit, my words
    when they speak me, my thoughts when they think me,
        my treason engendered by traitors beyond me,
            my life when they murder by means of my
                hands, my death when they live me.

I am not yet born; rehearse me
In the parts I must play and the cues I must take when
    old men lecture me, bureaucrats hector me, mountains
        frown at me, lovers laugh at me, the white
            waves call me to folly and the desert calls
                me to doom and the beggar refuses
                    my gift and my children curse me.

I am not yet born; O hear me,
Let not the man who is beast or who thinks he is God
    come near me.

I am not yet born; O fill me
With strength against those who would freeze my
    humanity, would dragoon me into a lethal automaton,

3

would make me a cog in a machine, a thing with
one face, a thing, and against all those
who would dissipate my entirety, would
blow me like thistledown hither and
thither or hither and thither
like water held in the
hands would spill me.

Let them not make me a stone and let them not spill me.
Otherwise kill me.

WILLIAM SHAKESPEARE

from Henry IV, Part I, Act III, Scene I

Glendower   At my nativity
The front of heaven was full of fiery shapes,
Of burning cressets, and at my birth
The frame and huge foundation of the earth
Shak'd like a coward.

Hotspur   Why, so it would have done
At the same season, if your mother's cat
Had but kitten'd, though yourself had never been born.

Glendower   I say the earth did shake when I was born.

Hotspur   And I say the earth was not of my mind,
If you suppose as fearing you it shook.

Glendower   The heavens were all on fire, the earth did
tremble.

Hotspur   O, then the earth shook to see the heavens on fire,
And not in fear of your nativity.
Diseased nature oftentimes breaks forth
In strange eruptions; oft the teeming earth
Is with a kind of colic pinch'd and vex'd
By the imprisoning of unruly wind
Within her womb, which, for enlargement striving,
Shakes the old beldam earth and topples down
Steeples and moss-grown towers. At your birth

Our grandam earth, having this distemp'rature,
In passion shook.
endower   Cousin, of many men
    I do not bear these crossings. Give me leave
    To tell you once again that at my birth
    The front of heaven was full of fiery shapes,
    The goats ran from the mountains, and the herds
    Were strangly clamorous to the frighted fields.
    These signs have mark'd me extraordinary,
    And all the courses of my life do show
    I am not in the roll of common men.
    Where is he living, clipp'd in with the sea
    That chides the banks of England, Scotland, Wales,
    Which calls me pupil, or hath read to me?
    And bring him out that is but woman's son
    Can trace me in the tedious ways of art
    And hold me pace in deep experiments.
otspur   I think there's no man speaks better Welsh.

ILLIAM BLAKE

Infant Joy

(*Innocence*)

'I have no name:
I am but two days old.'
What shall I call thee?
'I happy am,
Joy is my name.'
Sweet joy befall thee!

Pretty Joy!
Sweet Joy, but two days old!
Sweet Joy I call thee.
Thou dost smile,
I sing the while,
Sweet joy befall thee!

5

Infancy

My father got on his horse and went to the field.
My mother stayed sitting and sewing.
My little brother slept.
A small boy alone under the mango trees,
I read the story of Robinson Crusoe,
the long story that never comes to an end.

At noon, white with light, a voice that had learned
lullabies long ago in the slave-quarters – and never
    forgot –
called us for coffee.
Coffee blacker than the old black woman
delicious coffee
good coffee.

My mother stayed sitting and sewing
watching me:
Shh – don't wake the boy.
She stopped the cradle when a mosquito had lit
and gave a sigh . . . how deep!
Away off there my father went riding
through the farm's endless wastes.

And I didn't know that my story
was prettier than that of Robinson Crusoe.

translated from the Portuguese by Elizabeth Bishop

North(west)ern

I was twelve as in the 12-bar blues, sick
for the Southeast, marooned on the North Wales coast,
a crotchet, my tongue craving the music
of Welsh, Scouse or Manc; entering the outpost

of Colwyn Bay Pier, midsummer, noon,
niteclub for those of us with the deep ache
of adolescence, when I heard that tune.
Named it in one. Soul. My heart was break

dancing on the road to Wigan Casino,
Northern Soul mecca, where transatlantic bass
beat blacker than blue in glittering mono

then back via Southport, Rhyl to the time, place
I bit the Big Apple. Black. Impatient. Young.
A string of pips exploding on my tongue.

MURIEL RUKEYSER

Then I Saw What the Calling Was

All the voices of the wood called 'Muriel!'
but it was soon solved;   it was nothing, it was not for me.
The words were a little like Mortal and More and Endure
and a word like Real, a sound like Health or Hell.
Then I saw what the calling was : it was the road I
    traveled, the clear
time and these colors of orchards, gold behind gold and the full
shadow behind each tree and behind each slope.   Not to me
the calling, but to anyone, and at last I saw : where
the road lay through sunlight and many voices and the marvel
orchards, not for me, not for me, not for me.
I came into my clear being; uncalled, alive, and sure.
Nothing was speaking to me, but I offered and all was well.

And then I arrived at the powerful green hill.

Waiting To Go On

I turned the pages slowly, listening for the car,
till my father was young again, a soldier,
or throwing back his head
on slicked back Derby Days before the war.
I stared at all that fame and handsomeness
and thought they were the same.
Good looks were everything where I came from.
They made you laugh. They made you have a tan.
They made you speak with conviction.
'Such a nice young man!' my mother used to say.
'So good looking!' I didn't agree with her,
but I searched my face for signs of excellence,
turning up my collar in the long mirror on the stairs
and flourishing a dress sword at myself:
'Hugh Williams, even more handsome in Regency!'
The sound of wheels on the drive
meant I had about one minute
to put everything back where I'd found it
and come downstairs as myself.

BERTOLT BRECHT

Of Poor B.B.

I

I, Bertolt Brecht, came out of the black forests.
My mother moved me into the cities as I lay
Inside her body. And the coldness of the forests
Will be inside me till my dying day.

II

In the asphalt city I'm at home. From the very start
Provided with every last sacrament:
With newspapers. And tobacco. And brandy.
To the end mistrustful, lazy and content.

III

I'm polite and friendly to people. I put on
A hard hat because that's what they do.
I say: they are animals with a quite peculiar smell
And I say: does it matter? I am too.

IV

Before noon on my empty rocking chairs
I'll sit a woman or two, and with an untroubled eye
Look at them steadily and say to them:
Here you have someone on whom you can't rely.

V

Towards evening it's men that I gather round me
And then we address one another as 'gentlemen'.
They're resting their feet on my table tops
And say: things will get better for us. And I don't ask when.

VI

In the grey light before morning the pine trees piss
And their vermin, the birds, raise their twitter and cheep.
At that hour in the city I drain my glass, then throw
The cigar butt away and worriedly go to sleep.

VII

We have sat, an easy generation
In houses held to be indestructible
(Thus we built those tall boxes on the island of Manhattan
And those thin aerials that amuse the Atlantic swell).

VIII

Of those cities will remain what passed through them, the
  wind!
The house makes glad the eater: he clears it out.
We know that we're only tenants, provisional ones
And after us there will come: nothing worth talking
  about.

In the earthquakes to come, I very much hope
I shall keep my cigar alight, embittered or no
I, Bertolt Brecht, carried off to the asphalt cities
From the black forests inside my mother long ago.

translated from the German by Michael Hamburger

CHRISTOPHER REID

One for the Footnotes

Born in Hong Kong in 1949,
Christopher Reid was soon observed to shine
in the fields of nappy-wetting and ululation.
The leading baby of his generation,
he founded what became known as the Infantile School,
whose principal tenet, scorn for every rule,
inspired a brief literary Pentecost.
Sadly, his early efforts are now lost,
as is his output from the next two years
of experimentation with bawling, tantrums, tears
and other non-verbal forms of expression. The lure
of words, however, distracted him from this pure
line of enquiry, and one can only regret
his falling under the spell of the alphabet,
which led to such work of his as survives: obscene
botches, travesties of what might have been.

WILLIAM WORDSWORTH

from The Prelude, Book I (1805)

O there is blessing in this gentle breeze
That blows from the green fields and from the clouds
And from the sky: it beats against my cheek,
And seems half-conscious of the joy it gives.
O welcome messenger! O welcome friend!
A captive greets thee, coming from a house

Of bondage, from yon city's walls set free,
A prison where he hath been long immured.
Now I am free, enfranchised and at large,
May fix my habitation where I will.
What dwelling shall receive me? in what vale
Shall be my harbour? underneath what grove
Shall I take up my home? and what sweet stream
Shall with its murmurs lull me to my rest?
The earth is all before me. With a heart
Joyous, nor scared at its own liberty,
I look about; and should the guide I choose
Be nothing better than a wandering cloud,
I cannot miss my way. I breathe again!
Trances of thought and mountings of the mind
Come fast upon me: it is shaken off,
As by miraculous gift 'tis shaken off,
That burden of my own unnatural self,
The heavy weight of many a weary day
Not mine, and such as were not made for me.
Long months of peace (if such bold word accord
With any promises of human life),
Long months of ease and undisturbed delight
Are mine in prospect; whither shall I turn,
By road or pathway, or through open field,
Or shall a twig or any floating thing
Upon the river point me out my course?

   Enough that I am free; for months to come
May dedicate myself to chosen tasks;
May quit the tiresome sea and dwell on shore,
If not a settler on the soil, at least
To drink wild water, and to pluck green herbs,
And gather fruits fresh from their native tree.
Nay more, if I may trust myself, this hour
Hath brought a gift that consecrates my joy;
For I, methought, while the sweet breath of heaven
Was blowing on my body, felt within

A corresponding mild creative breeze,
A vital breeze which travelled gently on
O'er things which it had made, and is become
A tempest, a redundant energy,
Vexing its own creation. 'Tis a power
That does not come unrecognized, a storm,
Which, breaking up a long-continued frost,
Brings with it vernal promises, the hope
Of active days, of dignity and thought,
Of prowess in an honourable field,
Pure passions, virtue, knowledge, and delight,
The holy life of music and of verse.

JO SHAPCOTT

Phrase Book

I'm standing here inside my skin,
which will do for a Human Remains Pouch
for the moment. Look down there (up here).
Quickly. Slowly. This is my own front room

where I'm lost in the action, live from a war,
on screen. I am an Englishwoman, I don't understand you
What's the matter? You are right. You are wrong.
Things are going well (badly). Am I disturbing you?

TV is showing bliss as taught to pilots:
Blend, Low silhouette, Irregular shape, Small,
Secluded. (Please write it down. Please speak slowly.)
Bliss is how it was in this very room

when I raised my body to his mouth,
when he even balanced me in the air,
or at least I thought so and yes the pilots say
yes they have caught it through the Side-Looking

Airborne Radar, and through the J-Stars.
I am expecting a gentleman (a young gentleman,

two gentlemen, some gentlemen). Please send him
(them) up at once. This is really beautiful.

Yes they have seen us, the pilots, in the Kill Box
on their screens, and played the routine for
getting us Stealthed, that is, Cleansed, to you and me,
Taken Out. They know how to move into a single room

like that, to send in with Pinpoint Accuracy, a hundred
    Harms.
I have two cases and a cardboard box. There is another
bag there. I cannot open my case – look out,
the lock is broken. Have I done enough?

Bliss, the pilots say, is for evasion
and escape. What's love in all this debris?
Just one person pounding another into dust,
into dust. I do not know the word for it yet.

Where is the British Consulate? Please explain.
What does it mean? What must I do? Where
can I find? What have I done? I have done
nothing. Let me pass please. I am an Englishwoman.

BEN JONSON

Ode to Himself

Where dost thou careless lie,
    Buried in ease and sloth?
Knowledge that sleeps doth die;
And this security,
    It is the common moth,
That eats on wits, and arts, and oft destroys them both.

Are all the Aonian springs
    Dried up? lies Thespia waste?
Doth Clarius' harp want strings,
That not a nymph now sings?

Or droop they as disgraced,
To see their seats and bowers by chattering pies defaced?

If hence thy silence be,
    As 'tis too just a cause,
Let this thought quicken thee:
Minds that are great and free
    Should not on fortune pause,
'Tis crown enough to virtue still, her own applause.

What though the greedy fry
    Be taken with false baits
Of worded balladry
And think it poesy?
    They die with their conceits,
And only piteous scorn upon their folly waits.

Then take in hand thy lyre,
    Strike in thy proper strain;
With Japhet's line, aspire
Sol's chariot for new fire,
    To give the world again:
Who aided him will thee, the issue of Jove's brain.

And since our dainty age
    Cannot endure reproof,
Make not thyself a page
To that strumpet the Stage,
    But sing high and aloof,
Safe from the wolf's black jaw, and the dull ass's hoof.

WALTER DE LA MARE

Napoleon

'What is the world, O soldiers?
    It is I:
I, this incessant snow,
    This northern sky;

> Soldiers, this solitude
>   Through which we go
>   Is I.'

ANS MAGNUS ENZENSBERGER

historical process

the bay is frozen up
the trawlers are ice-bound.
so what.
you are free.
you can lie down.
you can get up again.
it doesn't matter about your name.
you can disappear.
and return.
that's possible.
a fighter howls across the island.
even when a man dies
letters still come for him.
there isn't much to be lost or thwarted.
you can sleep
that's possible.
the ice-breaker will be here by the morning.
then the trawlers will leave.
the channel they follow is narrow.
it freezes up again by the morning.
so what.
it doesn't matter about your name.

translated from the German by Michael Hamburger

The Form

I remember the form of my guilt
the blackness of the dotted line
on the white paper. Name, okay.
Nationality? Pen poised to begin
Hand encircling paper, eyes wandering

Friend looks up from frowning at the form
of her search. Well, Name filled in
Nationality Trinidadian. Hers, a simple
assertion. I hold my breath, hoping
not to be reminded that I, complete with

Irish name, like hers, am not yet Grenadian
but still British. Her own pen poised
she struggles with another mammoth problem.
Race? She looks at my hand, over and around
at the pencilled African. Giggles, grins,

says with a kind of questioning awe, I put
Black. We shrug, look at each other, caught
in this dilemma of expressing some belonging.
Aspiring social-scientists, we look at the next
dotted line on the tutor's form. Social strata?

You put Lower class? We giggle. We grin.
Sitting on the balcony, encircled by the walls
of the region's university, two of the privileged
few, unsure of much, sure of search. Feeling
the birth pains of moulding a future belonging.

I remember the form of the past
foretelling the shape of things to come.

I Am Man-made

I am man-made.
My father made me,
softened and pulled me,
thumbed me full of crescents.

I am man-made.
My teachers made me,
threw and turned me,
textured me with scratches.

I am man-made.
The Devil made me,
moistened and coiled me,
fired me, glazed me
blue-black and green.

Now they are gone,
by whom shall I be seen?

DENISE RILEY

No

All the towels are red
the navy towel and the black
blood-soaked
and the white dress has slipped
to the bloodied floor.

This one you lose you could not love.
You were deceived, your flat blood knew
to open its bright and factual eye.
This that you leak you never grew.

The officer is at the scarlet door.
Here is his evidence. Some body lied.
That body's mine but I am it.
And I am it and I have lied.

ANNE FINCH, COUNTESS OF WINCHILSEA

On Myself

Good heaven, I thank thee, since it was designed
I should be framed but of the weaker kind,
That yet my soul is rescued from the love
Of all those trifles which their passions move.
Pleasures, and praise, and plenty, have with me
But their just value. If allowed they be,
Freely and thankfully as much I taste
As will not reason or religion waste.
If they're denied, I on myself can live,
And slight those aids unequal chance does give:
When in the sun, my wings can be displayed;
And in retirement I can bless the shade.

JUAN RAMÓN JIMÉNEZ

I Am Not I

I am not I.
        I am this one
Walking beside me whom I do not see,
Whom at times I manage to visit,
And at other times I forget.
The one who remains silent when I talk,
The one who forgives, sweet, when I hate,
The one who takes a walk when I am indoors,
The one who will remain standing when I die.

translated from the Spanish by Robert Bly

from Song of Myself

Who goes there! hankering, gross, mystical, nude?
How is it I extract strength from the beef I eat?

What is a man anyhow? What am I? and what are you?
All I mark as my own you shall offset it with your own,
Else it were time lost listening to me.

I do not snivel that snivel the world over,
That months are vacuums and the ground but wallow and
    filth,
That life is a suck and a sell, and nothing remains at the
    end but threadbare crape and tears.

Whimpering and truckling fold with powders for invalids
    ... conformity goes to the fourth-removed,
I cock my hat as I please indoors or out.

Shall I pray? Shall I venerate and be ceremonious?
I have pried through the strata and analyzed to a hair,
And counselled with doctors and calculated close and
    found no sweeter fat than sticks to my own bones.

In all people I see myself, none more and not one a
    barleycorn less,
And the good or bad I say of myself I say of them.

And I know I am solid and sound,
To me the converging objects of the universe perpetually
    flow,
All are written to me, and I must get what the writing
    means.

And I know I am deathless,
I know this orbit of mine cannot be swept by a carpenter's
    compass,
I know I shall not pass like a child's carlacue cut with a
    burnt stick at night.

I know I am august,
I do not trouble my spirit to vindicate itself or be
    understood,
I see that the elementary laws never apologize,
I reckon I behave no prouder than the level I plant my
    house by after all.

I exist as I am, that is enough,
If no other in the world be aware I sit content,
And if each and all be aware I sit content.

One world is aware, and by far the largest to me, and that is
    myself,
And whether I come to my own today or in ten thousand
    or ten million years,
I can cheerfully take it now, or with equal cheerfulness I
    can wait.

My foothold is tenon'd and mortis'd in granite,
I laugh at what you call dissolution,
And I know the amplitude of time.

FERNANDO PESSOA

I See Boats Moving

    I see boats moving on the sea.
    Their sails, like wings of what I see,
Bring me a vague inner desire to be
Who I was without knowing what it was.
So all recalls my home self and, because
It recalls that, what I am aches in me.

    translated from the Portuguese by Jonathan Griffin

Bleep

I am the unreal voice speaking.
I will not be told I am real.
I care for the inauthentic, the disingenuous.
Deceit makes me shiver with glee.
I fall for false tears, false modesty,
false eyelashes, false teeth.
I enjoy seeing them sitting in a mouth
watching a soap on TV, pearly
as Hollywood can be, big white falsies.
Square, unreadable and slightly odd.
Wigs with synthetic hair, I hold dear.
Plastic hips. Silicone chips.
The wee tuck here and there.
I adore the plucked eyebrow,
shocked and bare, feigning surprise
at you there. I dote on everything false
from the moment I wake up from my faked sleep
for the rest of the fabricated day.
Bleached skin, shrunk arse,
wee tits, tiny hips, nae chin.
There's nothing like women faking it.
See my nose, it used to be a tomato.

JOHN CLARE

'I Am'

I

I am – yet what I am, none cares or knows;
    My friends forsake me like a memory lost: –
I am the self-consumer of my woes; –
    They rise and vanish in oblivion's host,
Like shadows in love's frenzied stifled throes: –
And yet I am, and live – like vapours tost

2

Into the nothingness of scorn and noise, –
　　Into the living sea of waking dreams,
Where there is neither sense of life or joys,
　　But the vast shipwreck of my lifes esteems;
Even the dearest, that I love the best
Are strange – nay, rather stranger than the rest.

3

I long for scenes, where man hath never trod
　　A place where woman never smiled or wept
There to abide with my Creator, God;
　　And sleep as I in childhood, sweetly slept,
Untroubling, and untroubled where I lie,
The grass below – above the vaulted sky.

JAMES FENTON

The Ideal

This is where I came from.
I passed this way.
This should not be shameful
Or hard to say.

A self is a self.
It is not a screen.
A person should respect
What he has been.

This is my past
Which I shall not discard.
This is the ideal.
This is hard.

I and I

Been so long since a strange woman has slept in my bed.
Look how sweet she sleeps, how free must be her dreams.
In another lifetime she must have owned the world, or
    been faithfully wed
To some righteous king who wrote psalms beside moonlit
    streams.

I and I
In creation where one's nature neither honors nor
    forgives.
I and I
One says to the other, no man sees my face and lives.

Think I'll go out and go for a walk,
Not much happenin' here, nothin' ever does.
Besides, if she wakes up now, she'll just want me to talk
I got nothin' to say, 'specially about whatever was.

I and I
In creation where one's nature neither honors nor
    forgives.
I and I
One says to the other, no man sees my face and lives.

Took an untrodden path once, where the swift don't win
    the race,
It goes to the worthy, who can divide the word of truth.
Took a stranger to teach me, to look into justice's beautiful
    face
And to see an eye for an eye and a tooth for a tooth.

I and I
In creation where one's nature neither honors nor
    forgives.
I and I
One says to the other, no man sees my face and lives.

Outside of two men on a train platform there's nobody in
    sight,
They're waiting for spring to come, smoking down the
    track.
The world could come to an end tonight, but that's all
    right.
She should still be there sleepin' when I get back.

I and I
In creation where one's nature neither honors nor
    forgives.
I and I
One says to the other, no man sees my face and lives.

Noontime, and I'm still pushin' myself along the road, the
    darkest part,
Into the narrow lanes, I can't stumble or stay put.
Someone else is speakin' with my mouth, but I'm listening
    only to my heart.
I've made shoes for everyone, even you, while I still go
    barefoot.

I and I
In creation where one's nature neither honors nor
    forgives.
I and I
One says to the other, no man sees my face and lives.

PATRICIA BEER

Autobiography

I sailed through many waters,
Cold following warm because I moved
Though Arctic and equator were steady.

Harbours sank as I discarded them,
Landmarks melted into the sky
When I needed them no longer.

I left behind all weathers.
I passed dolphins, flying-fish and seagulls
That are ships in their own stories.

ROBERT LOWELL

Words for Muffin, a Guinea-Pig

'Of late they leave the light on in my entry
so I won't scare, though I never scare in the dark;
I bless this arrow that flies from wall to window . . .
five years and a nightlight given me to breathe –
Heidegger said spare time is ecstasy. . .
I am not scared, although my life was short;
my sickly breathing sounded like dry leather.
Mrs. Muffin! It clicks. I had my day.
You'll paint me like Cromwell with all my warts:
small mop with a tumor and eyes too popped for thought.
I was a rhinoceros when jumped by my sons.
I ate and bred, and then I only ate,
my life zenithed in the Lyndon Johnson 'sixties . . .
this short pound God threw on the scales, found wanting.'

WELDON KEES

Robinson

The dog stops barking after Robinson has gone.
His act is over. The world is a gray world,
Not without violence, and he kicks under the grand piano,
The nightmare chase well under way.

The mirror from Mexico, stuck to the wall,
Reflects nothing at all. The glass is black.
Robinson alone provides the image Robinsonian.

Which is all of the room – walls, curtains,
Shelves, bed, the tinted photograph of Robinson's first
    wife,

Rugs, vases, panatellas in a humidor.
They would fill the room if Robinson came in.

The pages in the books are blank,
The books that Robinson has read. That is his favorite
    chair,
Or where the chair would be if Robinson were here.

All day the phone rings. It could be Robinson
Calling. It never rings when he is here.

Outside, white buildings yellow in the sun.
Outside, the birds circle continuously
Where trees are actual and take no holiday.

YEHUDA AMICHAI

I Lost My Identity Card

I lost my identity card.
I have to write out my curriculum vitae
all over again for many offices, one copy to God
and one to the devil. I remember
the photo taken thirty-three years ago
at a wind-scorched junction in the Negev.

My eyes were prophets then, but my body had no idea
what was happening to it or where it belonged.

You often say, This is the place,
This happened right here, but it's not the place,
you just think so and live in error,
an error whose eternity is greater
than the eternity of truth.

As the years go by, my life keeps filling up with names
like abandoned cemeteries
or like an absurd history class
or a telephone book in a foreign city.

And death is when someone keeps calling you
and calling you
and you no longer turn around to see
who it is.

translated from the Hebrew by the author

SYLVIA PLATH

Ariel

Stasis in darkness.
Then the substanceless blue
Pour of tor and distances.

God's lioness,
How one we grow,
Pivot of heels and knees! – The furrow

Splits and passes, sister to
The brown arc
Of the neck I cannot catch,

Nigger-eye
Berries cast dark
Hooks—

Black sweet blood mouthfuls,
Shadows.
Something else

Hauls me through air—
Thighs, hair;
Flakes from my heels.

White
Godiva, I unpeel—
Dead hands, dead stringencies.

And now I
Foam to wheat, a glitter of seas.
The child's cry

Melts in the wall.
And I
Am the arrow,

The dew that flies
Suicidal, at one with the drive
Into the red

Eye, the cauldron of morning.

THOMAS HARDY

The Self-Unseeing

Here is the ancient floor,
Footworn and hollowed and thin,
Here was the former door
Where the dead feet walked in.

She sat here in her chair,
Smiling into the fire;
He who played stood there,
Bowing it higher and higher.

Childlike, I danced in a dream;
Blessings emblazoned that day;
Everything glowed with a gleam;
Yet we were looking away!

Home

WARD THOMAS

The New House

Now first, as I shut the door,
    I was alone
In the new house; and the wind
    Began to moan.

Old at once was the house,
    And I was old;
My ears were teased with the dread
    Of what was foretold,

Nights of storm, days of mist, without end;
    Sad days when the sun
Shone in vain: old griefs and griefs
    Not yet begun.

All was foretold me; naught
    Could I foresee;
But I learned how the wind would sound
    After these things should be.

ATTHEW SWEENEY

The House

The house had a dozen bedrooms,
each of them cold, and the wind
battered the windows and blew down
power-lines to leave the house dark.
Rats lived in the foundations,
sending scouts under the stairs
for a year or two, and once
a friendly ghost was glimpsed
at the foot of a bed. Downhill
half a mile was the Atlantic,
with its ration of the drowned –
one of whom visited the house,

carried there on a door.
It hosted dry corpses, too,
with nostrils huge to a child,
but never a murder –
except the lambs bled dry
in the yard outside. Sunlight
never took over the interior,
and after dark the cockroaches
came from under a cupboard
to be eaten by the dog.
Crows were always sitting
on the wires, planning nests
in the chimneys, and a shotgun
sometimes blew a few away.
Neighbours never entered
as often as in other houses,
but it did have a piano upstairs.
And I did grow up there.

BERTOLT BRECHT

A New House

Back in my country after fifteen years of exile
I have moved into a fine house.
Here I have hung
My Nō masks and picture scroll representing the Doubt.
Every day, as I drive through the ruins, I am reminded
Of the privileges to which I owe this house. I hope
It will not make me patient with the holes
In which so many thousands huddle. Even now
On top of the cupboard containing my manuscripts
My suitcase lies.

translated from the German by Michael Hamburger

Home

Has canary-yellow curtains, so expensive
At certain times they become unaffordable,
Cost too much patience. A cartoon voice:

'I'm leaving, Elmer.' That's home also, sometimes;
The Eden a person can't go back to. Still . . .
If you don't leave it, it's only a world;

If you never return, just a place like any other.
Home isn't the *Blue Guide*, the A–Z
I only need for those ten thousand streets

Not one of which has Alice Wales in it.
At home you bolt on the new pine headboard,
Crying. You build from your tears

A hydroponicum; bitter-sweet nutrition
Becomes the address we ripen in like fruit
No one thought would grow here. Home

Is where we hang up our clothes and surnames
Without thought. Home is the instruction: dream home.
An architecture of faint clicks, and smells that haven't yet
    quite.

We grow old in it. Like children, it keeps us young,
Every evening being twenty-one again
With the key in the door, coming back from the library

You're shouting upstairs to me, telling me what you are
In the simplest of words, that I want you to go on repeating
Like a call-sign. You are shouting, 'I'm home.'

The Candle Indoors

Some candle clear burns somewhere I come by.
I muse at how its being puts blissful back
With yellowy moisture mild night's blear-all black,
Or to-fro tender trambeams truckle at the eye.
By that window what task what fingers ply,
I plod wondering, a-wanting, just for lack
Of answer the eagerer a-wanting Jessy or Jack
There God to aggrandize, God to glorify. –

Come you indoors, come home; your fading fire
Mend first and vital candle in close heart's vault:
You there are master, do your own desire;
What hinders? Are you beam-blind, yet to a fault
In a neighbour deft-handed? are you that liar
And, cast by conscience out, spendsavour salt?

IAN HAMILTON FINLAY

Orkney Interior

Doing what the moon says, he shifts his chair
Closer to the stove and stokes it up
With the very best fuel, a mixture of dried fish
And tobacco he keeps in a bucket with crabs

Too small to eat. One raises its pincer
As if to seize hold of the crescent moon
On the calendar which is almost like a zodiac
With inexplicable and pallid blanks. Meanwhile

A lobster is crawling towards the clever
Bait that is set inside the clock
On the shelf by the wireless – an inherited dried fish
Soaked in whisky and carefully trimmed

With potato flowers from the Golden Wonders
The old man grows inside his ears.
Click! goes the clock-lid, and the unfortunate lobster
Finds itself a prisoner inside the clock,

An adapted cuckoo-clock. It shows no hours, only
Tides and moons and is fitted out
With two little saucers, one of salt and one of water
For the lobster to live on while, each quarter-tide,

It must stick its head through the tiny trapdoor
Meant for the cuckoo. It will be trained to read
The broken barometer and wave its whiskers
To Scottish Dance Music, till it grows too old.

Then the old man will have to catch himself another
    lobster.
Meanwhile he is happy and takes the clock
Down to the sea. He stands and oils it
In a little rock pool that reflects the moon.

SEAMUS HEANEY

from Glanmore Revisited

THE SKYLIGHT

You were the one for skylights. I opposed
Cutting into the seasoned tongue-and-groove
Of pitch pine. I liked it low and closed,
Its claustrophobic, nest-up-in-the-roof
Effect. I liked the snuff-dry feeling,
The perfect, trunk-lid fit of the old ceiling.
Under there, it was all hutch and hatch.
The blue slates kept the heat like midnight thatch.

But when the slates came off, extravagant
Sky entered and held surprise wide open.
For days I felt like an inhabitant
Of that house where the man sick of the palsy

Was lowered through the roof, had his sins forgiven
Was healed, took up his bed and walked away.

W. B. YEATS

from Meditations in Time of Civil War

I   ANCESTRAL HOUSES

Surely among a rich man's flowering lawns,
Amid the rustle of his planted hills,
Life overflows without ambitious pains;
And rains down life until the basin spills,
And mounts more dizzy high the more it rains
As though to choose whatever shape it wills
And never stoop to a mechanical
Or servile shape, at others' beck and call.

Mere dreams, mere dreams! Yet Homer had not sung
Had he not found it certain beyond dreams
That out of life's own self-delight had sprung
The abounding glittering jet; though now it seems
As if some marvellous empty sea-shell flung
Out of the obscure dark of the rich streams,
And not a fountain, were the symbol which
Shadows the inherited glory of the rich.

Some violent bitter man, some powerful man
Called architect and artist in, that they,
Bitter and violent men, might rear in stone
The sweetness that all longed for night and day,
The gentleness none there had ever known;
But when the master's buried mice can play,
And maybe the great-grandson of that house,
For all its bronze and marble, 's but a mouse.

O what if gardens where the peacock strays
With delicate feet upon old terraces,
Or else all Juno from an urn displays
Before the indifferent garden deities;

O what if levelled lawns and gravelled ways
Where slippered Contemplation finds his ease
And Childhood a delight for every sense,
But take our greatness with our violence?

What if the glory of escutcheoned doors,
And buildings that a haughtier age designed,
The pacing to and fro on polished floors
Amid great chambers and long galleries, lined
With famous portraits of our ancestors;
What if those things the greatest of mankind
Consider most to magnify, or to bless,
But take our greatness with our bitterness?

DONALD DAVIE

Heigh-ho on a Winter Afternoon

There is a heigh-ho in these glowing coals
By which I sit wrapped in my overcoat
As if for a portrait by Whistler. And there is
A heigh-ho in the bird that noiselessly
Flew just now past my window, to alight
On winter's moulding, snow; and an alas,
A heigh-ho and a desultory chip,
Chip, chip on stone from somewhere down below.

Yes I have 'mellowed', as you said I would,
And that's a heigh-ho too for any man;
Heigh-ho that means we fall short of alas
Which sprigs the grave of higher hopes than ours.
Yet heigh-ho too has its own luxuries,
And salts with courage to be jocular
Disreputable sweets of wistfulness,
By deprecation made presentable.

What should we do to rate the long alas
But skeeter down a steeper gradient?
And then some falls are still more fortunate,

The meteors spent, the tragic heroes stunned
Who go out like a light. But here the chip,
Chip, chip will flake the stone by slow degrees,
For hour on hour the fire will gutter down,
The bird will call at longer intervals.

ROBERT LOUIS STEVENSON

'My house, I say . . .'

My house, I say. But hark to the sunny doves
That make my roof the arena of their loves,
That gyre about the gable all day long
And fill the chimneys with their murmurous song:
Our house, they say; and *mine*, the cat declares
And spreads his golden fleece upon the chairs;
And *mine* the dog, and rises stiff with wrath
If any alien foot profane the path.
So too the buck that trimmed my terraces,
Our whilome gardener, called the garden his;
Who now, deposed, surveys my plain abode
And his late kingdom, only from the road.

SAMUEL TAYLOR COLERIDGE

Frost at Midnight

The Frost performs its secret ministry,
Unhelped by any wind. The owlet's cry
Came loud – and hark, again! loud as before.
The inmates of my cottage, all at rest,
Have left me to that solitude, which suits
Abstruser musings: save that at my side
My cradled infant slumbers peacefully.
'Tis calm indeed! so calm, that it disturbs
And vexes meditation with its strange
And extreme silentness. Sea, hill, and wood,
This populous village! Sea, and hill, and wood,

With all the numberless goings on of life,
Inaudible as dreams! the thin blue flame
Lies on my low burnt fire, and quivers not;
Only that film, which fluttered on the grate,
Still flutters there, the sole unquiet thing.
Methinks, its motion in this hush of nature
Gives it dim sympathies with me who live,
Making it a companionable form,
Whose puny flaps and freaks the idling Spirit
By its own moods interprets, every where
Echo or mirror seeking of itself,
And makes a toy of Thought.

             But O! how oft,
How oft, at school, with most believing mind,
Presageful, have I gazed upon the bars,
To watch that fluttering *stranger*! and as oft
With unclosed lids, already had I dreamt
Of my sweet birth-place, and the old church-tower,
Whose bells, the poor man's only music, rang
From morn to evening, all the hot Fair-day,
So sweetly, that they stirred and haunted me
With a wild pleasure, falling on mine ear
Most like articulate sounds of things to come!
So gazed I, till the soothing things I dreamt
Lulled me to sleep, and sleep prolonged my dreams!
And so I brooded all the following morn,
Awed by the stern preceptor's face, mine eye
Fixed with mock study on my swimming book:
Save if the door half opened, and I snatched
A hasty glance, and still my heart leaped up,
For still I hoped to see the *stranger*'s face,
Townsman, or aunt, or sister more beloved,
My play-mate when we both were clothed alike!

Dear Babe, that sleepest cradled by my side,
Whose gentle breathings, heard in this deep calm,
Fill up the interspersèd vacancies
And momentary pauses of the thought!
My babe so beautiful! it thrills my heart
With tender gladness, thus to look at thee,
And think that thou shalt learn far other lore
And in far other scenes! For I was reared
In the great city, pent 'mid cloisters dim,
And saw nought lovely but the sky and stars.
But *thou*, my babe! shalt wander like a breeze
By lakes and sandy shores, beneath the crags
Of ancient mountain, and beneath the clouds,
Which image in their bulk both lakes and shores
And mountain crags: so shalt thou see and hear
The lovely shapes and sounds intelligible
Of that eternal language, which the God
Utters, who from eternity doth teach
Himself in all, and all things in himself.
Great universal Teacher! he shall mould
Thy spirit, and by giving make it ask.

Therefore all seasons shall be sweet to thee,
Whether the summer clothe the general earth
With greenness, or the redbreast sit and sing
Betwixt the tufts of snow on the bare branch
Of mossy apple-tree, while the nigh thatch
Smokes in the sun-thaw; whether the eave-drops fall
Heard only in the trances of the blast,
Or if the secret ministry of frost
Shall hang them up in silent icicles,
Quietly shining to the quiet Moon.

Hotels like Houses

She is the one who takes a shine
to ceilings and to floors,
whose eye finds room for every line
scratched on the wardrobe doors.

She thinks in terms of thick red rope
around the bed, a plaque
above the hardened bathroom soap.
He's always first to pack.

If their affair has awkward spells,
what's bound to cause the rows is
that he treats houses like hotels
and she, hotels like houses.

Sweat

I sit in the hot room and I sweat,
I see the cool pane bedew with me,
My skin breathes out and pearls the windowpane,
Likes it and clings to it. She comes in,
She loves me and she loves our children too,
And still the sweat is trickling down the pane,
The breath of life makes cooling streaks
And wobbles down the pane. We breathe and burn,
We burn, all together in a hot room,
Our sweat is smoking down the windowpane,
Marks time. I smoke, I stir, and there I write
PR, BR, a streaming heart.
The sun strikes at it down a wide hollow shaft;
Birds swing on the beams, boil off the grass.

Silence

My father used to say,
'Superior people never make long visits,
have to be shown Longfellow's grave
or the glass flowers at Harvard.
Self-reliant like the cat –
that takes its prey to privacy,
the mouse's limp tail hanging like a shoelace from its
    mouth –
they sometimes enjoy solitude,
and can be robbed of speech
by speech which has delighted them.
The deepest feeling always shows itself in silence;
not in silence, but restraint.'
Nor was he insincere in saying, 'Make my house your inn.'
Inns are not residences.

PHILIP LARKIN

Home is so Sad

Home is so sad. It stays as it was left,
Shaped to the comfort of the last to go
As if to win them back. Instead, bereft
Of anyone to please, it withers so,
Having no heart to put aside the theft

And turn again to what it started as,
A joyous shot at how things ought to be,
Long fallen wide. You can see how it was:
Look at the pictures and the cutlery.
The music in the piano stool. That vase.

Rooms

I remember rooms that have had their part
In the steady slowing down of the heart.
The room in Paris, the room at Geneva,
The little damp room with the seaweed smell,
And that ceaseless maddening sound of the tide –
    Rooms where for good or for ill – things died.
But there is the room where we (two) lie dead,
Though every morning we seem to wake and might just as
      well seem to sleep again
    As we shall somewhere in the other quieter, dustier bed
    Out there in the sun – in the rain.

'Sweet—safe—Houses . . .'

Sweet—safe—Houses—
Glad—gay—Houses—
Sealed so stately tight—
Lids of Steel—on Lids of Marble—
Locking Bare feet out—

Brooks of Plush—in Banks of Satin—
Not so softly fall
As the laughter—and the whisper—
From their People Pearl—

No Bald Death—affront their Parlors—
No Bold Sickness come
To deface their Stately Treasures—
Anguish—and the Tomb—

Hum by—in Muffled Coaches—
Lest they—wonder Why—
Any—for the Press of Smiling—
Interrupt—to die—

ROBERT MINHINNICK

The House

I lie across the rafters of the loft
Holding the torch. From the junction box
Wires twist into darkness, a crumbling
Skein of red and black under sackcloth
Of webs. For three stifling hours

In the attic's heat I have cursed
This challenge, frustrated by
Electricity – the merciless current
That will not come. And the silence
Of the house offers no clue. Matching

Myself against its fifty years,
The solid rooms and gables of this redbrick
Terrace, I must establish my own
Permanence. For territory is not
Bought or sold but fought over: it is

The first instinct, the small, unremarkable
Warfare of our lives. Yet crouched in this
Hot attic room my sweat has turned to ice.
The torchbeam's yellow cylinder
Identifies the dust, shapes from life

That have served their time and been abandoned
By the house. And I stare, fascinated,
At the dead. The faces of those who once called
This house home. Like them, like this frail
Blade of light, the house has swallowed me.

PHILIPPE JACCOTTET

Interior

I have been trying for a long time to live
here in this room I pretend to like

with its table, its thoughtless objects,
its window wide to the dawn leaves.
A blackbird throbs in the ivy; light
everywhere polishes off the ancient dark.

I would gladly believe the bad times are done,
that this is my home, that the sun will shine,
were it not for the spider in the dust
at the foot of the bed, strayed in from the garden.
I should have trampled it harder, you would think
it was still weaving a trap for my delicate ghost.

translated from the French by Derek Mahon

ROBERT FROST

The Hill Wife

I   LONELINESS
Her Word
One ought not to have to care
     So much as you and I
Care when the birds come round the house
     To seem to say good-by;

Or care so much when they come back
     With whatever it is they sing;
The truth being we are as much
     Too glad for the one thing

As we are too sad for the other here –
     With birds that fill their breasts
But with each other and themselves
     And their built or driven nests.

II   HOUSE FEAR
Always – I tell you this they learned –
Always at night when they returned
To the lonely house from far away,

45

To lamps unlighted and fire gone gray,
They learned to rattle the lock and key
To give whatever might chance to be,
Warning and time to be off in flight:
And preferring the out- to the indoor night,
They learned to leave the house door wide
Until they had lit the lamp inside.

III   THE SMILE
Her Word
I didn't like the way he went away.
That smile! It never came of being gay.
Still he smiled – did you see him? – I was sure!
Perhaps because we gave him only bread
And the wretch knew from that that we were poor.
Perhaps because he let us give instead
Of seizing from us as he might have seized.
Perhaps he mocked at us for being wed,
Or being very young (and he was pleased
To have a vision of us old and dead).
I wonder how far down the road he's got.
He's watching from the woods as like as not.

IV   THE OFT-REPEATED DREAM
She had no saying dark enough
    For the dark pine that kept
Forever trying the window latch
    Of the room where they slept.

The tireless but ineffectual hands
    That with every futile pass
Made the great tree seem as a little bird
    Before the mystery of glass!

It never had been inside the room,
    And only one of the two
Was afraid in an oft-repeated dream
    Of what the tree might do.

V THE IMPULSE

It was too lonely for her there,
    And too wild,
And since there were but two of them,
    And no child,

And work was little in the house,
    She was free,
And followed where he furrowed field,
    Or felled tree.

She rested on a log and tossed
    The fresh chips,
With a song only to herself
    On her lips.

And once she went to break a bough
    Of black alder.
She strayed so far she scarcely heard
    When he called her –

And didn't answer – didn't speak –
    Or return.
She stood, and then she ran and hid
    In the fern.

He never found her, though he looked
    Everywhere,
And he asked at her mother's house
    Was she there.

Sudden and swift and light as that
    The ties gave,
And he learned of finalities
    Besides the grave.

ROBERT BROWNING

Love in a Life

I

Room after room,
I hunt the house through
We inhabit together.
Heart, fear nothing, for, heart, thou shalt find her –
Next time, herself! – not the trouble behind her
Left in the curtain, the couch's perfume!
As she brushed it, the cornice-wreath blossomed anew:
Yon looking-glass gleamed at the wave of her feather.

II

Yet the day wears,
And door succeeds door;
I try the fresh fortune –
Range the wide house from the wing to the centre.
Still the same chance! she goes out as I enter.
Spend my whole day in the quest, – who cares?
But 'tis twilight, you see, – with such suites to explore,
Such closets to search, such alcoves to importune!

ALFRED, LORD TENNYSON

from In Memoriam

Dark house, by which once more I stand
    Here in the long unlovely street,
    Doors, where my heart was used to beat
So quickly, waiting for a hand,

A hand that can be clasp'd no more –
    Behold me, for I cannot sleep,
    And like a guilty thing I creep
At earliest morning to the door.

He is not here; but far away
   The noise of life begins again,
   And ghastly thro' the drizzling rain
On the bald streets breaks the blank day.

TER PORTER

The Easiest Room in Hell

At the top of the stairs is a room
one may speak of only in parables.

It is the childhood attic,
the place to go when love has worn away,
the origin of the smell of self.

We came here on a clandestine visit
and in the full fire of indifference.

We sorted out books and let the children
sleep here away from creatures.

From its windows, ruled by willows,
the flatlands of childhood stretched
to the watermeadows.

It was the site of a massacre,
of the running down of the body
to less even than the soul,
the tribe's revenge on everything.

It was the heart of England
where the ballerinas were on points
and locums laughed through every evening.

Once it held all the games,
Inconsequences, Misalliance, Frustration,
even *Mendacity, Adultery* and *Manic Depression*.

49

But that was just its alibi,
all along it was home,
a home away from home.

Having such a sanctuary
we who parted here
will be reunited here.

You asked in an uncharacteristic note,
'Dwell I but in the suburbs
of your good pleasure?'

I replied, 'To us has been allowed
the easiest room in hell.'

Once it belonged to you,
now it is only mine.

DEREK MAHON

A Refusal to Mourn

He lived in a small farm-house
At the edge of a new estate.
The trim gardens crept
To his door, and car engines
Woke him before dawn
On dark winter mornings.

All day there was silence
In the bright house. The clock
Ticked on the kitchen shelf,
Cinders moved in the grate,
And a warm briar gurgled
When the old man talked to himself;

But the door-bell seldom rang
After the milkman went,
And if a shirt-hanger
Knocked in an open wardrobe

That was a strange event
To be pondered on for hours

While the wind thrashed about
In the back garden, raking
The roof of the hen-house,
And swept clouds and gulls
Eastwards over the lough
With its flap of tiny sails.

Once a week he would visit
An old shipyard crony,
Inching down to the road
And the blue country bus
To sit and watch sun-dappled
Branches whacking the windows

While the long evening shed
Weak light in his empty house,
On the photographs of his dead
Wife and their six children
And the Missions to Seamen angel
In flight above the bed.

'I'm not long for this world,'
Said he on our last evening,
'I'll not last the winter,'
And grinned, straining to hear
Whatever reply I made;
And died the following year.

In time the astringent rain
Of those parts will clean
The words from his gravestone
In the crowded cemetery
That overlooks the sea
And his name be mud once again

And his boilers lie like tombs
In the mud of the sea bed
Till the next ice age comes
And the earth he inherited
Is gone like Neanderthal Man
And no records remain.

But the secret bred in the bone
On the dawn strand survives
In other times and lives,
Persisting for the unborn
Like a claw-print in concrete
After the bird has flown.

LOUIS MACNEICE

House on a Cliff

Indoors the tang of a tiny oil lamp. Outdoors
The winking signal on the waste of sea.
Indoors the sound of the wind. Outdoors the wind.
Indoors the locked heart and the lost key.

Outdoors the chill, the void, the siren. Indoors
The strong man pained to find his red blood cools,
While the blind clock grows louder, faster. Outdoors
The silent moon, the garrulous tides she rules.

Indoors ancestral curse-cum-blessing. Outdoors
The empty bowl of heaven, the empty deep.
Indoors a purposeful man who talks at cross
Purposes, to himself, in a broken sleep.

Ruins of a Great House

though our longest sun sets at right declensions and
makes but winter arches, it cannot be long before we lie
down in darkness, and have our light in ashes . . .
BROWNE: Urn Burial

Stones only, the *disjecta membra* of this Great House,
Whose moth-like girls are mixed with candledust,
Remain to file the lizard's dragonish claws;
The mouths of those gate cherubs streaked with stain.
Axle and coachwheel silted under the muck
Of cattle droppings.
                              Three crows flap for the trees,
And settle, creaking the eucalyptus boughs.
A smell of dead limes quickens in the nose
The leprosy of Empire.

                    'Farewell, green fields
                    Farewell, ye happy groves!'
Marble as Greece, like Faulkner's south in stone,
Deciduous beauty prospered and is gone;
But where the lawn breaks in a rash of trees
A spade below dead leaves will ring the bone
Of some dead animal or human thing
Fallen from evil days, from evil times.

It seems that the original crops were limes
Grown in the silt that clogs the river's skirt;
The imperious rakes are gone, their bright girls gone,
The river flows, obliterating hurt.
I climbed a wall with the grill ironwork
Of exiled craftsmen, protecting that great house
From guilt, perhaps, but not from the worm's rent,
Nor from the padded cavalry of the mouse.
And when a wind shook in the limes I heard

What Kipling heard; the death of a great empire, the abu
Of ignorance by Bible and by sword.

A green lawn, broken by low walls of stone
Dipped to the rivulet, and pacing, I thought next
Of men like Hawkins, Walter Raleigh, Drake,
Ancestral murderers and poets, more perplexed
In memory now by every ulcerous crime.
The world's green age then was a rotting lime
Whose stench became the charnel galleon's text.
The rot remains with us, the men are gone.
But, as dead ash is lifted in a wind,
That fans the blackening ember of the mind,
My eyes burned from the ashen prose of Donne.

Ablaze with rage, I thought
Some slave is rotting in this manorial lake,
And still the coal of my compassion fought:
That Albion too, was once
A colony like ours, 'Part of the continent, piece of the mair
Nook-shotten, rook o'er blown, deranged
By foaming channels, and the vain expense
Of bitter faction.
                All in compassion ends
So differently from what the heart arranged:
'as well as if a manor of thy friend's . . .'

CHRISTINA ROSSETTI

At Home

When I was dead, my spirit turned
    To seek the much frequented house:
I passed the door, and saw my friends
    Feasting beneath green orange boughs;
From hand to hand they pushed the wine,
    They sucked the pulp of plum and peach;

They sang, they jested, and they laughed.
    For each was loved of each.

I listened to their honest chat:
    Said one: 'Tomorrow we shall be
Plod plod along the featureless sands
    And coasting miles and miles of sea.'
Said one: 'Before the turn of tide
    We will achieve the eyrie-seat.'
Said one: 'Tomorrow shall be like
    Today, but much more sweet.'

'Tomorrow,' said they, strong with hope,
    And dwelt upon the pleasant way:
'Tomorow,' cried they one and all,
    While no one spoke of yesterday.
Their life stood full at blessed noon;
    I, only I, had passed away:
'Tomorrow and today,' they cried;
    I was of yesterday.

I shivered comfortless, but cast
    No chill across the tablecloth;
I all-forgotten shivered, sad
    To stay and yet to part how loth:
I passed from the familiar room,
    I who from love had passed away,
Like the remembrance of a guest
    That tarrieth but a day.

Town

We are Going

for Grannie Coolwell

They came in to the little town
A semi-naked band subdued and silent,
All that remained of their tribe.
They came here to the place of their old bora ground
Where now the many white men hurry about like ants.
Notice of estate agent reads: 'Rubbish May Be Tipped
    Here'.
Now it half covers the traces of the old bora ring.
They sit and are confused, they cannot say their thoughts:
'We are as strangers here now, but the white tribe are the
    strangers.
We belong here, we are of the old ways.
We are the corroboree and the bora ground,
We are the old sacred ceremonies, the laws of the elders.
We are the wonder tales of Dream Time, the tribal legends
    told.
We are the past, the hunts and the laughing games, the
    wandering camp fires.
We are the lightning-bolt over Gaphembah Hill
Quick and terrible,
And the Thunderer after him, that loud fellow.
We are the quiet daybreak paling the dark lagoon.
We are the shadow-ghosts creeping back as the camp fires
    burn low.
We are nature and the past, all the old ways
Gone now and scattered.
The scrubs are gone, the hunting and the laughter.
The eagle is gone, the emu and the kangaroo are gone
    from this place.
The bora ring is gone.
The corroboree is gone.
And we are going.'

Late Winter Morning on the Palisades

Candle in the throat of maple
alive in wet bark
like a soldering flame as the sun lifts
over Manhattan's shoulder,

the yard for a minute, no more,
washed in an antique gold,
a kind of cathedral light filtering down
on squirrels

digging up turf. The earth,
after a fortnight's thaw,
loosens, loosening some more
until a musty bouquet

digs a small trench in us, light
playing on pebbles and clods,
traceries in clay.
    Suddenly car doors,
jets and *the brutal slaying in Queens* –

morning rinsing the shadows,
pouring out day.

EZRA POUND

In a Station of the Metro

The apparition of these faces in the crowd;
Petals on a wet, black bough.

Metropolitan

In cities there are tangerine briefcases on the down-platform and jet parkas on the up-platform; in the mother of cities there is equal anxiety at all terminals.

West a business breast, North a morose jig, East a false escape, South steam in milk.

The centres of cities move westwards; the centre of the mother of cities has disappeared.

North the great cat, East the great water, South the great fire, West the great arrow.

In cities the sons of women become fathers; in the mother of cities the daughters of men have failed to become mothers.

East the uneager fingers, South the damp cave, West the chained ankle, North the rehearsed cry.

Cities are built for trade, where women and men may freely through knowing each other become more like themselves; the mother of cities is built for government, where women and men through fearing each other become more like each other than they care to be.

South the short, West the soap, North the sheets, East the shivers.

In cities the church fund is forever stuck below blood heat; in the mother of cities the church is a community arts centre.

West the Why-not, North the Now-then, East the End-product, South the Same-again.

In cities nobody can afford the price; in the mother of cities nobody dares to ask the price.

North the telephone smile, East the early appointment, South the second reminder, West the hanging button.

In cities the jealous man is jealous because he is himself i⟶
his imagination unfaithful; in the mother of cities th⟶
jealous man is jealous because he reads the magazines.

East the endless arrival, South the astounding statistic,
West the wasted words, North the night of nights.

In cities we dream about our desires; in the mother of citie⟶
we dream about our dreams.

MONIZA ALVI

Story of a City

I could tell you the story of a city –
how I seduced it in the afternoon.
The silenced birds were tangled in its hair.

I tried to stroke its million arms, its domes,
swept off some dust and sweetened it with rain,
unwound the suffocating scarves of dirt,

pounded it like a drum, like carnival time,
watched it stretch until it burst
with rhythm, paint and revelry and song.

Calming the city, subduing it in my house,
I thought I'd store it high up on a shelf,
or slip it in my pocket like a pen.

I begged on its behalf – a coin, a stroke of luck –
then left it in the dark recesses of a shop
steadily receding to another continent,

retrieved its deserts, chasms, embryos,
its open squares and theatre steps,
observed its networks running in my hands.

I started to examine how it seemed to be
just stuffed and stuffed inside itself.
Though once I cracked it open like an egg –

heard the river roaring free, the named
and nameless threats, the interlocking worlds.
At night I lie with this uncharted city.

It turns to me and murmurs in its sleep
I need you. Make of me what you can –
my suburbs of ideas, my flames, my empty spaces.

THOM GUNN

In Praise of Cities

I

Indifferent to the indifference that conceived her,
Grown buxom in disorder now, she accepts
– Like dirt, strangers, or moss upon her churches –
Your tribute to the wharf of circumstance,
Rejected sidestreet, formal monument . . .
And, irresistible, the thoroughfare.

You welcome in her what remains of you;
And what is strange and what is incomplete
Compels a passion without understanding,
For all you cannot be.

II

        Only at dawn
You might escape, she sleeps then for an hour:
Watch where she hardly breathes, spread out and cool,
Her pavements desolate in the dim dry air.

III

You stay. Yet she is occupied, apart.
Out of a mist the river turns to see
Whether you follow still. You stay. At evening
Your blood gains pace even as her blood does.

IV

Casual yet urgent in her love making,
She constantly asserts her independence:
Suddenly turning moist pale walls upon you
– Your own designs, peeling and unachieved –
Or her whole darkness hunching in an alley.
And all at once you enter the embrace
Withheld by day while you solicited.
She wanders lewdly, whispering her given name,
Charing Cross Road, or Forty-Second Street:
The longest streets, desire that never ends,
Familiar and inexplicable, wearing
Cosmetic light a fool could penetrate.
She presses you with her hard ornaments,
Arcades, late movie shows, the piled lit windows
Of surplus stores. Here she is loveliest;
Extreme, material, and the work of man.

DOUGLAS DUNN

On Roofs of Terry Street

Television aerials, Chinese characters
In the lower sky, wave gently in the smoke.

Nest-building sparrows peck at moss,
Urban flora and fauna, soft, unscrupulous.

Rain drying on the slates shines sometimes.
A builder is repairing someone's leaking roof,

He kneels upright to rest his back,
His trowel catches the light and becomes precious.

Composed Upon Westminster Bridge, September 3, 1802

Earth has not anything to show more fair:
Dull would he be of soul who could pass by
A sight so touching in its majesty:
This City now doth, like a garment, wear
The beauty of the morning; silent, bare,
Ships, towers, domes, theatres, and temples lie
Open unto the fields, and to the sky;
All bright and glittering in the smokeless air.
Never did sun more beautifully steep
In his first splendour, valley, rock, or hill;
Ne'er saw I, never felt, a calm so deep!
The river glideth at his own sweet will:
Dear God! the very houses seem asleep;
And all that mighty heart is lying still!

JOHN BETJEMAN

Parliament Hill Fields

Rumbling under blackened girders, Midland, bound for
    Cricklewood,
Puffed its sulphur to the sunset where that Land of
    Laundries stood.
Rumble under, thunder over, train and tram alternate go,
Shake the floor and smudge the ledger, Charrington, Sells,
    Dale and Co.,
Nuts and nuggets in the window, trucks along the lines
    below.

When the Bon Marché was shuttered, when the feet were
    hot and tired,
Outside Charrington's we waited, by the 'STOP HERE IF
    REQUIRED',

Launched aboard the shopping basket, sat precipitately
   down,
Rocked past Zwanziger the baker's, and the terrace
   blackish brown,
And the curious Anglo-Norman parish church of Kentish
   Town.

Till the tram went over thirty, sighting terminus again,
Past municipal lawn tennis and the bobble-hanging plane;
Soft the light suburban evening caught our ashlar-
   speckled spire,
Eighteen-sixty Early English, as the mighty elms retire
Either side of Brookfield Mansions flashing fine French-
   window fire.

Oh the after-tram-ride quiet, when we heard a mile
   beyond,
Silver music from the bandstand, barking dogs by
   Highgate Pond;
Up the hill where stucco houses in Virginia creeper drown –
And my childish wave of pity, seeing children carrying
   down
Sheaves of drooping dandelions to the courts of Kentish
   Town.

SEAN O'BRIEN

The Park by the Railway

Where should we meet but in this shabby park
Where the railings are missing and the branches black?
Industrial pastoral, our circuit
Of grass under ash, long-standing water
And unimportant sunsets flaring up
Above the half-dismantled fair. Our place
Of in-betweens, abandoned viaducts
And modern flowers, dock and willowherb,
Lost mongrels, birdsong scratching at the soot

Of the last century. Where should we be
But here, my industrial girl? Where else
But this city beyond conservation?
I win you a ring at the rifle range
For the twentieth time, but you've chosen
A yellow, implausible fish in a bag
That you hold to one side when I kiss you.
Sitting in the waiting-room in darkness
Beside the empty cast-iron fireplace,
In the last of the heat the brick gives off,
Not quite convinced there will be no more trains,
At the end of a summer that never began
Till we lost it, we cannot believe
We are going. We speak, and we've gone.
You strike a match to show the china map
Of where the railways ran before us.
Coal and politics, invisible decades
Of rain, domestic love and failing mills
That ended in a war and then a war
Are fading into what we are: two young
Polite incapables, our tickets bought
Well in advance, who will not starve, or die
Of anything but choice. Who could not choose
To live this funeral, lost August left
To no one by the dead, the ghosts of us.

AMY CLAMPITT

Real Estate

Something there is that doesn't
love a Third Avenue tenement,

that wants it gone the way the El
went. Façade a typical example

of red-brick eclectic, its five dozen
windows half now behind blank tin,

scrollwork lintels of strange parentage,
fire escapes' curling-iron birdcage,

are an anomaly among high-rise elevators,
besieged by Urban Relocation (Not A

Governmental Agency). Holdout tenants
confer, gesticulating, by storefronts

adapted only to an anxious present – Le
Boudoir, Le Shampoo, Le Retro (if passé

is chic, is chic passé?). One gelded
pawnshop, until last week, still brooded,

harboring, among tag ends of pathos,
several thirty-year-old umbrellas.

Regularly twice a day, the lingering wraith
within stepped out to shake her dustcloth.

That's done now. She advertised a sale.
Still nothing moved. Finally, a U-Haul

truck carted everything off somewhere.
Hail, real estate! Bravo, entrepreneur!

JOHN DAVIDSON

A Northern Suburb

Nature selects the longest way,
    And winds about in tortuous grooves;
A thousand years the oaks decay;
    The wrinkled glacier hardly moves.

But here the whetted fangs of change
    Daily devour the old demesne –
The busy farm, the quiet grange,
    The wayside inn, the village green.

In gaudy yellow brick and red,
　　With rooting pipes, like creepers rank,
The shoddy terraces o'erspread
　　Meadow, and garth, and daisied bank.

With shelves for rooms the houses crowd,
　　Like draughty cupboards in a row –
Ice-chests when wintry winds are loud,
　　Ovens when summer breezes blow.

Roused by the fee'd policeman's knock,
　　And sad that day should come again,
Under the stars the workmen flock
　　In haste to reach the workmen's train.

For here dwell those who must fulfil
　　Dull tasks in uncongenial spheres,
Who toil through dread of coming ill,
　　And not with hope of happier years –

The lowly folk who scarcely dare
　　Conceive themselves perhaps misplaced,
Whose prize for unremitting care
　　Is only not to be disgraced.

ROY FISHER

from City

Walking through the suburb at night, as I pass the dentist's house I hear a clock chime a quarter, a desolate brassy sound. I know where it stands, on the mantelpiece in the still surgery. The chime falls back into the house, and beyond it, without end. Peace.

I sense the simple nakedness of these tiers of sleeping men and women beneath whose windows I pass. I imagine it in its own setting, a mean bathroom in a house no longer new, a bathroom with plank panelling, painted a peculiar shade of green by an amateur, and badly preserved. It is full of steam, so much as to obscure the yellow light and hide the high, patched ceiling. In this dream, standing quiet, the private image of the householder or his wife, damp and clean.

I see this as it might be floating in the dark, as if the twinkling point of a distant street-lamp had blown in closer, swelling and softening to a foggy oval. I can call up a series of such glimpses that need have no end, for they are all the bodies of strangers. Some are deformed or diseased, some are ashamed, but the peace of humility and weakness is there in them all.

I have often felt myself to be vicious, in living so much by the eye, yet among so many people. I can be afraid that the egg of light through which I see these bodies might present itself as a keyhole. Yet I can find no sadism in the way I see them now. They are warm-fleshed, yet their shapes have the minuscule, remote morality of some mediaeval woodcut of the Expulsion: an eternally startled Adam, a permanently bemused Eve. I see them as homunculi, moving privately each in a softly lit fruit in a nocturnal tree. I can consider without scorn or envy the well-found bedrooms I pass, walnut and rose-pink, altars of tidy, dark-haired women, bare-backed, wifely. Even in these I can see order.

I come quite often now upon a sort of ecstasy, a rag of light blowing among the things I know, making me feel I am not the one for whom it was intended, that I have inadvertently been looking through another's eyes and have seen what I cannot receive.

from The Sydney Highrise Variations

THE FLIGHT FROM MANHATTAN

It is possible the heights of this view are a museum
though the highrise continues desultorily along some
    ridges,

> canned Housing, Strata Title,
> see-through Office Space,
> upright bedsteads of Harbour View,
> residential soviets,

the cranes have all but vanished from the central upsurge.

> Hot-air money-driers,
> towering double entry,
> Freud's cobwebbed poem
> with revolving restaurant,

they took eighty years to fly here from Manhattan
these variant towers. By then, they were arriving
    everywhere.

> In the land of veneers,
> of cladding, of Cape Codding
> (I shall have Cape Codded)
> they put on heavy side.

The iron ball was loose in the old five-storey city
clearing bombsites for them. They rose like nouveaux
    accents
and stilled, for a time, the city's conversation.

> Their arrival paralleled
> the rise of the Consumers
> gazing through themselves
> at iconoclasms, wines,
> Danish Modern ethics.

Little we could love expanded to fill the spaces
of high glazed prosperity. An extensive city

that had long contained the dimensions of heaven and hell
couldn't manage total awe at the buildings of the Joneses.

> Their reign coincided
> with an updraft of ideology,
> that mood in which the starving
> spirit is fed upon the heart.

Employment and neckties and ruling themes ascended
into the towers. But they never filled them.
Squinting at them through the salt
and much-washed glass of her history, the city kept her
flavour
fire-ladder high, rarely above three storeys.

In ambitious battle at length, she began to hedge
the grilles of aspiration. To limit them to standing
on economic grounds. With their twists of sculpture.

On similar grounds we are stopped here, still surveying
the ridgy plain of houses. Enormous. England's buried
Gulag.
The stacked entrepôt, great city of the Australians.

W. H. AUDEN

Brussels in Winter

Wandering through cold streets tangled like old string,
Coming on fountains rigid in the frost,
Its formula escapes you; it has lost
The certainty that constitutes a thing.

Only the old, the hungry and the humbled
Keep at this temperature a sense of place,
And in their misery are all assembled;
The winter holds them like an Opera-House.

Ridges of rich apartments loom to-night
Where isolated windows glow like farms,
A phrase goes packed with meaning like a van,

A look contains the history of man,
And fifty francs will earn a stranger right
To take the shuddering city in his arms.

T. S. ELIOT

Preludes

I

The winter evening settles down
With smell of steaks in passageways.
Six o'clock.
The burnt-out ends of smoky days.
And now a gusty shower wraps
The grimy scraps
Of withered leaves about your feet
And newspapers from vacant lots;
The showers beat
On broken blinds and chimney-pots,
And at the corner of the street
A lonely cab-horse steams and stamps.

And then the lighting of the lamps.

II

The morning comes to consciousness
Of faint stale smells of beer
From the sawdust-trampled street
With all its muddy feet that press
To early coffee-stands.

With the other masquerades
That time resumes,
One thinks of all the hands

That are raising dingy shades
In a thousand furnished rooms.

III

You tossed a blanket from the bed,
You lay upon your back, and waited;
You dozed, and watched the night revealing
The thousand sordid images
Of which your soul was constituted;
They flickered against the ceiling.
And when all the world came back
And the light crept up between the shutters,
And you heard the sparrows in the gutters,
You had such a vision of the street
As the street hardly understands;
Sitting along the bed's edge, where
You curled the papers from your hair,
Or clasped the yellow soles of feet
In the palms of both soiled hands.

IV

His soul stretched tight across the skies
That fade behind a city block,
Or trampled by insistent feet
At four and five and six o'clock;
And short square fingers stuffing pipes,
And evening newspapers, and eyes
Assured of certain certainties,
The conscience of a blackened street
Impatient to assume the world.

I am moved by fancies that are curled
Around these images, and cling:
The notion of some infinitely gentle
Infinitely suffering thing.

Wipe your hand across your mouth, and laugh;
The worlds revolve like ancient women
Gathering fuel in vacant lots.

S. GRAHAM

The Night City

Unmet at Euston in a dream
Of London under Turner's steam
Misting the iron gantries, I
Found myself running away
From Scotland into the golden city.

I ran down Gray's Inn Road and ran
Till I was under a black bridge.
This was me at nineteen
Late at night arriving between
The buildings of the City of London.

And then I (O I have fallen down)
Fell in my dream beside the Bank
Of England's wall to bed, me
With my money belt of Northern ice.
I found Eliot and he said yes

And sprang into a Holmes cab.
Boswell passed me in the fog
Going to visit Whistler who
Was with John Donne who had just seen
Paul Potts shouting on Soho Green.

Midnight. I hear the moon
Light chiming on St Paul's.

The City is empty. Night
Watchmen are drinking their tea.

The Fire had burnt out.
The Plague's pits had closed
And gone into literature.

Between the big buildings
I sat like a flea crouched
In the stopped works of a watch.

CAROL ANN DUFFY

Foreign

Imagine living in a strange, dark city for twenty years.
There are some dismal dwellings on the east side
and one of them is yours. On the landing, you hear
your foreign accent echo down the stairs. You think
in a language of your own and talk in theirs.

Then you are writing home. The voice in your head
recites the letter in a local dialect; behind that
is the sound of your mother singing to you,
all that time ago, and now you do not know
why your eyes are watering and what's the word for this.

You use the public transport. Work. Sleep. Imagine one
   night
you saw a name for yourself sprayed in red
against a brick wall. A hate name. Red like blood.
It is snowing on the streets, under the neon lights,
as if this place were coming to bits before your eyes.

And in the delicatessen, from time to time, the coins
in your palm will not translate. Inarticulate,
because this is not home, you point at fruit. Imagine
that one of you says *Me not know what these people mean.*
It like they only go to bed and dream. Imagine that.

Street Song

Pink Lane, Strawberry Lane, Pudding Chare:
someone is waiting, I don't know where;
hiding among the nursery names,
he wants to play peculiar games.

In Leazes Terrace or Leazes Park
someone is loitering in the dark,
feeling the giggles rise in his throat
and fingering something under his coat.

He could be sidling along Forth Lane
to stop some girl from catching her train,
or stalking the grounds of the RVI
to see if a student nurse goes by.

In Belle Grove Terrace or Fountain Row
or Hunter's Road he's raring to go –
unless he's the quiet shape you'll meet
on the cobbles in Back Stowell Street.

Monk Street, Friars Street, Gallowgate
are better avoided when it's late.
Even in Sandhill and the Side
there are shadows where a man could hide.

So don't go lightly along Darn Crook
because the Ripper's been brought to book.
Wear flat shoes, and be ready to run:
remember, sisters, there's more than one.

LINTON KWESI JOHNSON

Di Great Insohreckshan

it woz in april nineteen eighty wan
doun inna di ghetto af Brixtan
dat di babylan dem cauz such a frickshan

77

dat it bring about a great insohreckshan
an it spread all ovah di naeshan
it woz truly an histarical occayshan

it woz event af di year
an I wish I ad been dere
wen wi run riat all ovah Brixtan
wen wi mash-up plenty police van
wen wi mash-up di wicked wan plan
wen wi mash-up di Swamp Eighty Wan
fi wha?
fi mek di rulah dem andahstan
dat wi naw tek noh more a dem oppreshan

wi nevvah bun di lanlaad
wen wi run riat all ovah Brixtan
wen wi mash-up plenty police van
wen wi mash-up di wicked wan plan
wen wi mash-up di swamp eighty wan

dem seh wi comandeer cyar
an wi ghaddah ammunishan
wi bill wi baricade
an di wicked ketch afraid
wi sen out wi scout
fi goh fine dem whereabout
den wi faam-up wi passi
an wi mek wi raid

well now dem run gaan goh plan countah-ackshan
but di plastic bullit an di waatah cannan
will bring a blam-blam
will bring a blam-blam
nevvah mine Scarman
will bring a blam-blam

Leningrad

I've come back to my city. These are my own old tears,
my own little veins, the swollen glands of my childhood.

So you're back. Open wide. Swallow
the fish-oil from the river lamps of Leningrad.

Open your eyes. Do you know this December day,
the egg-yolk with the deadly tar beaten into it?

Petersburg! I don't want to die yet!
You know my telephone numbers.

Petersburg! I've still got the addresses:
I can look up dead voices.

I live on back stairs, and the bell,
torn out nerves and all, jangles in my temples.

And I wait till morning for guests that I love,
and rattle the door in its chains.

> translated from the Russian by Clarence Brown and
> W. S. Merwin

Naked Town

On the plain that town flat like an iron sheet
with mutilated hand of its cathedral a pointing claw
with pavements the colour of intestines houses stripped of
    their skin
the town beneath a yellow wave of sun
a chalky wave of moon

o town what a town tell me what's the name of that town
under what star on what road

about people: they work at the slaughter-house in an
    immense building
of raw concrete blocks around them the odour of blood
and the penitential psalm of animals Are there poets the
    (silent poets)
there are troops a big rattle of barracks on the outskirts
on Sunday beyond the bridge in prickly bushes on cold
    sand
on rusty grass girls receive soldiers
there are as well some places dedicated to dreams The
    cinema
with a white wall on which splash the shadows of the
    absent
little halls where alcohol is poured into glass thin and
    thick
there are also dogs at last hungry dogs that howl
and in that fashion indicate the borders of the town Ame

so you still ask what's the name of that town
which deserves biting anger where is that town
on the cords of what winds beneath what column of air
and who lives there people with the same skin as ours
or people with our faces or

    translated from the Polish by Czeslaw Milosz and Peter Dale Sco

C. P. CAVAFY

The City

You said, 'I will go to another land, I will go to another se
Another city will be found, a better one than this.
Every effort of mine is a condemnation of fate;
and my heart is – like a corpse – buried.
How long will my mind remain in this wasteland.
Wherever I turn my eyes, wherever I may look
I see black ruins of my life here,
where I spent so many years destroying and wasting.'

You will find no new lands, you will find no other seas.
The city will follow you. You will roam the same
streets. And you will age in the same neighborhoods;
and you will grow gray in these same houses.
Always you will arrive in this city. Do not hope for any
      other –
There is no ship for you, there is no road.
As you have destroyed your life here
in this little corner, you have ruined it in the entire world.

translated from the Greek by Edmund Kelley and Philip Sherard

IZABETH BISHOP

Night City
(*From the plane*)

No foot could endure it,
shoes are too thin.
Broken glass, broken bottles,
heaps of them burn.

Over those fires
no one could walk:
those flaring acids
and variegated bloods.

The city burns tears.
A gathered lake
of aquamarine
begins to smoke.

The city burns guilt.
– For guilt-disposal
the central heat
must be this intense.

Diaphanous lymph,
bright turgid blood,

spatter outward
in clots of gold

to where run, molten,
in the dark environs
green and luminous
silicate rivers.

A pool of bitumen
one tycoon
wept by himself,
a blackened moon.

Another cried
a skyscraper up.
Look! Incandescent,
its wires drip.

The conflagration
fights for air
in a dread vacuum.
The sky is dead.

(Still, there are creatures,
careful ones, overhead.
They set down their feet, they walk
green, red; green, red.)

Land

from The Prelude, Book I (1805)

    Fair seed-time had my soul, and I grew up
Foster'd alike by beauty and by fear;
Much favor'd in my birthplace, and no less
In that beloved Vale to which, erelong,
I was transplanted. Well I call to mind
('Twas at an early age, ere I had seen
Nine summers) when upon the mountain slope
The frost and breath of frosty wind had snapp'd
The last autumnal crocus, 'twas my joy
To wander half the night among the Cliffs
And the smooth Hollows, where the woodcocks ran
Along the open turf. In thought and wish
That time, my shoulder all with springes hung,
I was a fell destroyer. On the heights
Scudding away from snare to snare, I plied
My anxious visitation, hurrying on,
Still hurrying, hurrying onward; moon and stars
Were shining o'er my head; I was alone,
And seem'd to be a trouble to the peace
That was among them. Sometimes it befel
In these night-wanderings, that a strong desire
o'erpower'd my better reason, and the bird
Which was the captive of another's toils
Became my prey; and, when the deed was done
I heard among the solitary hills
Low breathings coming after me, and sounds
Of undistinguishable motion, steps
Almost as silent as the turf they trod.
Nor less in springtime when on southern banks
The shining sun had from his knot of leaves
Decoy'd the primrose flower, and when the Vales
And woods were warm, was I a plunderer then
In the high places, on the lonesome peaks

Where'er, among the mountains and the winds,
The Mother Bird had built her lodge. Though mean
My object, and inglorious, yet the end
Was not ignoble. Oh! when I have hung
Above the raven's nest, by knots of grass
And half-inch fissures in the slippery rock
But ill sustain'd, and almost, as it seem'd,
Suspended by the blast which blew amain,
Shouldering the naked crag; Oh! at that time,
While on the perilous ridge I hung alone,
With what strange utterance did the loud dry wind
Blow through my ears! the sky seem'd not a sky
Of earth, and with what motion mov'd the clouds!

FAUSTIN CHARLES

Landscape

Love the land!
Feel the earth-pulse beating
In the earth-shaking Caribbean;
Worship the root-gods swelling
Mighty Silk-Cotton, poui and ginger lily
And the hibiscus trailing our destiny.
The mountain-scape swims sweetly
In the soothing river-light;
Sun panting on tree-top spotlights the caterpillar
Eating a star-apple inside out.
Caress the blue-scape, eyes peeling wide open
The bat suckling a bursting sapodilla.
When the moon is full, the crabs come out to play,
The breadfruit gives birth, bursting into rosy cheeks,
And the murmur from surrounding hills,
Hails the newborn trumpeter;
The sweet voiced bees honey the blossoms
On the shading immortelle
With an enchanting rhythm.

Love the land!
Come back to the ancient castle covered with stars,
Garlanded by birds and threaded in red wood;
The swaying cedar signals all with the melodic bamboo
Calling! calling!
When all the grasses have sprouted
And a spray of sandflies ride the leaves
And ponder the next biting session,
Listen to the night-worm gnawing the cane-root!
Listen to the golden grasshopper chirping
In the magic garden!
Listen to the cricket! Singing in the forest
Where the souls of the ancients chant through dove-calls.
Listen to the soil as it charms its children!
Return to the land!
Reclaim the children!

OBERT DUNCAN

Often I Am Permitted to Return to a Meadow

as if it were a scene made-up by the mind,
that is not mine, but is a made place,

that is mine, it is so near to the heart,
an eternal pasture folded in all thought
so that there is a hall therein

that is a made place, created by light
wherefrom the shadows that are forms fall.

Wherefrom fall all architectures I am
I say are likenesses of the First Beloved
whose flowers are flames lit to the Lady.

She it is Queen Under The Hill
whose hosts are a disturbance of words within words
that is a field folded.

It is only a dream of the grass blowing
east against the source of the sun
in an hour before the sun's going down

whose secret we see in a children's game
of ring a round of roses told.

Often I am permitted to return to a meadow
as if it were a given property of the mind
that certain bounds hold against chaos,

that is a place of first permission,
everlasting omen of what is.

DYLAN THOMAS

Poem in October

It was my thirtieth year to heaven
Woke to my hearing from harbour and neighbour wood
   And the mussel pooled and the heron
         Priested shore
         The morning beckon
With water praying and call of seagull and rook
And the knock of sailing boats on the net webbed wall
   Myself to set foot
      That second
In the still sleeping town and set forth.

My birthday began with the water-
Birds and the birds of the winged trees flying my name
   Above the farms and the white horses
      And I rose
     In rainy autumn
And walked abroad in a shower of all my days.
High tide and the heron dived when I took the road
   Over the border
      And the gates
Of the town closed as the town awoke.

A springful of larks in a rolling
Cloud and the roadside bushes brimming with whistling
　　Blackbirds and the sun of October
　　　　　　Summery
　　On the hill's shoulder,
Here were fond climates and sweet singers suddenly
Come in the morning where I wandered and listened
　　To the rain wringing
　　　　Wind blow cold
　　In the wood faraway under me.

　Pale rain over the dwindling harbour
And over the sea wet church the size of a snail
　　With its horns through mist and the castle
　　　　Brown as owls
　　But all the gardens
Of spring and summer were blooming in the tall tales
Beyond the border and under the lark full cloud.
　　There could I marvel
　　　　My birthday
　　Away but the weather turned around.

　It turned away from the blithe country
And down the other air and the blue altered sky
　　Streamed again a wonder of summer
　　　　With apples
　　Pears and red currants
And I saw in the turning so clearly a child's
Forgotten mornings when he walked with his mother
　　Through the parables
　　　　Of sun light
　　And the legends of the green chapels

　And the twice told fields of infancy
That his tears burned my cheeks and his heart moved in
　　mine.
　These were the woods the river and sea
　　　　Where a boy

In the listening
Summertime of the dead whispered the truth of his joy
To the trees and the stones and the fish in the tide.
And the mystery
Sang alive
Still in the water and singingbirds.

And there could I marvel my birthday
Away but the weather turned around. And the true
Joy of the long dead child sang burning
In the sun.
It was my thirtieth
Year to heaven stood there then in the summer noon
Though the town below lay leaved with October blood.
O may my heart's truth
Still be sung
On this high hill in a year's turning.

PATRICK KAVANAGH

Epic

I have lived in important places, times
When great events were decided, who owned
That half a rood of rock, a no-man's land
Surrounded by our pitchfork-armed claims.
I heard the Duffys shouting 'Damn your soul'
And old McCabe stripped to the waist, seen
Step the plot defying blue cast-steel –
'Here is the march along these iron stones'
That was the year of the Munich bother. Which
Was more important? I inclined
To lose my faith in Ballyrush and Gortin
Till Homer's ghost came whispering to my mind
He said: I made the Iliad from such
A local row. Gods make their own importance.

Discoverers of Chile

From the north Almagro brought his crushed ember.
And over the territory, between explosion and sunset,
he bent, day and night, as over a chart.
Shadow of thorns, shadow of thistle and wax,
the Spaniard meeting with his dry figure,
watching the sombre strategies of the terrain.
Night, snow, and sand make up the form
of my thin country,
all silence lies in its long line,
all foam flows from its marine beard,
all coal covers it with mysterious kisses.
Gold burns in its fingers like an ember
and silver illuminates like a green moon
its thickened shadow of a sullen planet.
The Spaniard seated by the rose one day,
by the olive oil, by the wine, by the antique sky,
did not imagine this point of choleric stone
being born from under the dung of the sea eagle.

translated from the Spanish by Anthony Kerrigan

W. R. RODGERS

Field Day

The old farmer, nearing death, asked
To be carried outside and set down
Where he could see a certain field
'And then I will cry my heart out,' he said.

It troubles me, thinking about that man;
What shape was the field of his crying
In Donegal?

I remember a small field in Down, a field
Within fields, shaped like a triangle.

I could have stood there and looked at it
All day long.

And I remember crossing the frontier between
France and Spain at a forbidden point, and seeing
A small triangular field in Spain,
And stopping

Or walking in Ireland down any rutted by-road
To where it hit the highway, there was always
At this turning-point and abuttment
A still centre, a V-shape of grass
Untouched by cornering traffic,
Where country lads larked at night.

I think I know what the shape of the field was
That made the old man weep.

MIRIAM WADDINGTON

Popular Geography

Miami is one big yellow
pantsuit where the ocean
is louder than the sighs
of old age; Chicago is
a huge hot gun sending
smoke into the sky for
1000 miles to Winnipeg;
New York is a bright sharp
hypodermic needle and the
Metropolitan Opera singing
Wagner on winter afternoons,
and my own Toronto is an
Eaton's charge account adding
to the music in a Henry Moore
skating rink; Montreal was
once an Iroquois city huddled
around a mountain under a cross

and now is the autoroute to
an Olympic dream; everything
has changed, all the cities
are different, but Manitoba
oh Manitoba, you are still
a beautiful green grain
elevator storing the sunlight
and growing out of the black
summer earth.

NORMAN MACCAIG

Summer Farm

Straws like tame lightnings lie about the grass
And hang zigzag on hedges. Green as glass
The water in the horse-trough shines.
Nine ducks go wobbling by in two straight lines.

A hen stares at nothing with one eye,
Then picks it up. Out of an empty sky
A swallow falls and, flickering through
The barn, dives up again into the dizzy blue.

I lie, not thinking, in the cool, soft grass,
Afraid of where a thought might take me – as
This grasshopper with plated face
Unfolds his legs and finds himself in space.

Self under self, a pile of selves I stand
Threaded on time, and with metaphysic hand
Lift the farm like a lid and see
Farm within farm, and in the centre, me.

WALLACE STEVENS

Anecdote of the Jar

I placed a jar in Tennessee,
And round it was, upon a hill.

It made the slovenly wilderness
Surround that hill.

The wilderness rose up to it,
And sprawled around, no longer wild.
The jar was round upon the ground
And tall and of a port in air.

It took dominion everywhere.
The jar was gray and bare.
It did not give of bird or bush,
Like nothing else in Tennessee.

T. S. ELIOT

from Landscapes

CAPE ANN

O quick quick quick, quick hear the song-sparrow,
Swamp-sparrow, fox-sparrow, vesper-sparrow
At dawn and dusk. Follow the dance
Of the goldfinch at noon. Leave to chance
The Blackburnian warbler, the shy one. Hail
With shrill whistle the note of the quail, the bob-white
Dodging by bay-bush. Follow the feet
Of the walker, the water-thrush. Follow the flight
Of the dancing arrow, the purple martin. Greet
In silence the bullbat. All are delectable. Sweet sweet
   sweet
But resign this land at the end, resign it
To its true owner, the tough one, the sea-gull.

The palaver is finished.

Home-thoughts, from Abroad

I

Oh, to be in England
Now that April's there,
And whoever wakes in England
Sees, some morning, unaware,
That the lowest boughs and the brushwood sheaf
Round the elm-tree bole are in tiny leaf,
While the chaffinch sings on the orchard bough
In England – now!

II

And after April, when May follows,
And the whitethroat builds, and all the swallows!
Hark, where my blossomed pear-tree in the hedge
Leans to the field and scatters on the clover
Blossoms and dewdrops – at the bent spray's edge –
That's the wise thrush; he sings each song twice over,
Lest you should think he never could recapture
The first fine careless rapture!
And though the fields look rough with hoary dew,
All will be gay when noontide wakes anew
The buttercups, the little children's dower
– Far brighter than this gaudy melon-flower!

ELIZABETH BARRETT BROWNING

from Aurora Leigh, Book I

Ofter we walked only two
If cousin Romney pleased to walk with me.
We read, or talked, or quarrelled, as it chanced.
We were not lovers, nor even friends well-matched:
Say rather, scholars upon different tracks,
And thinkers disagreed, he, overfull
Of what is, and I, haply, overbold

For what might be.
　　　　　　But then the thrushes sang,
And shook my pulses and the elms' new leaves;
At which I turned, and held my finger up,
And bade him mark that, howsoe'er the world
Went ill, as he related, certainly
The thrushes still sang in it. At the word
His brow wold soften, – and he bore with me
In melancholy patience, not unkind,
While breaking into voluble ecstasy
I flattered all the beauteous country round,
As poets use, the skies, the clouds, the fields.
The happy violets hiding from the roads
The primroses run down to, carrying gold;
The tangled hedgerows, where the cows push out
Impatient horns and tolerant churning mouths
'Twixt dripping ash-boughs, – hedgerows all alive
With birds and gnats and large white butterflies
Which look as if the May-flower had caught life
And palpitated forth upon the wind;
Hills, vales, woods, netted in a silver mist,
Farms, granges, doubled up among the hills;
And cattle grazing in the watered vales,
And cottage-chimneys smoking from the woods,
And cottage-gardens smelling everywhere,
Confused with smell of orchards. 'See,' I said,
'And see! is God not with us on the earth?
And shall we put Him down by aught we do?
Who says there's nothing for the poor and vile
Save poverty and wickedness? behold!'
And ankle-deep in English grass I leaped
And clapped my hands, and called all very fair.

IVOR GURNEY

Cotswold Ways

One comes across the strangest things in walks:
Fragments of Abbey tithe-barns fixed in modern
And Dutch-sort houses where the water baulks
Weired up, and brick kilns broken among fern,
Old troughs, great stone cisterns bishops might have
    blessed
Ceremonially, and worthy mounting-stones;
Black timber in red brick, queerly placed
Where Hill stone was looked for – and a manor's bones
Spied in the frame of some wisteria'd house
And mill-falls and sedge pools and Saxon faces;
Stream-sources happened upon in unlikely places,
And Roman-looking hills of small degree
And the surprise of dignity of poplars
At a road end, or the white Cotswold scars,
Or sheets spread white against the hazel tree.
Strange the large difference of up-Cotswold ways;
Birdlip climbs bold and treeless to a bend,
Portway to dim wood-lengths without end,
And Crickley goes to cliffs are the crown of days.

JOSEPH BRODSKY

from In England

STONE VILLAGES

The stone-built villages of England.
A cathedral bottled in a pub window.
Cows dispersed across the fields.
Monuments to kings.

A man in a moth-eaten suit
sees a train off, heading, like everything here, for the sea,
smiles at his daughter, leaving for the East.
A whistle blows.

And the endless sky over the tiles
grows bluer as swelling birdsong fills.
And the clearer the song is heard,
the smaller the bird.

translated from the Russian by Alan Myers

MICHAEL LONGLEY

Landscape

Here my imagination
Tangles through a turfstack
Like skeins of sheep's wool:
Is a bull's horn silting
With powdery seashells.

I am clothed, unclothed
By racing cloud shadows,
Or else disintegrate
Like a hillside neighbour
Erased by sea mist.

A place of dispersals
Where the wind fractures
Flight-feathers, insect wings
And rips thought to tatters
Like a fuchsia petal.

For seconds, dawn or dusk,
The sun's at an angle
To read inscriptions by:
The splay of the badger
And the otter's skidmarks

Melting into water
Where a minnow flashes:
A mouth drawn to a mouth
Digests the glass between
Me and my reflection.

from On a Raised Beach

I must get into this stone world now.
Ratchel, striae, relationships of tesserae,
    Innumerable shades of grey,
    Innumerable shapes,
And beneath them all a stupendous unity,
Infinite movement visibly defending itself
Against all the assaults of weather and water,
Simultaneously mobilised at full strength
At every point of the universal front,
    Always at the pitch of its powers,
    The foundation and end of all life.
I try them with the old Norn words – hraun
Duss, rønis, queedaruns, kollyarum:
They hvarf from me in all directions
Over the hurdifell – klett, millya, hellya, hellyina bretta,
Hellyina wheeda, hellyina grø, bakka, ayre, –
    and lay my world in kolgref.
This is no heap of broken images.
Let men find the faith that builds mountains
Before they seek the faith that moves them. Men cannot
   hope
To survive the fall of the mountains
Which they will no more see than they saw their rise
Unless they are more concentrated and determined,
Truer to themselves and with more to be true to,
Than these stones, and as inerrable as they are.
Their sole concern is that what can be shaken
Shall be shaken and disappear
And only the unshakable be left.
What hardihood in any man has part or parcel in the
   latter?
It is necessary to make a stand and maintain it forever.

These stones go through Man, straight to God, if there is
    one.
What have they not gone through already?
Empires, civilisations, aeons. Only in them
If in anything, can His creation confront Him.
They came so far out of the water and halted forever.
That larking dallier, the sun, has only been able to play
With superficial by-products since;
The moon moves the waters backwards and forwards,
But the stones cannot be lured an inch farther
Either on this side of eternity or the other.
Who thinks God is easier to know than they are?
Trying to reach men any more, any otherwise, than they
    are?
These stones will reach us long before we reach them.
Cold, undistracted, eternal and sublime.

WALT WHITMAN

This Compost

I

Something startles me where I thought I was safest,
I withdraw from the still woods I loved,
I will not go now on the pastures to walk,
I will not strip the clothes from my body to meet my lover
    the sea,
I will not touch my flesh to the earth as to other flesh to
    renew me.

O how can it be that the ground itself does not sicken?
How can you be alive you growths of spring?
How can you furnish health you blood of herbs, roots,
    orchards, grain?
Are they not continually putting distemper'd corpses
    within you?
Is not every continent work'd over and over with sour
    dead?

Where have you disposed of their carcasses?
Those drunkards and gluttons of so many generations?
Where have you drawn off all the foul liquid and meat?
I do not see any of it upon you to-day, or perhaps I am
    deceiv'd,
I will run a furrow with my plough, I will press my spade
    through the sod and turn it up underneath,
I am sure I shall expose some of the foul meat.

11

Behold this compost! behold it well!
Perhaps every mite has once form'd part of a sick person –
    yet behold!
The grass of spring covers the prairies,
The bean bursts noiselessly through the mould in the
    garden,
The delicate spear of the onion pierces upward,
The apple-buds cluster together on the apple-branches,
The resurrection of the wheat appears with pale visage
    out of its graves,
The tinge awakes over the willow-tree and the mulberry-
    tree,
The he-birds carol mornings and evenings while the she-
    birds sit on their nests,
The young of poultry break through the hatch'd eggs,
The new-born of animals appear, the calf is dropt from the
    cow, the colt from the mare,
Out of its little hill faithfully rise the potato's dark green
    leaves,
Out of its hill rises the yellow maize-stalk, the lilacs bloom
    in the dooryards,
The summer growth is innocent and disdainful above all
    those strata of sour dead.

What chemistry!
That the winds are really not infectious,

That this is no cheat, this transparent green-wash of the
    sea which is so amorous after me,
That it is safe to allow it to lick my naked body all over wi
    its tongues,
That it will not endanger me with the fevers that have
    deposited themselves in it,
That all is clean forever and forever,
That the cool drink from the well tastes so good,
That blackberries are so flavorous and juicy,
That the fruits of the apple-orchard and the
    orange-orchard, that melons, grapes, peaches, plums
    will none of them poison me,
That when I recline on the grass I do not catch any diseas
Though probably every spear of grass rises out of what
    was once a catching disease.

Now I am terrified at the Earth, it is that calm and patien
It grows such sweet things out of such corruptions,
It turns harmless and stainless on its axis, with such
    endless successions of diseas'd corpses,
It distills such exquisite winds out of such infused fetor,
It renews with such unwitting looks its prodigal, annual
    sumptuous crops,
It gives such divine materials to men, and accepts such
    leavings from them at last.

EDWARD THOMAS

Digging

To-day I think
Only with scents, – scents dead leaves yield,
And bracken, and wild carrot's seed,
And the square mustard field;

Odours that rise
When the spade wounds the root of tree,

Rose, currant, raspberry, or goutweed,
Rhubarb or celery;

The smoke's smell, too,
Flowing from where a bonfire burns
The dead, the waste, the dangerous,
And all to sweetness turns.

It is enough
To smell, to crumble the dark earth,
While the robin sings over again
Sad songs of Autumn mirth.

OHN CLARE

from The Moors

Far spread the moory ground a level scene,
Bespread with rush and one eternal green,
That never felt the rage of blundering plough
Though centuries wreathed Spring's blossoms on its
    brow,
Still meeting plains that stretched them far away
In unchecked shadows of green, brown and grey.
Unbounded freedom ruled the wandering scene
Nor fence of ownership crept in between
To hide the prospect of the following eye;
Its only bondage was the circling sky.
One mighty flat undwarfed by bush and tree
Spread its faint shadow of immensity
And lost itself, which seemed to eke its bounds,
In the blue mist the horizon's edge surrounds.
Now this sweet vision of my boyish hours,
Free as Spring clouds and wild as Summer flowers,
Is faded all – a hope that blossomed free
And hath been once no more shall ever be.
Enclosure came and trampled on the grave
Of labour's rights and left the poor a slave;

And memory's pride, ere want to wealth did bow,
Is both the shadow and the substance now.
The sheep and cows were free to range as then
Where change might prompt, nor felt the bonds of men.
Cows went and came with evening, morn and night
To the wild pasture as their common right
And sheep, unfolded with the rising sun,
Heard the swains shout and felt their freedom won,
Tracked the red fallow field and heath and plain,
Then met the brook and drank and roamed again –
The brook that dribbled on as clear as glass
Beneath the roots they hid among the grass –
While the glad shepherd traced their tracks along,
Free as the lark and happy as her song.
But now all's fled and flats of many a dye
That seemed to lengthen with the following eye,
Moors losing from the sight, far, smooth and blea,
Where swopt the plover in its pleasure free,
Are vanished now with commons wild and gay
As poets' visions of life's early day . . .
Each little tyrant with his little sign
Shows, where man claims, earth glows no more divine.
On paths to freedom and to childhood dear
A board sticks up to notice 'no road here'
And on the tree with ivy overhung
The hated sign by vulgar taste is hung
As though the very birds should learn to know
When they go there they must no further go.
Thus, with the poor, scared freedom bade good bye
And much they feel it in the smothered sign,
And birds and trees and flowers without a name
All sighed when lawless law's enclosure came;
And dreams of plunder in such rebel schemes
Have found too truly that they were but dreams.

Men against Trees

I note that the deforestation of Brazil
      is going ahead at a cracking pace.
Valiant feats of giant-toppling! Disgrace
      to the ancient Empire of Chlorophyll!

Nature's strongholds surrender one by one.
      Even here at home, the fight
continues quietly; men roam about at night
      snapping saplings – and not just for fun.

Burger boxes and buckled lager cans
      stuff the guts of older trees.
On more technical missions, auxiliaries
      steal forth in trucks and vans.

I saw one last week on a daylight job:
      reversing under the boughs of an ash,
he tore a limb and left an enormous gash.
      You had to admire the insouciant slob!

STANLEY KUNITZ

The War against the Trees

The man who sold his lawn to Standard Oil
Joked with his neighbours come to watch the show
While the bulldozers, drunk with gasoline,
Tested the virtue of the soil
Under the branchy sky
By overthrowing first the privet-row.

Forsythia-forays and hydrangea-raids
Were but preliminaries to a war
Against the great-grandfathers of the town,
So freshly lopped and maimed.

They struck and struck again,
And with each elm a century went down.

All day the hireling engines charged the trees,
Subverting them by hacking underground
In grub-dominions, where dark summer's mole
Rampages through his halls,
Till a northern seizure shook
Those crowns, forcing the giants to their knees.

I saw the ghosts of children at their games
Racing beyond their childhood in the shade,
And while the green world turned its death-foxed page
And a red wagon wheeled,
I watched them disappear
Into the suburbs of their grievous age.

Ripped from the craters much too big for hearts
The club-roots bared their amputated coils,
Raw gorgons matted blind, whose pocks and scars
Cried Moon! on a corner lot
One witness-moment, caught
In the rear-view mirrors of the passing cars.

THOMAS HARDY

Overlooking the River Stour

The swallows flew in the curves of an eight
    Above the river-gleam
    In the wet June's last beam:
Like little crossbows animate
The swallows flew in the curves of an eight
    Above the river-gleam.

Planing up shavings of crystal spray
    A moor-hen darted out
    From the bank thereabout,

And through the stream-shine ripped his way;
Planing up shavings of crystal spray
    A moor-hen darted out.

Closed were the kingcups; and the mead
    Dripped in monotonous green,
    Though the day's morning sheen
Had shown it golden and honeybee'd;
Closed were the kingcups; and the mead
    Dripped in monotonous green.

And never I turned my head, alack,
    While these things met my gaze
    Through the pane's drop-drenched glaze,
To see the more behind my back . . .
O never I turned, but let, alack,
    These less things hold my gaze!

A. E. HOUSMAN

'Tell me not here . . .'

Tell me not here, it needs not saying,
    What tune the enchantress plays
In aftermaths of soft September
    Or under blanching mays,
For she and I were long acquainted
    And I knew all her ways.

On russet floors, by waters idle,
    The pine lets fall its cone;
The cuckoo shouts all day at nothing
    In leafy dells alone;
And traveller's joy beguiles in autumn
    Hearts that have lost their own.

On acres of the seeded grasses
    The changing burnish heaves;
Or marshalled under moons of harvest

Stand still all night the sheaves;
Or beeches strip in storms for winter
    And stains the wind with leaves.

Possess, as I possessed a season,
    The countries I resign,
Where over elmy plains the highway
    Would mount the hills and shine,
And full of shade the pillared forest
Would murmur and be mine.

For nature, heartless, witless nature,
    Will neither care nor know
What stranger's feet may find the meadow
    And trespass there and go,
Nor ask amid the dews of morning
    If they are mine or no.

WILLIAM CARLOS WILLIAMS

Raleigh Was Right

We cannot go to the country
for the country will bring us
        no peace
What can the small violets tell us
that grow on furry stems in
the long grass among lance shaped
        leaves?

Though you praise us
and call to mind the poets
who sung of our loveliness
it was long ago!
long ago! when country people
would plow and sow with
flowering minds and pockets
        at ease —
if ever this were true.

Not now. Love itself a flower
with roots in a parched ground.
Empty pockets make empty heads.
Cure it if you can but
do not believe that we can live
today in the country
for the country will bring us
     no peace.

R. S. THOMAS

Welsh Landscape

To live in Wales is to be conscious
At dusk of the spilled blood
That went to the making of the wild sky,
Dyeing the immaculate rivers
In all their courses.
It is to be aware,
Above the noisy tractor
And hum of the machine
Of strife in the strung woods,
Vibrant with sped arrows.
You cannot live in the present,
At least not in Wales.
There is the language for instance,
The soft consonants
Strange to the ear.
There are cries in the dark at night
As owls answer the moon,
And thick ambush of shadows,
Hushed at the fields' corners.
There is no present in Wales,
And no future;
There is only the past,
Brittle with relics,
Wind-bitten towers and castles

With sham ghosts;
Mouldering quarries and mines;
And an impotent people,
Sick with inbreeding,
Worrying the carcase of an old song.

GEOFFREY HILL

from An Apology for the Revival of Church Architecture in England

II IDYLLS OF THE KING

The pigeon purrs in the wood; the wood has gone;
dark leaves that flick to silver in the gust,
and the marsh-orchids and the heron's nest,
goldgrimy shafts and pillars of the sun.

Weightless magnificence upholds the past.
Cement recesses smell of fur and bone
and berries wrinkle in the badger-run
and wiry heath-fern scatters its fresh rust.

'O clap your hands' so that the dove takes flight,
bursts through the leaves with an untidy sound,
plunges its wings into the green twilight

above this long-sought and forsaken ground,
the half-built ruins of the new estate,
warheads of mushrooms round the filter-pond.

PAUL CELAN

Draft of a Landscape

Circular graves, below. In
four-beat time the year's pace on
the steep steps around them.

Lavas, basalts, glowing
stone from the world's heart.

Wellspring tuff
where light grew for us, before
our breath.

Oilgreen, soaked with sea spray the
impassable hour. Toward
the centre, grey,
a stone saddle, and on it,
dented and charred,
the animal forehead with
its radiant blaze.

translated from the German by Michael Hamburger

SYLVIA PLATH

Sheep in Fog

The hills step off into whiteness.
People or stars
Regard me sadly, I disappoint them.

The train leaves a line of breath.
O slow
Horse the color of rust,

Hooves, dolorous bells –
All morning the
Morning has been blackening,

A flower left out.
My bones hold a stillness, the far
Fields melt my heart.

They threaten
To let me through to a heaven
Starless and fatherless, a dark water.

Swineherd

'When all this is over,' said the swineherd,
'I mean to retire, where
Nobody will have heard about my special skills
And conversation is mainly about the weather.

I intend to learn how to make coffee, at least as well
As the Portuguese lay-sister in the kitchen
And polish the brass fenders every day.
I want to lie awake at night
Listening to cream crawling to the top of the jug
And the water lying soft in the cistern.

I want to see an orchard where the trees grow in straight
  lines
And the yellow fox finds shelter between the navy-blue
  trunks,
Where it gets dark early in summer
And the apple-blossom is allowed to wither on the bough.'

W. S. GRAHAM

The Stepping Stones

I have my yellow boots on to walk
Across the shires where I hide
Away from my true people and all
I can't put easily into my life.

So you will see I am stepping on
The stones between the runnels getting
Nowhere nowhere. It is almost
Embarrassing to be alive alone.

Take my hand and pull me over from
The last stone on to the moss and

The three celandines. Now my dear
Let us go home across the shires.

RAYMOND CARVER

Late Fragment

And did you get what
you wanted from this life, even so?
I did.
And what did you want?
To call myself beloved, to feel myself
beloved on the earth.

Work

You will be hearing from us shortly

You feel adequate to the demands of this position?
What qualities do you feel you
Personally have to offer?

                                             Ah

Let us consider your application form.
Your qualifications, though impressive, are
Not, we must admit, precisely what
We had in mind. Would you care
To defend their relevance?

                                         Indeed

Now your age. Perhaps you feel able
To make your own comment about that,
Too? We are conscious ourselves
Of the need for a candidate with precisely
The right degree of immaturity.

                                    So glad we agree

And now a delicate matter: your looks.
You do appreciate this work involves
Contact with the actual public? Might they,
Perhaps, find your appearance
Disturbing?

                                       Quite so

And your accent. That is the way
You have always spoken, is it? What
Of your education? Were
You educated? We mean, of course,
Where were you educated?

                                  And how

Much of a handicap is that to you,
Would you say?

           Married, children,
We see. The usual dubious
Desire to perpetuate what had better
Not have happened at all. We do not
Ask what domestic disasters shimmer
Behind that vaguely unsuitable address.

And you were born – ?

                                 Yes. Pity.

So glad we agree.

GEOFFREY LEHMANN

Tools

Man's tools
are the last stronghold
of something ancient.
You can fool the consumer
but not the workman.
He'll make use
of a newer, more powerful tool,
but the brace-and-bit doesn't change.

In department stores
with their wilderness
of veneers, synthetic wood and plastic brass
give me a counter
of hammers with real wood handles
or spirit levels of solid wood and brass –
or my cattle cane,
its handle plaited with hide
hanging on the veranda
among my rifles.

I spray my tree
with a long thin pump of brass
that can reach among the branches,
elegantly,
a design that's not changed for years.

On a hot day
the metal chills your hand
as the spray flows through.

The tools are tenacious.
My spanners will be able to take
the nuts off spacecraft.

ELAINE FEINSTEIN

Father

The wood trade in his hands
at sixtyone back at the sawbench,
my stubborn father sands and planes
birchwood for kitchen chairs.

All my childhood he was a rich man
unguarded purchaser
of salmon trout, off-season strawberries
and spring in Switzerland.

Bully to prudish aunts
whose niggard habits taught them to assess
honest advantage, without rhetoric:
his belly laughter overbore their tutting.

Still boss of his own shop
he labours in the chippings without grudge
loading the heavy tables,
shabby and powerful as an old bus.

A Suffolk Dairy Song

He.   If you with me will go, my love,
     You shall see a pretty show, my love,
       Let dame say what she will;
     And if you will have me, my love,
     I will have thee, my love,
       So let the milk pail stand still.

She. Since you have said so, my love,
     Longer I will go, my love,
       Let dame say what she will;
     If you will have me, my love,
     I will have thee, my love,
       So let the milk pail stand still.

PATRICIA BEER

The Healer

He could have charmed the warts off Cromwell.
I have seen the pure, peeled hands
Of those he cured.

Poor Mary Tudor
With Philip/Calais written on her heart
And her false pregnancies
Would have been more difficult.

He does not have to touch.
One day he simply stood like dawn
On top of a hedge up Kentisbeare
And ringworm faded from a herd of cattle.
I saw this happen.

He says he failed only once,
That was with his wife's migraine.

Thoughts After Ruskin

Women reminded him of lilies and roses.
Me they remind rather of blood and soap,
Armed with a warm rag, assaulting noses,
Ears, neck, mouth and all the secret places:

Armed with a sharp knife, cutting up liver,
Holding hearts to bleed under a running tap,
Gutting and stuffing, pickling and preserving,
Scalding, blanching, broiling, pulverizing,
– All the terrible chemistry of their kitchens.

Their distant husbands lean across mahogany
And delicately manipulate the market,
While safe at home, the tender and the gentle
Are killing tiny mice, dead snap by the neck,
Asphyxiating flies, evicting spiders,
Scrubbing, scouring aloud, disturbing cupboards,
Committing things to dustbins, twisting, wringing,
Wrists red and knuckles white and fingers puckered,
Pulpy, tepid. Steering screaming cleaners
Around the snags of furniture, they straighten
And haul out sheets from under the incontinent
And heavy old, stoop to importunate young,
Tugging, folding, tucking, zipping, buttoning,
Spooning in food, encouraging excretion,
Mopping up vomit, stabbing cloth with needles,
Contorting wool around their knitting needles,
Creating snug and comfy on their needles.

Their huge hands! their everywhere eyes! their voices
Raised to convey across the hullabaloo,
Their massive thighs and breasts dispensing comfort,
Their bloody passages and hairy crannies,
Their wombs that pocket a man upside down!

And when all's over, off with overalls,
Quickly consulting clocks, they go upstairs,
Sit and sigh a little, brushing hair,
And somehow find, in mirrors, colours, odours,
Their essences of lilies and of roses.

MATTHEW MITCHELL

Printing Jenny

Printing Bibles is Jenny's daily chore,
Or rather, stacking wads of India paper
As the press revolves them out galore.

Today it's Genesis and all that caper –
Catch a modern girl listening to snakes! –
Still it's a job and, viewed through the vapour

Of four o'clock tea, has got what it takes,
That is, nice pay, nice hours, no coming the boss.
Only an hour before knock-off, which makes

Three-quarters really, then off to the Cross
To meet Dan with his guitar and scooter,
Who says her lips are sweet as candy-floss.

Jenny's not sure these tight jeans really suit her
But for pillions and jive they're ideal.
Dan's picked up lots of tunes without a tutor.

Silly of him last month to go and steal.
He says he got that passionate in clink!
But, as the mags say, how to know love's real?

There's Rachel, who was told she'd get a mink:
She's had the kid adopted and she's back
On Cost Accounting, but it makes you think.

Jenny chucks the last heap on the binding stack:
Scriptures for those whose faith is on the cool,
For those who burn or twist upon the rack,

For many a bell-resounding mission school,
For best-seller export to the States:
She leaves them with her mug, her only tool,

And hurls her sixteen summers through the gates.

RITA DOVE

The Great Palaces of Versailles

Nothing nastier than a white person!
She mutters as she irons alterations
in the backroom of Charlotte's Dress Shoppe.
The steam rising from a cranberry wool
comes alive with perspiration
and stale Evening of Paris.
Swamp she born from, swamp
she swallow, swamp she got to sink again.

The iron shoves gently
into a gusset, waits until
the puckers bloom away. Beyond
the curtain, the white girls are all
wearing shoulder pads to make their faces
delicate. That laugh would be Autumn,
tossing her hair in imitation of Bacall.

Beulah had read in the library
how French ladies at court would tuck
their fans in a sleeve
and walk in the gardens for air. Swaying
among lilies, lifting shy layers of silk,
they dropped excrement as daintily
as handkerchieves. Against all rules
she had saved the lining from a botched coat
to face last year's gray skirt. She knows
whenever she lifts a knee
she flashes crimson. That seems legitimate;

but in the book she had read
how the *cavaliere* amused themselves
wearing powder and perfume and spraying
yellow borders knee-high on the stucco
of the *Orangerie*.

A hanger clatters
in the front of the shoppe.
Beulah remembers how
even Autumn could lean into a settee
with her ankles crossed, sighing
I need a man who'll protect me
while smoking her cigarette down to the very end.

WILLIAM WORDSWORTH

The Solitary Reaper

Behold her, single in the field,
Yon solitary Highland Lass!
Reaping and singing by herself;
Stop here, or gently pass!
Alone she cuts and binds the grain,
And sings a melancholy strain;
O listen! for the Vale profound
Is overflowing with the sound.

No Nightingale did ever chaunt
More welcome notes to weary bands
Of travellers in some shady haunt,
Among Arabian sands:
A voice so thrilling ne'er was heard
In spring-time from the Cuckoo-bird,
Breaking the silence of the seas
Among the farthest Hebrides.

Will no one tell me what she sings? –
Perhaps the plaintive numbers flow

For old, unhappy, far-off things,
And battles long ago:
Or is it some more humble lay,
Familiar matter of today?
Some natural sorrow, loss, or pain,
That has been, and may be again?

Whate'er the theme, the Maiden sang
As if her song could have no ending;
I saw her singing at her work,
And o'er the sickle bending; –
I listened, motionless and still;
And, as I mounted up the hill,
The music in my heart I bore,
Long after it was heard no more.

JLLY HOLDEN

Photograph of Haymaker, 1890

It is not so much the image of the man
that's moving – he pausing from his work
to whet his scythe, trousers tied
below the knee, white shirt lit by
another summer's sun, another century's –
as the sight of the grasses beyond
his last laid swathe, so living yet
upon the moment previous to death;
for as the man stooping straightened up
and bent again they died before his blade.

Sweet hay and gone some seventy years ago
and yet they stand before me in the sun,
stems damp still where their neighbours' fall
uncovered them, succulent and straight,
immediate with moon-daisies.

GILLIAN CLARKE

Hay-making

You know the hay's in
when gates hang slack
in the lanes. These hot nights
the fallen fields lie open
under the moon's clean sheets.

The homebound road is
sweet with the liquors
of the grasses, air
green with the pastels
of stirred hayfields.

Down at Fron Felen
in the loaded barn
new bales displace
stale darknesses. Breathe.
Remember finding
first kittens, first love
in the scratch of the hay,
our sandals filled with seeds.

HANNAH HOCKEY

Sampler Poem

These lines I here present unto the Sight
Of you, my Friends, to shew how I can work
My M^{rs} unto me hath shewn her skill
And here's the Product of my Hand and Needle

The Needle, an Instrument tho' small
Is of great Use and benefit to all
Trust rather to your Fingers ends
Then to the Promises of Friends.

Hannah Hockey End this Sampler in The
13 year of her Age in the Year of our Lord
1798 Work'd at Mrs Champion's School Shapwick.

RACE NICHOLS

Waterpot

The daily going out
and coming in
always being hurried
along
like like . . . cattle

In the evenings
returning from the fields
she tried hard to walk
like a woman

she tried very hard
pulling herself erect
with every three or four
steps
pulling herself together
holding herself like
royal cane

And the overseer
hurrying them along
in the quickening darkness

And the overseer sneering
them along in the quickening
darkness

sneered at the pathetic –
the pathetic display
of dignity

O but look
there's a waterpot growing
from her head

SUJATA BHATT

Muliebrity

I have thought so much about the girl
who gathered cow-dung in a wide, round basket
along the main road passing by our house
and the Radhavallabh temple in Maninagar.
I have thought so much about the way she
moved her hands and her waist
and the smell of cow-dung and road-dust and wet canna
    lilies,
the smell of monkey breath and freshly washed clothes
and the dust from crows' wings which smells different –
and again the smell of cow-dung as the girl scoops
it up, all these smells surrounding me separately
and simultaneously – I have thought so much
but have been unwilling to use her for a metaphor,
for a nice image – but most of all unwilling
to forget her or to explain to anyone the greatness
and the power glistening through her cheekbones
each time she found a particularly promising
mound of dung –

EDNA ST VINCENT MILLAY

Men Working

Charming, the movement of girls about a May-pole in
    May,
Weaving the coloured ribbons in and out,
Charming; youth is charming, youth is fair.

But beautiful the movement of men striking pikes
Into the end of a black pole, and slowly

Raising it out of the damp grass and up into the air.
The clean strike of the pike into the pole: beautiful.

Joe is the boss; but Ed or Bill will say,
'No, Joe'; we can't get it that way –
We've got to take it from here. Are you okay
On your side, Joe?' 'Yes,' says the boss. 'Okay.'

The clean strike of the pike into the pole – *'That's it!'*
'Ground your pikes!'

The grounded pikes about the rising black pole, beautiful.
'Ed, you'd better get under here with me!' 'I'm
Under!'
'That's it!'
'Ground your pikes!'

Joe says, 'Now, boys, don't heave
Too hard – we've got her – but you, Ed, you and Mike,
You'll have to hold her from underneath while Bill
Shifts his pike – she wants to fall downhill;
We've got her all right, but we've got her on a slight
Slant.'
'That's it!' – 'Mike,
About six feet lower this time.'
'That's it!'

'Ground your pikes!'

One by one the pikes are moved about the pole, more
    beautiful
Than coloured ribbons weaving.

The clean strike of the pike into the pole; each man
Depending on the skill
And the balance, both of body and of mind,
Of each of the others: in the back of each man's mind
The respect for the pole: it is forty feet high, and weighs
Two thousand pounds.

In the front of each man's mind: 'She's going to go
Exactly where we want her to go: this pole
Is going to go into that seven-foot hole we dug
For her
To stand in.'

This was in the deepening dusk of a July night.
They were putting in the poles: bringing the electric ligh

A. B. ('BANJO') PATERSON

Shearing at Castlereagh

The bell is set a-ringing, and the engine gives a toot,
There's five-and-thirty shearers here a-shearing for the
loot,
So stir yourselves, you penners-up, and shove the sheep
along –
The musterers are fetching them a hundred thousand
strong –
And make your collie dogs speak up; what would the
buyers say
In London if the wool was late this year from Castlereagh

The man that 'rung' the Tubbo shed is not the ringer her
That stripling from the Cooma-side can teach him how to
shear.
They trim away the ragged locks, and rip the cutter goes
And leaves a track of snowy fleece from brisket to the nos
It's lovely how they peel it off with never stop nor stay,
They're racing for the ringer's place this year at
Castlereagh.

The man that keeps the cutters sharp is growling in his
cage,
He's always in a hurry; and he's always in a rage –
'You clumsy-fisted mutton-heads, you'd turn a fellow sick
You pass yourselves as shearers, you were born to swing
pick.

Another broken cutter here, that's two you've broke
    today.'
It's lovely how they peel it off with never stop nor stay.

The youngsters picking up the fleece enjoy the merry din,
They throw the classer up the fleece, he throws it to the
    bin;
The pressers standing by the rack are waiting for the wool,
There's room for just a couple more, the press is nearly full;
Now jump upon the lever, lads, and heave and heave
    away,
Another bale of golden fleece is branded 'Castlereagh'.

LEN GINSBERG

The Bricklayer's Lunch Hour

Two bricklayers are setting the walls
of a cellar in a new dug out patch
of dirt behind an old house of wood
with brown gables grown over with ivy
on a shady street in Denver. It is noon
and one of them wanders off. The young
subordinate bricklayer sits idly for
a few minutes after eating a sandwich
and throwing away the paper bag. He
has on dungarees and is bare above
the waist; he has yellow hair and wears
a smudged but still bright red cap
on his head. He sits idly on top
of the wall on a ladder that is leaned
up between his spread thighs, his head
bent down, gazing uninterestedly at
the paper bag on the grass. He draws
his hand across his breast, and then
slowly rubs his knuckles across the
side of his chin, and rocks to and fro

131

on the wall. A small cat walks to him
along the top of the wall. He picks
it up, takes off his cap, and puts it
over the kitten's body for a moment.
Meanwhile it is darkening as if to rain
and the wind on top of the trees in the
street comes through almost harshly.

RUTH PADEL

Builders

I meet them in cycles
    in houses I inhabit, paint,
        and leave. They sit in my dusty futures,
            tired – Colin, Rodney, Steve,

talking of homes they'll build
    for themselves one day.
        They are ruthless of course.
            A danger to marriage, creepers,

bare feet, patience, dogs.
    They gassed the house last week.
        But I like the way they change
            how you see, so casually

and for ever. They speak of resting –
    of sockets, skirting-boards and living-space –
        with assurance and tough hands.
            Then they move on. I find them later
                in an unforeseeable place.

NORMAN CAMERON

Public-House Confidence

Well, since you're from the other side of town,
I'll tell you how I hold a soft job down,

In the designing-rooms and laboratory
I'm dressed in overalls, and so pretend
To be on business from the factory.
The workmen think I'm from the other end.
The in-betweens and smart commission-men
Believe I must have some pull with the boss.
So, playing off the spanner against the pen
I never let the rumour get across
Of how I am no use at all to either
And draw the pay of both for doing neither.

OMAS TRANSTRÖMER

On the Outskirts of Work

In the middle of work
we start longing fiercely for wild greenery,
for the Wilderness itself, penetrated only
by the thin civilisation of the telephone wires.

*

The moon of leisure circles the planet Work
with its mass and weight. – That's how they want it.
When we are on the way home the ground pricks up its
    ears.
The underground listens to us via the grass-blades.

*

Even in this working day there is a private calm.
As in a smoky inland area where a canal flows:
THE BOAT appears unexpectedly in the traffic
or glides out behind the factory, a white vagabond.

*

One Sunday I walk past an unpainted new building
standing before a grey wet surface.

It is half finished. The wood has the same light colour
as the skin on someone bathing.

   *

Outside the lamps the September night is totally dark.
When the eyes adjust, there is faint light
over the ground where large snails glide out
and the mushrooms are as numerous as the stars.

translated from the Swedish by Robin Fulton

MURIEL RUKEYSER

Alloy

This is the most audacious landscape. The gangster's
stance with his gun smoking and out is not so
vicious as this commercial field, its hill of glass.

Sloping as gracefully as thighs, the foothills
narrow to this, clouds over every town
finally indicate the stored destruction.

Crystalline hill: a blinded field of white
murdering snow, seamed by convergent tracks;
the travelling cranes reach for the silica.

And down the track, the overhead conveyor
slides on its cable to the feet of chimneys.
Smoke rises, not white enough, not so barbaric.

Here the severe flame speaks from the brick throat,
electric furnaces produce this precious, this clean,
annealing the crystals, fusing at last alloys.

Hottest for silicon, blast furnaces raise flames,
spill fire, spill steel, quench the new shape to freeze,
tempering it to perfected metal.

Forced through this crucible, a million men.
Above this pasture, the highway passes those
who curse the air, breathing their fear again.

The roaring flowers of the chimney-stacks
less poison, at their lips in fire, than this
dust that is blown from off the field of glass;

blows and will blow, rising over the mills,
crystallized and beyond the fierce corrosion
disintegrated angel on these hills.

ED HUGHES

Dehorning

Bad-tempered bullying bunch, the horned cows
Among the unhorned. Feared, spoilt.
Cantankerous at the hay, at assemblies, at crowded
Yard operations. Knowing their horn-tips' position
To a fraction, every other cow knowing it too.
Like their own tenderness. Horning of bellies, hair-tufting
Of horn-tips. Handy levers. But
Off with the horns.
So there they all are in the yard –
The pick of the bullies, churning each other
Like thick fish in a bucket, churning their mud.
One by one, into the cage of the crush: the needle,
A roar not like a cow – more like a tiger,
Blast of air down a cavern, and long, long
Beginning in pain and ending in terror – then the next.
The needle between the horn and the eye, so deep
Your gut squirms for the eyeball twisting
In its pink-white fastenings of tissue. This side and that.
Then the first one anaesthetized, back in the crush.
The bulldog pincers in the septum, stretched full strength,
The horn levered right over, the chin pulled round
With the pincers, the mouth drooling, the eye

Like a live eye caught in a pan, like the eye of a fish
Imprisoned in air. Then the cheese cutter
Of braided wire, and stainless steel peg handles,
Aligned on the hair-bedded root of the horn, then leanin
Backward full weight, pull-punching backwards,
Left right left right and the blood leaks
Down over the cheekbone, the wire bites
And buzzes, the ammonia horn-burn smokes
And the cow groans, roars shapelessly, hurls
Its half-ton commotion in the tight cage. Our faces
Grimace like faces in the dentist's chair. The horn
Rocks from its roots, the wire pulls through
The last hinge of hair, the horn is heavy and free,
And a water-pistol jet of blood
Rains over the one who holds it – a needle jet
From the white-rasped and bloody skull-crater. Then
    tweezers
Twiddle the artery nozzle, knotting it enough,
And purple antiseptic squirts a cuttlefish cloud over it
Then the other side the same. We collect
A heap of horns. The floor of the crush
Is a trampled puddle of scarlet. The purple-crowned cattle
The bullies, with suddenly no horns to fear,
Start ramming and wrestling. Maybe their heads
Are still anaesthetized. A new order
Among the hornless. The bitchy high-headed
Straight-back brindle, with her Spanish bull trot,
and her head-shaking snorting advance and her crazy
    spirit,
Will have to get maternal. What she's lost
In weapons, she'll have to make up for in tits.
But they've all lost one third of their beauty.

'Mother wept . . .'

Mother wept, and father sighed;
    With delight a-glow
Cried the lad, 'To-morrow,' cried,
    'To the pit I go.'

Up and down the place he sped, –
    Greeted old and young;
Far and wide the tidings spread;
    Clapt his hands and sung.

Came his cronies; some to gaze
    Wrapt in wonder; some
Free with counsel; some with praise;
    Some with envy dumb.

'May he,' many a gossip cried,
    'Be from peril kept;'
Father hid his face and sighed,
    Mother turned and wept.

ALAN GOULD

Demolisher

By six he's started. I wake to a wince and arrh,
the animal protests of my neighbour's iron roof.
Behind a cypress-dark, the February sky

is blue as gin. The house is nineteen twenties;
he moves along its apex removing it,
and at this hour he's higher than the sun,

flexing a torso of cinnamon brown, his singlet
dangling whitely from his belt. Slav
or Italian, perhaps, he applies that rigid serpent,

the pinch-bar, to open unconsidered caches
of darkness. His work is wholly restoration –
he is recovering horizons, and

with the long arm of Archimedes, bringing
sunlight to gulf the spiders' vertical suburbs,
dense as hairballs in their sudden light.

So ridge-cap, gutter, sheet iron are grimaced free
from battens; sheets of fibro drop-shatter,
nails, clenched in the pinch-bar's single knuckle,

come out with a sigh. By lunchtime the house
is a birdcage of timbers; by evening it's gone,
and the man sits, gleaming like resin,

rolling cigarettes, drinking water,
looking through a gap at new hills,
peering down the shaft he's made in sixty years.

WILLIAM BLAKE

The Chimney Sweeper

When my mother died I was very young,
And my father sold me while yet my tongue
Could scarcely cry 'weep 'weep, 'weep 'weep!
so your chimneys I sweep, and in soot I sleep.

There's little Tom Dacre, who cried when his head,
That curled like a lamb's back, was shaved; so I said,
'Hush Tom, never mind it, for when your head's bare,
You know that the soot cannot spoil your white hair.'

And so he was quiet, and that very night,
As Tom was asleeping he had such a sight –
That thousands of sweepers, Dick, Joe, Ned, and Jack,
Were all of them locked up in coffins of black;

And by came an angel, who had a bright key,
And he opened the coffins and set them all free;
Then down a green plain leaping, laughing they run,
And wash in a river and shine in the sun.

Then naked and white, all their bags left behind,
They rise upon clouds and sport in the wind.
And the angel told Tom, if he'd be a good boy,
He'd have God for his father and never want joy.

And so Tom awoke, and we rose in the dark,
And got with our bags and our brushes to work.
Though the morning was cold, Tom was happy and warm;
So if all do their duty, they need not fear harm.

ONY HARRISON

Working

Among stooped getters, grimy, knacker-bare,
head down thrusting a 3 cwt corf
turned your crown bald, your golden hair
chafed fluffy first and then scuffed off,
chick's back, then eggshell, that sunless white.
You strike sparks and plenty but can't see.
You've been underneath too long to stand the light.
You're lost in this sonnet for the bourgeoisie.

Patience Kershaw, bald hurryer, fourteen,
this wordshift and inwit's a load of crap
for dumping on a slagheap, I mean
th'art nobbut summat as wants raking up.

I stare into the fire. Your skinned skull shines.
I close my eyes. That makes a dark like mines.

Wherever hardship held its tongue the job
's breaking the silence of the worked-out-gob.

GERARD MANLEY HOPKINS

Felix Randal

Felix Randal the farrier, O is he dead then? my duty all
  ended,
Who have watched his mould of man, big-boned and
  hardy-handsome
Pining, pining, till time when reason rambled in it and
  some
Fatal four disorders, fleshed there, all contended?

Sickness broke him. Impatient, he cursed at first, but
  mended
Being anointed and all; though a heavenlier heart began
  some

Months earlier, since I had our sweet reprieve and ranson
Tendered to him. Ah well, God rest him all road ever he
  offended!

This seeing the sick endears them to us, us too it endears.
My tongue had taught thee comfort, touch had quenche
  thy tears,
Thy tears that touched my heart, child, Felix, poor Felix
  Randal;

How far from then forethought of, all thy more boisterous
  years,
When thou at the random grim forge, powerful amidst
  peers,
Didst fettle for the great grey drayhorse his bright and
  battering sandal!

SAMUEL TAYLOR COLERIDGE

Work Without Hope

All Nature seems at work. Slugs leave their lair –
The bees are stirring – birds are on the wing –

And Winter slumbering in the open air,
Wears on his smiling face a dream of Spring!
And I the while, the sole unbusy thing,
Nor honey make, nor pair, nor build, nor sing.

Yet well I ken the banks where amaranths blow,
Have traced the fount whence streams of nectar flow.
Bloom, O ye amaranths! bloom for whom ye may,
For me ye bloom not! Glide, rich streams, away!
With lips unbrightened, wreathless brow, I stroll:
And would you learn the spells that drowse my soul?
Work without Hope draws nectar in a sieve,
And Hope without an object cannot live.

ANONYMOUS

'I call upon the Creator . . .'

I call upon the Creator
Give me the vagina of a frog
That I may save my mother from the mortar
That I may save my mother from grinding the grain.
When my guests come home
O, when my guests come home
My mother is in the house
Only grain is boiling.
I wish I were born a girl in the clan Pajing
So that I might save my mother from the mortar
So that I might save my mother from grinding the grain.

Ngok Work Song

CHRISTOPHER LOGUE

'I've worked here all my life'

'I've worked here all my life.
The new machines need fewer hands
so this is my last week.

My job was threading up.
That is to say the sets came down the belt,
as they passed me by
I put a green wire through four yellow beads.

The belt went by for years.
And if I wasn't thinking other things
I used to wonder what its colour was.
The sets were packed so tight you couldn't see.

Last week when it stopped I found out.
It was black.'

BEN JONSON

On Chev'rill the Lawyer

No cause, nor client fat, will CHEV'RILL leese,
    But as they come, on both sides he takes fees,
And pleaseth both. For while he melts his greace
    For this: that winnes, for whom he holds his peace.

D. H. LAWRENCE

Wages

The wages of work is cash.
The wages of cash is want more cash.
The wages of want more cash is vicious competition.
The wages of vicious competition is – the world we live in.

The work-cash-want circle is the viciousest circle
that ever turned men into fiends.

Earning a wage is a prison occupation
and a wage-earner is a sort of gaol-bird.
Earning a salary is a prison overseer's job,
a gaoler instead of a gaol-bird.

Living on your income is strolling grandly outside the
    prison
in terror lest you have to go in. And since the work-prison
    covers
almost every scrap of the living earth, you stroll up and
    down
on a narrow beat, about the same as a prisoner taking his
    exercise.

This is called universal freedom.

C. H. SISSON

Money

I was led into captivity by the bitch business
Not in love but in what seemed a physical necessity
And now I cannot even watch the spring
The itch for subsistence having become responsibility.

Money the she-devil comes to us under many veils
Tactful at first, calling herself beauty
Tear away this disguise, she proposes paternal solicitude
Assuming the dishonest face of duty.

Suddenly you are in bed with a screeching tear-sheet
This is money at last without her night-dress
Clutching you against her fallen udders and sharp bones
In an unscrupulous and deserved embrace.

ANONYMOUS

The Great American Bum

Come all you jolly jokers,
And listen while I hum.
A story I'll relate to you
Of the great American Bum.
From the east, the west, the north, the south,

143

Like a swarm of bees we come,
We sleep in the dirt and wear a shirt
That is dirty and full of crumbs.

Oh, it's early in the morning,
And the dew is off the ground,
The bum arises from his nest
And gazes all around.
From the boxcar and the haystack,
He gazes everywhere,
He never turns back upon his track,
Until he gets a square.

I've beat my way from 'Frisco Bay
To the rockbound coast of Maine,
To Canada and Mexico,
Then wandered back again.
I've met town clowns and harness bulls,
As tough as a cop could be,
And I've been in every calaboose
In this Land of Liberty.

I've topped the spruce and worked the sluice,
And taken a turn at the plow,
I've searched for gold in the rain and cold,
And worked on a river scow,
I've dug the clam and built the dam,
And packed the elusive prune,
But my troubles pale when I hit the trail,
A-paddlin' my own balloon.

Oh a-standin' in the railroad yard,
A-waitin' for a train,
A-waitin' for a westbound freight,
But I think it's all in vain.
Goin' east they loaded,
Goin' west sealed tight.

I think we'll have to get aboard
The fast express to-night.

Oh lady, would you be kind enough
To give me somethin' to eat?
A piece of bread and butter,
And a ten foot slice of meat.
A piece of pie and custard,
To tickle my appetite,
For really I'm so hungry
I don't know where to sleep to-night.

I met a man the other day
I never had met before.
He asked me if I wanted a job
A-shovellin' iron ore.
I asked him what the wages were,
And he said, 'Ten cents a ton.'
I said: 'Old man, go chase yerself,
I'd rather be on the bum.'

Oh, a-sleepin' against the station
Is a trial and tribulation,
But that's our recommendation,
Hurrah, hurree, hurrum,
For we're three bums, three jolly old bums,
Who live like royal Turks,
We have good luck a-bummin' our chuck.
God bless the man that works!

PHILIP LARKIN

Toads

Why should I let the toad *work*
    Squat on my life?
Can't I use my wit as a pitchfork
    And drive the brute off?

Six days of the week it soils
    With its sickening poison –
Just for paying a few bills!
    That's out of proportion.

Lots of folk live on their wits:
    Lecturers, lispers,
Losels, loblolly-men, louts –
    They don't end as paupers;

Lots of folk live up lanes
    With fires in a bucket,
Eat windfalls and tinned sardines –
    They seem to like it.

Their nippers have got bare feet,
    Their unspeakable wives
Are skinny as whippets – and yet
    No one actually *starves*.

Ah, were I courageous enough
    To shout *Stuff your pension!*
But I know, all too well, that's the stuff
    That dreams are made on:

For something sufficiently toad-like
    Squats in me, too;
Its hunkers are heavy as hard luck,
    And cold as snow,

And will never allow me to blarney
    My way to getting
The fame and the girl and the money
    All at one sitting.

I don't say, one bodies the other
    One's spiritual truth;
But I do say it's hard to lose either,
    When you have both.

CAROL RUMENS

Jarrow

Nothing is left to dig, little to make.
Night has engulfed both firelit hall and sparrow.
Wind and car-noise pour across the Slake.
Nothing is left to dig, little to make
A stream of rust where a great ship might grow.
And where a union-man was hung for show
Nothing is left to dig, little to make.
Night has engulfed both firelit hall and sparrow.

STEPHEN KNIGHT

Voyage to the Bottom of the Sea

The trick (he tells me) is to sleep till twelve
    then watch the television.
In the corner of his murky bedroom
    there is always a swirl of colour:

T-shirts; smoke threading from an ashtray
    to the light; shoes; anemones thriving
on the wreck of the Torrey Canyon;
    our Chancellor raising the Budget box.

KATRINA PORTEOUS

Charlie Douglas

'We're gan' tyek hor off, th' morn,'
Said Charlie, squatting in his black-tarred hut;
And the other old fishermen muttered, spat, swore.
So after a thin night, cracked by storm,
I arrived by the harbour kilns at dawn,
Where the sour *Jane Douglas* smoked and heaved,
Rocking her burden of dans and creeves.
And Charlie, a tab in his toothless jaw,

Stared blindly out to Featherblaa',
Tiller in hand. And away she roared,
Her proud bows rising, blue and white,
The same cold colours as the changing light
Bowling over the wind-torn sea.
Now, all the creatures that creep below,
Lobster and nancy, crab and frone,
From many million years ago
Have secret places, and Charlie knows
The banks and hollows of every part.
He's learnt their lineaments by heart
And mapped the landscape beneath the sea.
O, I was the blind man then, not he.
Now Charlie's quiet. His words were few:
'Aah'll tell ye somethin'. Now this is true –
We're finished, hinny. The fishin's deed.
Them greet, muckle traa'lers – it's nowt but greed.
Whae, there's nae bloody chance for the fish t' breed . . .
An' the lobsters! Y' bugger! In wor day
W' hoyed aa' th' berried hens away!'
'And they don't do that now?' 'Darsay noo!'
As he spoke, I watched the steeple grow
Smaller, still smaller, marking where
His folk, for the last three-hundred years,
Were christened and married and laid to rest.
So I urged him to tell me of all the past,
That other, hidden, deep-sea floor;
And whatever I'd cherished in life before –
Home, friends – just then, I loved him more,
This crined old man of eighty-two;
I wanted to trawl him through and through
For all the mysteries he knew
About the sea, about the years.
I wanted to haul his memories free
Like a string of creeves from the troubled sea,
Shining with swad and water-beads.

But turning his fierce, blind gaze on me,
His eyes said, 'Hinny, ye'll nivvor see –
Ye divvin't tell them aa' ye kna
Or aal your stories in a day.'

dans: *marker buoys*; creeves: *crab or lobster pots*; nancy: *squat lobster*;
frone: *starfish*; berried hens: *female lobsters carrying eggs*; swad: *the
green, fringed seaweed that clings to ropes.*

IMON ARMITAGE

CV

Started, textiles, night shift,
no wheels, bussed it,
bus missed, thumbed it,
in my office sunbeam, fluffed it.

Shoe-shine, gofer, caddie,
bellboy, three bags full sir,
busker, juggler, bookie's runner,
move along there.

Sweatshop, mop and bucket,
given brush, shop floor,
slipped up, clocked in
half stoned, shown door.

Backwoodsman number, joiner,
timber, lumber, trouble,
axe fell, sacked for prank
with spirit-level bubble.

Sales rep, basic training,
car, own boss, P.A.,
commission, targets,
stuff that, cards same day.

Grant, small hours, square eyes,
half-arse O.U. student;

painting job, Forth Bridge
but made redundant.

Understudy, back legs panto horse,
put down, not suited;
broke in Doctor Martens
for police force, elbowed, booted.

Big break: trap shut, kickback,
fall guy, front man,
verbal contract, public admin,
quango stunt man,

collar felt, fair cop, threw hands in,
covered tracks up,
mea culpa, coughed, took flak
for every lash-up,

shredded trash, dug out top brass,
ate crap, digested orders,
sat on facts, last post
took rap for P.M.'s body odour;

rested, sick note,
self-certificated heart attack
but fit now, comeback,
job plan, welcome mat,

or out to grass, find door to lay me at.

STEPHEN SPENDER

'Moving through the silent crowd . . .'

Moving through the silent crowd
Who stand behind dull cigarettes,
These men who idle in the road,
I have the sense of falling light.

They lounge at corners of the street
And greet friends with a shrug of shoulder
And turn their empty pockets out,
The cynical gestures of the poor.

Now they've no work, like better men
Who sit at desks and take much pay
They sleep long nights and rise at ten
To watch the hours that drain away.

I'm jealous of the weeping hours
They stare through with such hungry eyes
I'm haunted by these images,
I'm haunted by their emptiness.

. S. THOMAS

Iago Prytherch

Iago Prytherch, forgive my naming you.
You are so far in your small fields
From the world's eye, sharpening your blade
On a cloud's edge, no one will tell you
How I made fun of you, or pitied either
Your long soliloquies, crouched at your slow
And patient surgery under the faint
November rays of the sun's lamp.

Made fun of you? That was their graceless
Accusation, because I took
Your rags for theme, because I showed them
Your thought's bareness; science and art,
The mind's furniture, having no chance
To install themselves, because of the great
Draught of nature sweeping the skull.

Fun? Pity? No word can describe
My true feelings. I passed and saw you
Labouring there, your dark figure

Marring the simple geometry
Of the square fields with its gaunt question.
My poems were made in its long shadow
Falling coldly across the page.

BERTOLT BRECHT

The Peasant's Concern is with His Field

The peasant's concern is with his field
He looks after his cattle, pays taxes
Produces children, to save on labourers, and
Depends on the price of milk.
The townspeople speak of love for the soil
Of healthy peasant stock and
Call peasants the backbone of the nation.

The townspeople speak of love for the soil
Of healthy peasant stock
And call peasants the backbone of the nation.

The peasant's concern is with his field
He looks after his cattle, pays taxes
Produces children, to save on labourers, and
Depends on the price of milk.

translated from the German by Michael Hamburger

BASIL BUNTING

What the Chairman told Tom

Poetry? It's a hobby.
I run model trains.
Mr Shaw there breeds pigeons.

It's not work. You don't sweat.
Nobody pays for it.
You *could* advertise soap.

Art, that's opera; or repertory –
The Desert Song.
Nancy was in the chorus.

But to ask for twelve pounds a week –
married, aren't you? –
you've got a nerve.

How could I look a bus conductor
in the face
if I paid you twelve pounds?

Who says it's poetry, anyhow?
My ten year old
can do it *and* rhyme.

I get three thousand and expenses,
a car, vouchers,
but I'm an accountant.

They do what I tell them,
my company.
What do *you* do?

Nasty little words, nasty long words,
it's unhealthy.
I want to wash when I meet a poet.

They're Reds, addicts,
all delinquents.
What you write is rot.

Mr Hines says so, and he's a schoolteacher,
he ought to know.
Go and find *work*.

BENJAMIN ZEPHANIAH

It's Work

I could hav been a builder
A painter or a swimmer
I dreamt of being a Rasta writer,
I fancied me a farmer
I could never be a barber
Once I was not sure about de future,
Got a sentence an I done it
Still me angry feelings groweth
Now I am jus a different fighter,
I sight de struggle up more clearly
I get younger yearly
An me black heart don't get no lighter.
I will not join de army
I would work wid malt an barley
But here I am checking me roots,
I could work de ital kitchen
But I won't cook dead chicken
An I won't lick nobody's boots,
Yes I could be a beggar
Maybe not a tax collector
But I could be a streetwise snob,
But I'll jus keep reciting de poems dat I am writing
One day I'll hav a proper job.

SAINT COLUMCILLE

'My hand is weary with writing'

My hand is weary with writing,
My sharp quill is not steady,
My slender-beaked pen jets forth
A black draught of shining dark-blue ink.

A stream of wisdom of blessed God
Springs from my fair-brown shapely hand:
On the page it squirts its draught
Of ink of the green-skinned holly.

My little dripping pen travels
Across the plain of shining books,
Without ceasing for the wealth of the great –
Whence my hand is weary with writing.

translated from the Irish by Kuno Meyer

TADEUSZ RÓŻEWICZ

Busy with Many Jobs

Busy with very urgent jobs
I forgot
one also has
to die

irresponsible
I kept neglecting that duty
or performed it
perfunctorily

as from tomorrow
things will be different

I'll start dying meticulously
wisely optimistically
without wasting time

translated from the Polish by Adam Czerniawski

Love

Still-life

Through the open French window the warm sun
lights up the polished breakfast table, laid
round a bowl of crimson roses, for one –
a service of Worcester porcelain, arrayed
near it a melon, peaches, figs, small hot
rolls in a napkin, fairy rack of toast,
butter in ice, high silver coffee-pot,
and, heaped on a silver salver, the morning's post.

She comes over the lawn, the young heiress,
from her early walk in her garden-wood,
feeling that life's a table set to bless
her delicate desires with all that's good,
that even the unopened future lies
like a love-letter, full of sweet surprise.

W. H. AUDEN

'May with its light behaving'

May with its light behaving
Stirs vessel, eye, and limb;
The singular and sad
Are willing to recover,
And to the swan-delighting river
The careless picnics come,
The living white and red.

The dead remote and hooded
In their enclosures rest; but we
From the vague woods have broken,
Forests where children meet
And the white angel-vampires flit;
We stand with shaded eye,
The dangerous apple taken.

The real world lies before us;
Animal motions of the young,
The common wish for death,
The pleasured and the haunted;
The dying master sinks tormented
In the admirers' ring,
The unjust walk the earth.

And love that makes impatient
The tortoise and the roe, and lays
The blonde beside the dark,
Urges upon our blood,
Before the evil and the good
How insufficient is
The endearment and the look.

JOHN CROWE RANSOM

Piazza Piece

– I am a gentleman in a dustcoat trying
To make you hear. Your ears are soft and small
And listen to an old man not at all,
They want the young men's whispering and sighing.
But see the roses on your trellis dying
And hear the spectral singing of the moon;
For I must have my lovely lady soon,
I am a gentleman in a dustcoat trying.

– I am a lady young in beauty waiting
Until my truelove comes, and then we kiss.
But what grey man among the vines is this
Whose words are dry and faint as in a dream?
Back from my trellis, Sir, before I scream!
I am a lady young in beauty waiting.

To Mistress Margaret Hussey

Merry Margaret,
   As midsummer flower,
Gentle as falcon
   Or hawk of the tower:
With solace and gladness,
Much mirth and no madness,
All good and no badness;
   So joyously,
   So maidenly,
   So womanly.

   Her demeaning
   In every thing,
   Far, far passing
   That I can indite,
   Or suffice to write
Of Merry Margaret
   As midsummer flower,
Gentle as falcon
   Or hawk of the tower
   And patient and still
   And as full of good will
   As fair Isaphill,
   Coliander
   Sweet pomander,
   Good Cassander,
   Steadfast of thought,
Well made, well wrought,
   Far may be sought
   Ere that he can find
   So courteous, so kind
As Merry Margaret,
   This midsummer flower

Gentle as falcon
　　Or hawk of the tower.

ANONYMOUS

Passing By

There is a Lady sweet and kind,
Was never face so pleased my mind;
I did but see her passing by,
And yet I love her till I die.

Her gesture, motion, and her smiles,
Her wit, her voice my heart beguiles,
Beguiles my heart, I know not why,
And yet I love her till I die.

Cupid is wingèd and doth range,
Her country so my love doth change:
But change she earth, or change she sky,
Yet will I love her till I die.

WENDY COPE

The Uncertainty of the Poet

*'The Tate Gallery yesterday announced that it had paid £1 million
for a Giorgio de Chirico masterpiece, The Uncertainty of the Poet.
It depicts a torso and a bunch of bananas.'*
Guardian, 2 April 1985

I am a poet.
I am very fond of bananas.

I am bananas.
I am very fond of a poet.

I am a poet of bananas.
I am very fond,

A fond poet of 'I am, I am' –
Very bananas,

Fond of 'Am I bananas,
Am I?' – a very poet.

Bananas of a poet!
Am I fond? Am I very?

Poet bananas! I am.
I am fond of a 'very'.

I am of very fond bananas.
Am I a poet?

ANDREW MARVELL

To His Coy Mistress

Had we but world enough, and time,
This coyness, Lady, were no crime.
We would sit down, and think which way
To walk, and pass our long love's day.
Thou by the Indian Ganges' side
Shouldst rubies find: I by the tide
Of Humber would complain. I would
Love you ten years before the flood:
And you should, if you please, refuse
Till the conversion of the Jews.
My vegetable love should grow
Vaster than empires, and more slow.
An hundred years should go to praise
Thine eyes, and on thy forehead gaze.
Two hundred to adore each breast:
But thirty thousand to the rest.
An age at least to every part,
And the last age should show your heart:
For, Lady, you deserve this state;
Nor would I love at lower rate.

But at my back I always hear
Time's wingèd chariot hurrying near:
And yonder all before us lie
Deserts of vast eternity.
Thy beauty shall no more be found;
Nor, in thy marble vault, shall sound
My echoing song: then worms shall try
That long-preserved virginity:
And your quaint honour turn to dust;
And into ashes all my lust.
The grave's a fine and private place,
But none, I think, do there embrace.
    Now, therefore, while the youthful glue
Sits on thy skin like morning dew,
And while thy willing soul transpires
At every pore with instant fires,
Now let us sport us while we may;
And now, like amorous birds of prey,
Rather at once our time devour,
Than languish in his slow-chapped power.
Let us roll all our strength, and all
Our sweetness, up into one ball:
And tear our pleasures with rough strife,
Thorough the iron grates of life.
Thus, though we cannot make our sun
Stand still, yet we will make him run.

KATHERINE PHILIPS

Friendship's Mystery: To My Dearest Lucasia

Come, my *Lucasia*, since we see
    That Miracles Men's faith do move,
By wonder and by prodigy
    To the dull angry world let's prove
    There's a Religion in our Love.

For though we were design'd t'agree,
    That Fate no liberty destroyes,
But our Election is as free
    As Angels, who with greedy choice
    Are yet determin'd to their joyes.

Our hearts are doubled by the loss,
    Here Mixture is Addition grown;
We both diffuse, we both ingross:
    And we whose minds are so much one,
    Never, yet ever are alone.

We court our own Captivity
    Than Thrones more great and innocent:
'Twere banishment to be set free,
    Since we wear fetters whose intent
    Not Bondage is, but Ornament.

Divided joyes are tedious found,
    And griefs united easier grow:
We are ourselves but by rebound,
    And all our Titles shuffled so,
    Both Princes, and both Subjects too.

Our Hearts are mutual Victims laid,
    While they (such power in Friendship lies)
Are Altars, Priests, and off'rings made:
    And each Heart which thus kindly dies,
    Grows deathless by the Sacrifice.

PAUL CELAN

Corona

Autumn eats its leaf out of my hand: we are friends.
From the nuts we shell time and we teach it to walk:
then time returns to the shell.

In the mirror it's Sunday,
in dream there is room for sleeping,
our mouths speak the truth.

My eye moves down to the sex of my loved one:
we look at each other,
we exchange dark words,
we love each other like poppy and recollection,
we sleep like wine in the conches,
like the sea in the moon's blood ray.

We stand by the window embracing, and people look up
    from the street:
it is time they knew!
It is time the stone made an effort to flower,
time unrest had a beating heart.
It is time it were time.

It is time.

translated from the German by Michael Hamburger

MARILYN HACKER

'O little one, this longing is the pits'

O little one, this longing is the pits.
I'm horny as a timber wolf in heat.
Three times a night, a tangle up the sheet.
I seem to flirt with everything with tits:
Karyn at lunch, who knows I think she's cute;
my ex, the D.A. on the Sex Crimes Squad;
Iva's gnarled, canny New England god-
mother, who was my Saturday night date.
I'm trying to take things one at a time:
situps at bedtime, less coffee, less meat,
more showers, till a remedy appears.
Since there's already quite enough Sex Crime,

I think I ought to be kept off the street.
What are you doing for the next five years?

GEOFFREY CHAUCER

from Troilus and Criseyde, Book II, lines 624–679

This Troilus sat on his baye steede,
Al armed, save his hed, full richely;
And wownded was his hors, and gan to blede,
On which he rood a pas ful softely.
But swich a knyghtly sighte, trewely,
As was on hym, was nought, withouten faille,
To loke on Mars, that god is of bataille.

So lik a man of armes and a knyght
He was to seen, fulfilled of heigh prowesse;
For bothe he hadde a body and a myght
To don that thing, as wel as hardynesse;
And ek to seen hym in his gere hym dresse,
So fressh, so yong, so weldy semed he,
It was an heven upon hym for to see.

His helm tohewen was in twenty places,
That by a tyssew heng his bak byhynde;
His sheeld todasshed was with swerdes and maces,
In which men myght many an arwe fynde
That thirled hadde horn and nerf and rynde;
And ay the peple cryde, 'Here cometh oure joye,
And, next his brother, holder up of Troye!'

For which he wex a litel reed for shame,
Whan he the peple upon hym herde cryen,
That to byholde it was a noble game,
How sobrelich he caste down his yën.
Criseÿda gan al his chere aspien,
And leet it so softe in hire herte synke,
That to hireself she seyde, 'Who yaf me drynke?'

167

For of hire owen thought she wex al reed,
Remembryng hire right thus, 'Lo, this is he
Which that myn uncle swerith he moot be deed,
But I on hym have mercy and pitee.'
And with that thought, for pure ashamed, she
Gan in hire hed to pulle, and that as faste,
Whil he and alle the peple forby paste;

And gan to caste and rollen up and down
Withinne hire thought his excellent prowesse,
And his estat, and also his renown,
His wit, his shap, and ek his gentilesse;
But moost hir favour was, for his distresse
Was al for hire, and thoughte it was a routhe
To sleen swich oon, if that he mente trouthe.

Now myghte som envious jangle thus:
'This was a sodeyn love; how myght it be
That she so lightly loved Troilus,
Right for the firste syghte, ye, parde?'
Now whoso seith so, mote he nevere ythe!
For every thyng, a gynnyng hath it nede
Er al be wrought, withowten any drede.

For I sey nought that she so sodeynly
Yaf hym hire love, but that she gan enclyne
To like hym first, and I have told yow whi;
And after that, his manhod and his pyne
Made love withinne hire herte for to myne;
For which, by proces and by good servyse,
He gat hire love, and in no sodeyn wyse.

weldy: *active*; thirled: *pierced*; nerf: *sinew*; pyne: *torment, suffering*

from The Dream Songs

Filling her compact & delicious body
with chicken páprika, she glanced at me
twice.
Fainting with interest, I hungered back
and only the fact of her husband & four other people
kept me from springing on her

or falling at her little feet and crying
'You are the hottest one for years of night
Henry's dazed eyes
have enjoyed, Brilliance.' I advanced upon
(despairing) my spumoni. – Sir Bones: is stuffed,
de world, wif feeding girls.

– Black hair, complexion Latin, jewelled eyes
downcast . . . The slob beside her feasts . . . What wonders
    is
she sitting on, over there?
The restaurant buzzes. She might as well be on Mars.
Where did it all go wrong? There ought to be a law against
    Henry.
– Mr Bones: there is.

ANONYMOUS

The Foggy Dew

When I was a batchelor early and young,
    I followed the weaving trade,
And all the harm ever I done,
    Was courting a servant maid.
I courted her the summer season,
    And part of the winter too,
And many a night I rolled her in my arms,
    All over the Foggy dew.

One night as I lay on my bed,
    As I laid fast asleep,
There came a pretty fair maid,
    And most bitterly did weep.
She wept she mourned she tore her hair,
    Crying, alas what shall I do,
This night I'm resolved to come to bed with you
    For fear of the Foggy dew.

It was in the first part of the night,
    We both did sport and play,
And in the latter part of the night,
    She slept in my arms till day.
When broad day-light did appear,
    She cried I am undone,
Hold your tongue you foolish girl,
    The Foggy dew is gone.

Suppose that we should have a child,
    It would cause us to smile,
Suppose that we should have another
    It would make us laugh awhile.
Suppose that we should have another,
    And another one too,
Would make you leave off your foolish tricks
    And think no more of the Foggy dew.

I love this young girl dearly,
    I loved her as my life,
Took this girl and married her,
    And made her my lawful wife.
Never told her of her faults,
    Nor never intend to do,
But every time she winks or smiles,
    She thinks of the Foggy dew.

Making Love

You wake up, and you do not know
where you are, or who you are
or what you are, the last light of the evening
coming up to the panes, not coming in,
the solid, slanted body of the desk
between the windows, its bird's-eye slightly
shining, here and there, in the wood. And you
try to think back, you cannot remember it,
it stands behind your mind, like a mountain,
at night, behind you, your pants are torn
or across the room or still dangling from one leg
like a heavy scarlet loop of the body, your
bra is half on or not on or you were naked to begin with,
you cannot remember, everything is changed.
Tomorrow, maybe, taking a child to school,
your foot in the air half off the curb you'll
see his mouth where it was and feel it and the
large double star of your two bodies,
but for now you are like the one in the crib,
you are everyone, right now,
the milky, greenish windows still as
sentinels, saying, *Don't worry,*
you will not remember, you will never know.

from The Eve of St Agnes

Then by the bed-side, where the faded moon
Made a dim, silver twilight, soft he set
A table, and, half anguish'd, threw thereon
A cloth of woven crimson, gold, and jet: –
O for some drowsy Morphean amulet!
The boisterous, midnight, festive clarion,

The kettle-drum, and far-heard clarionet,
  Affray his ears, though but in dying tone: –
The hall door shuts again, and all the noise is gone.

  And still she slept an azure-lidded sleep,
    In blanched linen, smooth, and lavender'd,
  While he from forth the closet brought a heap
    Of candied apple, quince, and plum, and gourd;
  With jellies soother than the creamy curd,
    And lucent syrops, tinct with cinnamon;
  Manna and dates, in argosy transferr'd
    From Fez; and spiced dainties, every one,
From silken Samarcand to cedar'd Lebanon.

  These delicates he heap'd with glowing hand
    On golden dishes and in baskets bright
  Of wreathed silver: sumptuous they stand
    In the retired quiet of the night,
  Filling the chilly room with perfume light. –
    'And now, my love, my seraph fair, awake!
  Thou art my heaven, and I thine eremite:
    Open thine eyes, for meek St Agnes' sake,
Or I shall drowse beside thee, so my soul doth ache.'

  Thus whispering, his warm, unnerved arm
    Sank in her pillow. Shaded was her dream
  By the dusk curtains: – 'twas a midnight charm
    Impossible to melt as iced stream:
  The lustrous salvers in the moonlight gleam;
    Broad golden fringe upon the carpet lies:
  It seem'd he never, never could redeem
    From such a stedfast spell his lady's eyes;
So mus'd awhile, entoil'd in woofed phantasies.

  Awakening up, he took her hollow lute, –
    Tumultuous, – and, in chords that tenderest be,
  He play'd an ancient ditty, long since mute,
    In Provence call'd 'La belle dame sans mercy':

Close to her ear touching the melody: –
Wherewith disturb'd, she utter'd a soft moan:
He ceased – she panted quick – and suddenly
Her blue affrayed eyes wide open shone:
Upon his knees he sank, pale as smooth-sculptured stone.

Her eyes were open, but she still beheld,
Now wide awake, the vision of her sleep:
There was a painful change, that nigh expell'd
The blisses of her dream so pure and deep
At which fair Madeline began to weep,
And moan forth witless words with many a sigh;
While still her gaze on Porphyro would keep;
Who knelt, with joined hands and piteous eye,
Fearing to move or speak, she look'd so dreamingly.

'Ah, Porphyro!' said she, 'but even now
Thy voice was at sweet tremble in mine ear,
Made tuneable with every sweetest vow;
And those sad eyes were spiritual and clear:
How chang'd thou art! how pallid, chill, and drear!
Give me that voice again, my Porphyro,
Those looks immortal, those complainings dear!
Oh leave me not in this eternal woe,
For if thou diest, my Love, I know not where to go.'

Beyond a mortal man impassion'd far
At these voluptuous accents, he arose,
Ethereal, flush'd, and like a throbbing star
Seen mid the sapphire heaven's deep repose;
Into her dream he melted, as the rose
Blendeth its odour with the violet, –
Solution sweet: meantime the frost-wind blows
Like Love's alarum pattering the sharp sleet
Against the window-panes; St Agnes' moon hath set.

Intimacy

Since I have seen you do those intimate things
that other men but dream of; lull asleep
the sinister dark forest of your hair
and tie the bows that stir on your calm breast
faintly as leaves that shudder in their sleep;
since I have seen your stocking swallow up,
a swift black wind, the flame of your pale foot,
and deemed your slender limbs so meshed in silk
sweet mermaid sisters drowned in their dark hair;
I have not troubled overmuch with food,
and wine has seemed like water from a well;
pavements are built of fire, grass of thin flames;
all other girls grow dull as painted flowers,
or flutter harmlessly like coloured flies
whose wings are tangled in the net of leaves
spread by frail trees that grow behind the eyes.

Muse

When I kiss you in all the folding places
of your body, you make that noise like a dog
dreaming, dreaming of the long run he makes
in answer to some jolt to his hormones,
running across landfills, running, running
by tips and shorelines from the scent of too much,
but still going with head up and snout
in the air because he loves it all
and has to get away. I have to kiss deeper
and more slowly – your neck, your inner arm,
the neat creases under your toes, the shadow
behind your knee, the white angles of your groin –

until you fall quiet because only then
can I get the damned words to come into my mouth.

CHRISTOPHER MARLOWE

from Hero and Leander

With that he stripped him to the ivory skin,
And crying, 'Love, I come,' leapt lively in.
Whereat the sapphire-visaged god grew proud,
And made his capering Triton sound aloud,
Imagining that Ganymede, displeased,
Had left the heavens; therefore on him he seized.
Leander strived, the waves about him wound,
And pulled him to the bottom, where the ground
Was strewed with pearl, and in low coral groves
Sweet singing mermaids sported with their loves
On heaps of heavy gold, and took great pleasure
To spurn in careless sort the shipwrack treasure.
For here the stately azure palace stood
Where kingly Neptune and his train abode.
The lusty god embraced him, called him love,
And swore he never should return to Jove.
But when he knew it was not Ganymede,
For under water he was almost dead,
He heaved him up, and looking on his face,
Beat down the bold waves with his triple mace,
Which mounted up, intending to have kissed him,
And fell in drops like tears because they missed him.
Leander being up, began to swim,
And, looking back, saw Neptune follow him;
Whereat aghast, the poor soul 'gan to cry,
'O let me visit Hero ere I die.'
The god put Helle's bracelet on his arm,
And swore the sea should never do him harm.
He clapped his plump cheeks, with his tresses played,
And smiling wantonly, his love betrayed.

He watched his arms, and as they opened wide
At every stroke, betwixt them would he slide
And steal a kiss, and then run out and dance,
And as he turned, cast many a lustful glance,
And threw him gaudy toys to please his eye,
And dive into the water, and there pry
Upon his breast, his thighs, and every limb,
And up again, and close beside him swim,
And talk of love. Leander made reply,
'You are deceived, I am no woman, I.'

ANNA WICKHAM

The Fired Pot

In our town, people live in rows.
The only irregular thing in the street is the steeple;
And where that points to, God only knows,
And not the poor disciplined people!

And I have watched the women growing old,
Passionate about pins, and pence, and soap,
Till the heart within my wedded breast grew cold,
And I lost hope.

But a young soldier came to our town,
He spoke his mind most candidly.
He asked me quickly to lie down,
And that was very good for me.

For though I gave him no embrace –
Remembering my duty –
He altered the expression of my face,
And gave me back my beauty.

Meeting Point

Time was away and somewhere else,
There were two glasses and two chairs
And two people with the one pulse
(Somebody stopped the moving stairs):
Time was away and somewhere else.

And they were neither up nor down;
The stream's music did not stop
Flowing through heather, limpid brown,
Although they sat in a coffee shop
And they were neither up nor down.

The bell was silent in the air
Holding its inverted poise –
Between the clang and clang a flower,
A brazen calyx of no noise:
The bell was silent in the air.

The camels crossed the miles of sand
That stretched around the cups and plates;
The desert was their own, they planned
To portion out the stars and dates:
The camels crossed the miles of sand.

Time was away and somewhere else.
The waiter did not come, the clock
Forgot them and the radio waltz
Came out like water from a rock:
Time was away and somewhere else.

Her fingers flicked away the ash
That bloomed again in tropic trees:
Not caring if the markets crash
When they had forests such as these,
Her fingers flicked away the ash.

God or whatever means the Good
Be praised that time can stop like this,
That what the heart has understood
Can verify in the body's peace
God or whatever means the Good.

Time was away and she was here
And life no longer what it was,
The bell was silent in the air
And all the room one glow because
Time was away and she was here.

ROBERT HERRICK

Upon Julia's Clothes

Whenas in silks my Julia goes,
Then, then, methinks, how sweetly flows
That liquefaction of her clothes!

Next, when I cast mine eyes and see
That brave vibration each way free,
– O how that glittering taketh me!

ROBERT BROWNING

Meeting at Night

I

The grey sea and the long black land;
And the yellow half-moon large and low;
And the startled little waves that leap
In fiery ringlets from their sleep,
As I gain the cove with pushing prow,
And quench its speed i' the slushy sand.

II

Then a mile of warm sea-scented beach;
Three fields to cross till a farm appears;

A tap at the pane, the quick sharp scratch
And blue spurt of a lighted match,
And a voice less loud, thro' its joys and fears,
Than the two hearts beating each to each!

CRISTINA ROSSETTI

A Birthday

My heart is like a singing bird
   Whose nest is in a watered shoot:
My heart is like an apple-tree
   Whose boughs are bent with thickset fruit;
My heart is like a rainbow shell
   That paddles in a halcyon sea;
My heart is gladder than all these
   Because my love is come to me.

Raise me a dais of silk and down;
   Hang it with vair and purple dyes;
Carve it in doves and pomegranates,
   And peacocks with a hundred eyes;
   Work it in gold and silver grapes,
     In leaves and silver fleurs-de-lys;
   Because the birthday of my life
     Is come, my love is come to me.

STEVIE SMITH

I Remember

It was my bridal night I remember,
An old man of seventy-three
I lay with my young bride in my arms,
A girl with t.b.
It was wartime, and overhead
The Germans were making a particularly heavy raid on
   Hampstead.

What rendered the confusion worse, perversely
Our bombers had chosen that moment to set out for
   Germany.
Harry, do they ever collide?
I do not think it has ever happened,
Oh my bride, my bride.

WILLIAM EMPSON

Aubade

Hours before dawn we were woken by the quake.
My house was on a cliff. The thing could take
Bookloads off shelves, break bottles in a row.
Then the long pause and then the bigger shake.
It seemed the best thing to be up and go.

And far too large for my feet to step by.
I hoped that various buildings were brought low.
The heart of standing is you cannot fly.

It seemed quite safe till she got up and dressed.
The guarded tourist makes the guide the test.
Then I said The Garden? Laughing she said No.
Taxi for her and for me healthy rest.
It seemed the best thing to be up and go.

The language problem but you have to try.
Some solid ground for lying could she show?
The heart of standing is you cannot fly.

None of these deaths were her point at all.
The thing was that being woken he would bawl
And finding her not in earshot he would know.
I tried saying Half an Hour to pay this call.
It seemed the best thing to be up and go.

I slept, and blank as that I would yet lie.
Till you have seen what a threat holds below,
The heart of standing is you cannot fly.

Tell me again about Europe and her pains,
Who's tortured by the drought, who by the rains.
Glut me with floods where only the swine can row
Who cuts his throat and let him count his gains.
It seemed the best thing to be up and go.

A bedshift flight to a Far Eastern sky.
Only the same war on a stronger toe.
The heart of standing is you cannot fly.

Tell me more quickly what I lost by this,
Or tell me with less drama what they miss
Who call no die a god for a good throw,
Who says after two aliens had one kiss
It seemed the best thing to be up and go.

But as to risings, I can tell you why.
It is on contradiction that they grow.
It seemed the best thing to be up and go.
Up was the heartening and the strong reply.
The heart of standing is we cannot fly.

ASKO POPA

The Love of the Quartz Pebble

He fell for a beautiful
A rounded blue-eyed
A frivolous endlessness

He is quite transformed
Into the white of her eye

Only she understands him
Only her embrace has
The shape of his desire
Dumb and boundless

All her shadows
He has captured in himself

He is blind in his love
And he sees
No other beauty
But her he loves
Who will cost him his head

translated from the Serbo-Croat by Anna Pennington

CHARLOTTE MEW

The Farmer's Bride

Three Summers since I chose a maid,
   Too young maybe – but more's to do
At harvest-time than bide and woo.
   When us was wed she turned afraid
Of love and me and all things human;
Like the shut of a winter's day
Her smile went out, and 'twadn't a woman –
   More like a little frightened fay.
      One night, in the Fall, she runned away.

'Out 'mong the sheep, her be,' they said,
'Should properly have been abed;
But sure enough she wadn't there
Lying awake with her wide brown stare.
So over seven-acre field and up-along across the down
We chased her, flying like a hare
Before our lanterns. To Church-Town
   All in a shiver and a scare
We caught her, fetched her home at last
   And turned the key upon her, fast.

She does the work about the house
As well as most, but like a mouse:
   Happy enough to chat and play
   With birds and rabbits and such as they,
   So long as men-folk keep away.

'Not near, not near!' her eyes beseech
When one of us comes within reach.
   The women say that beasts in stall
   Look round like children at her call.
   I've hardly heard her speak at all.
   Shy as a leveret, swift as he,
   Straight and slight as a young larch tree,
   Sweet as the first wild violets, she,
   To her wild self. But what to me?

The short days shorten and the oaks are brown,
   The blue smoke rises to the low grey sky,
One leaf in the still air falls slowly down,
   A magpie's spotted feathers lie
On the black earth spread white with rime,
The berries redden up to Christmas-time.
   What's Christmas-time without there be
   Some other in the house than we!

   She sleeps up in the attic there
   Alone, poor maid. 'Tis but a stair
Betwixt us. Oh! my God! the down,
The soft young down of her, the brown,
The brown of her – her eyes, her hair, her hair!

SIR WALTER SCOTT

'Proud Maisie . . .'

Proud Maisie is in the wood,
   Walking so early;
Sweet Robin sits on the bush,
   Singing so rarely.

'Tell me, thou bonny bird,
   When shall I marry me?'
– 'When six braw gentlemen
   Kirkward shall carry ye.'

'Who makes the bridal bed,
    Birdie say truly?'
– 'The gray-headed sexton
    That delves the grave duly.

'The glowworm o'er grave and stone
    Shall light thee steady;
The owl from the steeple sing
    Welcome, proud lady.'

NINA CASSIAN

Face to Face

I waited for this moment when, face to face
we are traveling toward a destination which separates us
face to face, with our features violently reciprocated,
with our hands exhausted by blood,
not daring to kiss, with our clothes not daring to turn red
with our mouths deserted by that word
that brings day and night into the world.
So, here we are, face to face, becoming more and more
    estranged,
alienating ourselves with our whole capacity of
    misunderstanding,
in a true species' adversity – so that,
when the train jerks us into each other's arms
we have the revelation of death
as, probably the mammoths had
when they leapt into the next era.

translated from the Romanian by Brenda Walker and
Andrea Deletant

To My Dear and Loving Husband

If ever two were one, then surely we,
If ever man were lov'd by wife, then thee;
If ever wife was happy in a man,
Compare with me ye women if you can.
I prize thy love more than whole mines of gold,
Or all the riches that the East doth hold.
My love is such that rivers cannot quench,
Nor aught but love from thee, give recompense.
Thy love is such I can no way repay,
The heavens reward thee manifold, I pray.
Then while we live, in love let's so persevere
That, when we live no more, we may live ever.

A Lyric Afterwards

There was a taut dryness all that summer
and you sat each day in the hot garden
until those uniformed comedians
filled the street with their big white ambulance,
fetching you and bringing you back to me.

Far from the sea of ourselves we waited
and prayed for the tight blue silence to give.
In your absence I climbed to a square room
where there were dried flowers, folders of sonnets
and crossword puzzles: call them musical

snuffboxes or mannered anachronisms,
they were all too uselessly intricate,
caskets of the dead spirit. Their bitter
constraints and formal pleasures were a style
of being perfect in despair; they spoke

with the vicious trapped crying of a wren.
But that is changed now, and when I see you
walking by the river, a step from me,
there is this great kindness everywhere:
now in the grace of the world and always.

ELIZABETH BISHOP

The Shampoo

The still explosions on the rocks,
the lichens, grow
by spreading, gray, concentric shocks.
They have arranged
to meet the rings around the moon, although
within our memories they have not changed.

And since the heavens will attend
as long on us,
you've been, dear friend,
precipitate and pragmatical;
and look what happens. For Time is
nothing if not amenable.

The shooting stars in your black hair
in bright formation
are flocking where,
so straight, so soon?
– Come, let me wash it in this big tin basin,
battered and shiny like the moon.

SEAMUS HEANEY

The Skunk

Up, black, striped and damasked like the chasuble
At a funeral Mass, the skunk's tail
Paraded the skunk. Night after night
I expected her like a visitor.

The refrigerator whinnied into silence.
My desk light softened beyond the verandah.
Small oranges loomed in the orange tree.
I began to be tense as a voyeur.

After eleven years I was composing
Love-letters again, broaching the word 'wife'
Like a stored cask, as if its slender vowel
Had mutated into the night earth and air

Of California. The beautiful, useless
Tang of eucalyptus spelt your absence.
The aftermath of a mouthful of wine
Was like inhaling you off a cold pillow.

And there she was, the intent and glamorous,
Ordinary, mysterious skunk,
Mythologized, demythologized,
Snuffing the boards five feet beyond me.

It all came back to me last night, stirred
By the sootfall of your things at bedtime,
Your head-down, tail-up hunt in a bottom drawer
For the black plunge-line nightdress.

EDWIN MUIR

The Confirmation

Yes, yours, my love, is the right human face.
I in my mind had waited for this long,
Seeing the false and searching for the true,
Then found you as a traveller finds a place
Of welcome suddenly amid the wrong
Valleys and rocks and twisting roads. But you,
What shall I call you? A fountain in a waste,
A well of water in a country dry,
Or anything that's honest and good, an eye
That makes the whole world bright. Your open heart,

Simple with giving, gives the primal deed,
The first good world, the blossom, the blowing seed,
The hearth, the steadfast land, the wandering sea,
Not beautiful or rare in every part,
But like yourself, as they were meant to be.

EDWARD DORN

Song

This afternoon was unholy, the sky
bright mixed with cloud wrath, I read Yeats,
then black, and their land of heart's desire
where beauty has no ebb

                            decay no flood
but joy is wisdom, time
an endless song

                       I kiss you
and the world begins to fade
I kiss you not, the world is not.
I would not give my soul to you yet
the desire inside me burns.
November. The eighteenth was the coldest
this season, encumbered with routine errands
out past the factory

                    black sulphur
and in the dense checks
of its burdensome smoke the intense yellow tanks,
hooded, there sat a smell of weak death

and we pass these days of our isolation
in our rigidly assigned shelters
heads bent in occupation
a couple of pointless daydreamers
smiles lit and thrown into the breeze,

   how artful can love
suffer in the cross streets of this town

marked simply by the clicking railroad
and scratch of the janitor's broom.

WILLIAM SHAKESPEARE

'Like as the waves ...'

Like as the waves make towards the pebbled shore,
So do our minutes hasten to their end,
Each changing place with that which goes before,
In sequent toil all forwards do contend.
Nativity once in the main of light,
Crawls to maturity, wherewith being crowned,
Crookéd eclipses 'gainst his glory fight,
And Time that gave, doth now his gift confound.
Time doth transfix the flourish set on youth,
And delves the parallels in beauty's brow,
Feeds on the rarities of nature's truth,
And nothing stands but for his scythe to mow.
   And yet to times in hope, my verse shall stand
   Praising thy worth, despite his cruel hand.

JOHN DONNE

Song

Sweetest love, I do not go
   For weariness of thee,
Nor in hope the world can show
   A fitter love for me;
     But since that I
Must die at last, 'tis best
To use myself in jest
   Thus by fainéd deaths to die.

Yesternight the sun went hence,
   And yet is here today,
He hath no desire nor sense,

Nor half so short a way:
    Then fear not me,
But believe that I shall make
Speedier journeys, since I take
    More wings and spurs than he.

O how feeble is man's power,
    That if good fortune fall,
Cannot add another hour,
    Nor a lost hour recall!
        But come bad chance,
And we join to it our strength,
And we teach it art and length,
    Itself o'er us to advance.

When thou sigh'st, thou sigh'st not wind,
    But sigh'st my soul away,
When thou weep'st, unkindly kind,
    My life's blood doth decay.
        It cannot be
That thou lov'st me, as thou say'st,
If in thine my life thou waste,
    Thou art the best of me.

Let not thy divining heart
    Forethink me any ill,
Destiny may take thy part,
    And may thy fears fulfil;

    But think that we
Are but turned aside to sleep;
They who one another keep
    Alive, ne'er parted be.

ROBERT GRAVES

Counting the Beats

You, love, and I,
(He whispers) you and I,
And if no more than only you and I
What care you or I?

Counting the beats,
Counting the slow heart beats,
The bleeding to death of time in slow heart beats,
Wakeful they lie.

Cloudless day,
Night, and a cloudless day;
Yet the huge storm will burst upon their heads one day
From a bitter sky.

Where shall we be,
(She whispers) where shall we be,
When death strikes home, O where then shall we be
Who were you and I?

Not there but here,
(He whispers) only here,
As we are, here, together, now and here,
Always you and I.

Counting the beats,
Counting the slow heart beats,
The bleeding to death of time in slow heart beats,
Wakeful they lie.

GEORGE MEREDITH

from Modern Love

In our old shipwrecked days there was an hour,
When in the firelight steadily aglow,

Joined slackly, we beheld the red chasm grow
Among the clicking coals. Our library-bower
That eve was left to us: and hushed we sat
As lovers to whom Time is whispering.
From sudden-opened doors we heard them sing:
The nodding elders mixed good wine with chat.
Well knew we that Life's greatest treasure lay
With us, and of it was our talk. 'Ah, yes!
Love dies!' I said: I never thought it less.
She yearned to me that sentence to unsay.
Then when the fire domed blackening, I found
Her cheek was salt against my kiss, and swift
Up the sharp scale of sobs her breast did lift: –
Now am I haunted by that taste! that sound!

DOM MORAES

Moz

I saw him turn to bluster, clutch his head,
The King of Moz, his thunders launched in vain:
The ageing Queen sank back into her bed,
Making one final gesture of disdain.

She flashed her eyes and passed beyond his yells,
Dying from her Moz, country of talking trees,
To strike a happy medium somewhere else,
The King came slowly to his royal knees.

A chirping twilight fell. She lay quietly.
Priests moved their hands and lips, imploring grace.
Her emptied eyes looked up, where in the sky
Two stars resumed their long vacated place.

Wordless, I closed my heart. Now I return,
Amazed that stone endures and rivers move,
And persecute my friends with smiles to learn
Their water rates, and have they been in love.

I clench my sleep upon a thought that springs
Out of a nervous kind of fixity:
The King pacing his bedroom, touching things,
Trying vaguely to conceive eternity.

NNE EVANS

Over!

A knight came prancing on his way,
And across the path a lady lay:
'Stoop a little and hear me speak!'
Then, 'You are strong, and I am weak:
 Ride over me now, and kill me.'

He opened wide his gay blue eyes,
Like one o'ermastered by surprise;
His cheek and brow grew burning red,
'Long looked-for, come at last,' she said,
 'Ride over me now, and kill me.'

Then softly spoke the knight, and smiled:
'Fair maiden, whence this mood so wild?'
'Smile on,' said she, 'my reign is o'er,
But do my bidding yet once more:
 Ride over me now, and kill me.'

He smote his steed of dapple-gray,
And lightly cleared her where she lay;
But still, as he sped on amain,
She murmured ever, 'Turn again:
 Ride over me now, and kill me.'

VICKI FEAVER

Lily Pond

Thinking of new ways to kill you
and bring you back from the dead,
I try drowning you in the lily pond –

holding your head down
until every bubble of breath
is squeezed from your lungs

and the flat leaves and spiky flowers
float over you like a wreath.
I sit on the stones until I'm numb,

until, among reflections of sky,
water-buttercups, spears of iris,
your face rises to the surface –

a face that was always puffy
and pale, so curiously unchanged.
A wind rocks the waxy flowers, curls

the edges of the leaves. Blue dragonflies
appear and vanish like ghosts.
I part the mats of yellow weed

and drag you to the bank, covering
your green algae-stained corpse
with a white sheet. Then, I lift the edge

and climb in underneath –
thumping your chest,
breathing into your mouth.

W. B. YEATS

No Second Troy

Why should I blame her that she filled my days
With misery, or that she would of late
Have taught to ignorant men most violent ways,
Or hurled the little streets upon the great,
Had they but courage equal to desire?
What could have made her peaceful with a mind
That nobleness made simple as a fire,
With beauty like a tightened bow, a kind

That is not natural in an age like this,
Being high and solitary and most stern?
Why, what could she have done, being what she is?
Was there another Troy for her to burn?

ROBERT LOWELL

'To Speak of the Woe That is In Marriage'

*It is the future generation that presses into being by means of these
exuberant feelings and supersensible soap bubbles of ours.*
SCHOPENHAUER

'The hot night makes us keep our bedroom windows open.
Our magnolia blossoms. Life begins to happen.
My hopped up husband drops his home disputes,
and hits the streets to cruise for prostitutes,
free-lancing out along the razor's edge.
This screwball might kill his wife, then take the pledge.
Oh the monotonous meanness of his lust. . . .
It's the injustice . . . he is so unjust –
whiskey-blind, swaggering home at five.
My only thought is how to keep alive.
What makes him tick? Each night now I tie
ten dollars and his car key to my thigh . . .
Gored by the climacteric of his want,
he stalls above me like an elephant.'

CAROL ANN DUFFY

Adultery

Wear dark glasses in the rain.
Regard what was unhurt
as though through a bruise.
Guilt. A sick, green tint.

New gloves, money tucked in the palms,
the handshake crackles. Hands

can do many things. Phone.
Open the wine. Wash themselves. Now

you are naked under your clothes all day,
slim with deceit. Only the once
brings you alone to your knees,
miming, more, more, older and sadder,

creative. Suck a lie with a hole in it
on the way home from a lethal, thrilling night
up against a wall, faster. Language
unpeels to a lost cry. You're a bastard.

Do it do it do it. Sweet darkness
in the afternoon; a voice in your ear
telling you how you are wanted,
which way, now. A telltale clock

wiping the hours from its face, your face
on a white sheet, gasping, radiant, yes.
Pay for it in cash, fiction, cab-fares back
to the life which crumbles like a wedding-cake.

Paranoia for lunch; too much
to drink, as a hand on your thigh
tilts the restaurant. You know all about love,
don't you. Turn on your beautiful eyes

for a stranger who's dynamite in bed, again
and again; a slow replay in the kitchen
where the slicing of innocent onions
scalds you to tears. Then, selfish autobiographical sleep

in a marital bed, the tarnished spoon of your body
stirring betrayal, your heart overripe at the core.
You're an expert, darling; your flowers
dumb and explicit on nobody's birthday.

So write the script – illness and debt,
a ring thrown away in a garden

no moon can heal, your own words
commuting to bile in your mouth, terror –

and all for the same thing twice. And all
for the same thing twice. You did it.
What. Didn't you. Fuck. Fuck. No. That was
the wrong verb. This is only an abstract noun.

PATRICIA BEER

The Letter

I have not seen your writing
For ages, nor have been fretting
To see it. As once, darling.

This letter will certainly be
About some book, written by you or by me.
You turned to other ghosts. So did I.

It stopped raining long ago
But drops caught up in the bough
Fall murderously on me now.

ROSEMARY TONKS

Badly-Chosen Lover

Criminal, you took a great piece of my life,
And you took it under false pretences,
That piece of time
– In the clear muscles of my brain
I have the lens and jug of it!
Books, thoughts, meals, days, and houses,
Half Europe, spent like a coarse banknote,
You took it – leaving mud and cabbage stumps.

And, Criminal, I damn you for it (very softly).
My spirit broke her fast on you. And, Turk,
You fed her with the breath of your neck

– In my brain's clear retina
I have the stolen love-behaviour.
Your heart, greedy and tepid, brothel-meat,
Gulped it, like a flunkey with erotica.
And very softly, Criminal, I *damn* you for it.

MICK IMLAH

Clio's

Am I to be blamed for the state of it now? – Surely not –
Her poor wee fractured soul that I loved for its lightness
    and left?
Now she rings up pathetically, not to make claims of me,
Only to be in her wild way solicitous:
'Do you know of a restaurant called *Clio's* – or something
    like that –
At number *forty-three* in its road or street, – and the owne
Is beautiful, rich and Italian – you see, I dreamt of it,
And I can't relax without telling you never to go there,
Divining, somehow, that for you the place is *danger* –'

(But I dine at Clio's every night, poor lamb.)

FLEUR ADCOCK

Against Coupling

I write in praise of the solitary act:
of not feeling a trespassing tongue
forced into one's mouth, one's breath
smothered, nipples crushed against the
ribcage, and that metallic tingling
in the chin set off by a certain odd nerve:

unpleasure. Just to avoid those eyes would help –
such eyes as a young girl draws life from,
listening to the vegetal
rustle within her, as his gaze

stirs polypal fronds in the obscure
sea-bed of her body, and her own eyes blur.

There is much to be said for abandoning
this no longer novel exercise –
for not 'participating in
a total experience' – when
one feels like the lady in Leeds who
had seen *The Sound of Music* eighty-six times;

or more, perhaps, like the school drama mistress
producing *A Midsummer Night's Dream*
for the seventh year running, with
yet another cast from 5B.
Pyramus and Thisbe are dead, but
the hole in the wall can still be troublesome.

I advise you, then, to embrace it without
encumbrance. No need to set the scene,
dress up (or undress), make speeches.
Five minutes of solitude are
enough – in the bath, or to fill
that gap between the Sunday papers and lunch.

ANONYMOUS

'O waly, waly . . .'

O waly waly up the bank,
    And waly waly down the brae,
And waly waly yon burn-side
    Where I and my Love wont to gae!
I leant my back unto an aik,
    I thought it was a trusty tree;
But first it bow'd, and snye it brak,
    Sae my true Love did lichtly me.

O waly waly, but love be bonny
    A little time while it is new;

But when 'tis auld, it waxeth cauld
    And fades awa' like morning dew.
O wherefore should I busk my head?
    Or wherefore should I kame my hair?
For my true Love has me forsook,
    And says he'll never loe me mair.

Now Arthur-seat sall be my bed;
    The sheets shall ne'er be prest by me:
Saint Anton's well sall be my drink,
    Since my true Love has forsaken me.
Marti'mas wind, when wilt thou blaw
    And shake the green leaves aff the tree?
O gentle Death, when wilt thou come?
    For of my life I am wearíe.

'Tis not the frost, that freezes fell,
    Nor blawing snaw's inclemencie;
'Tis not sic cauld that makes me cry,
    But my Love's heart grown cauld to me.
When we came in by Glasgow town
    We were a comely sight to see;
My Love was clad in the black velvét,
    And I myself in cramasie.

But had I wist, before I kist,
    That love had been sae ill to win;
I had lockt my heart in a case of gowd
    And pinn'd it with a siller pin.
And, O! if my young babe were born,
    And set upon the nurse's knee,
And I mysell were dead and gane,
    And the green grass growing over me!

'My life closed twice ...'

My life closed twice before its close –
It yet remains to see
If Immortality unveil
A third event to me

So huge, so hopeless to conceive
As these that twice befell.
Parting is all we know of heaven,
And all we need of hell.

The River-Merchant's Wife
A Letter

While my hair was still cut straight across my forehead
I played about the front gate, pulling flowers.
You came by on bamboo stilts, playing horse,
You walked about my seat, playing with blue plums.
And we went on living in the village of Chokan:
Two small people, without dislike or suspicion.

At fourteen I married My Lord you.
I never laughed, being bashful.
Lowering my head, I looked at the wall.
Called to, a thousand times, I never looked back.

At fifteen I stopped scowling,
I desired my dust to be mingled with yours
For ever and for ever and for ever.
Why should I climb the look out?

At sixteen you departed,
You went into far Ku-to-yen, by the river of swirling
    eddies,

And you have been gone five months.
The monkeys make sorrowful noise overhead.

You dragged your feet when you went out.
By the gate now, the moss is grown, the different mosses
Too deep to clear them away!
The leaves fall early this autumn, in wind.
The paired butterflies are already yellow with August
Over the grass in the West garden;
They hurt me. I grow older.
If you are coming down through the narrows of the river Kiang,
Please let me know beforehand,
And I will come out to meet you
        As far as Cho-fu-Sa.

    translated from the Chinese of Rihaku, 8th century

ANONYMOUS

Donal Og

It is late last night the dog was speaking of you;
the snipe was speaking of you in her deep marsh.
It is you are the lonely bird through the woods;
and that you may be without a mate until you find one.

You promised me, and you said a lie to me,
that you would be before me where the sheep are flocked;
I gave a whistle and three hundred cries to you,
and I found nothing there but a bleating lamb.

You promised me a thing that was hard for you,
a ship of gold under a silver mast;
twelve towns with a market in all of them,
and a fine white court by the side of the sea.

You promised me a thing that is not possible,
that you would give me gloves of the skin of a fish;

that you would give me shoes of the skin of a bird;
and a suit of the dearest silk in Ireland.

When I go by myself to the Well of Loneliness,
I sit down and I go through my trouble;
when I see the world and do not see my boy,
he that has an amber shade in his hair.

It was on that Sunday I gave my love to you;
the Sunday that is last before Easter Sunday.
And myself on my knees reading the Passion;
and my two eyes giving love to you for ever.

My mother said to me not to be talking with you today,
or tomorrow, or on the Sunday;
it was a bad time she took for telling me that;
it was shutting the door after the house was robbed.

My heart is as black as the blackness of the sloe,
or as the black coal that is on the smith's forge;
or as the sole of a shoe left in white halls;
it was you put the darkness over my life.

You have taken the east from me; you have taken the west
    from me;
you have taken what is before me and what is behind me;
you have taken the moon, you have taken the sun from
    me;
and my fear is great that you have taken God from me!

    translated from the Irish by Lady Augusta Gregory

IR THOMAS WYATT

'They flee from me . . .'

They flee from me that sometime did me seek,
    With naked foot stalking in my chamber.
I have seen them gentle, tame and meek,
    That now are wild and do not remember

That sometime they put themselves in danger
    To take bread at my hand; and now they range
    Busily seeking with a continual change.

Thankt be fortune, it hath been otherwise
    Twenty times better; but once, in special,
In thin array, after a pleasant guise,
    When her loose gown from her shoulders did fall,
    And she me caught in her arms long and small,
        Therewith all sweetly did me kiss,
        And softly said: 'Dear heart, how like you this?'

It was no dream; I lay broad waking:
    But all is turned thorough my gentleness
Into a strange fashion of forsaking;
    And I have leave to go of her goodness;
    And she also to use new-fangleness.
        But since that I so kindely am served,
        I fain would know what she hath deserved.

ROBERT BURNS

John Anderson

John Anderson my jo, John,
When we were first acquent
Your locks were like the raven,
Your bonnie brow was brent;
But now your brow is bald, John,
Your locks are like the snow;
But blessings on your frosty pow,
John Anderson my jo.

John Anderson my jo, John,
We clamb the hill thegither,
And mony a canty day, John,
We've had wi' ane anither:
Now we maun totter down, John,
But hand in hand we'll go,

And sleep thegither at the foot,
John Anderson my jo.

NONYMOUS

The Fisher Lad of Whitby

My love he was a fisher-lad, and when he came ashore
He always steer'd to me, to greet me at the door;
For he knew I loved him well, as any one could see,
And O but I was fain when he came a courting to me.

It was one lovely morning, one morning in May,
He took me in his boat to sail out on the bay;
Then he told me of his love, as he sat by my side,
And he said that in a month he would make me his bride.

That very afternoon a man of war came in the bay;
And the press-gang came along and took my lad away;
Put irons on his hands, and irons on his feet,
And they carried him aboard, to fight in the fleet.

My father often talks of the perils of the main,
And my mother says she hopes he will come back again:
But I know he never will, but in my dreams I see
His body lying low at the bottom of the sea.

The ships come sailing in, and the ships they sail away,
And the sailors sing their merry songs out on the bay;
But for me, my heart is breaking, and I only wish to be,
Lying low with my lover deep down in the sea.

When the house is all still, and every one asleep,
I sit upon my bed, and bitterly I weep;
And I think of my lover away down in the sea,
For he never, never more, will come again to me.

JOHN WILMOT, EARL OF ROCHESTER

A Song of a Young Lady to Her Ancient Lover

Ancient person, for whom I
All the flattering youth defy,
Long be it ere thou grow old,
Aching, shaking, crazy, cold;
    But still continue as thou art,
    Ancient person of my heart.

On thy withered lips and dry,
Which like barren furrows lie,
Brooding kisses I will pour
Shall thy youthful heat restore
(Such kind showers in autumn fall,
And a second spring recall);
    Nor from thee will ever part,
    Ancient person of my heart.

Thy nobler part, which but to name
In our sex would be counted shame,
By age's frozen grasp possessed,
From his ice shall be released,
And soothed by my reviving hand,
In former warmth and vigor stand.
All a lover's wish can reach
For thy joy my love shall teach,
And for thy pleasure shall improve
All that art can add to love.
    Yet still I love thee without art,
    Ancient person of my heart.

MIKLÓS RADNOTI

Naïve Song about the Wife

As she steps in the door clicks,
the many flowerpots start up tiptoe,

and in her hair a little sleepy blond
spot speaks, chirping, like a frightened sparrow.

The old electric cord lets out a shout,
it's rolling its heavy body toward her,
and it all spins, I can't even jot it down.

She just got home, was far away all day;
in her hand a huge poppy petal,
with it she chases death away from me.

translated from the Hungarian by Emery George

ELIZABETH JENNINGS

One Flesh

Lying apart now, each in a separate bed,
He with a book, keeping the light on late,
She like a girl dreaming of childhood,
All men elsewhere – it is as if they wait
Some new event: the book he holds unread,
Her eyes fixed on the shadows overhead.

Tossed up like flotsam from a former passion,
How cool they lie. They hardly ever touch,
Or if they do it is like a confession
Of having little feeling – or too much.
Chastity faces them, a destination
For which their whole lives were a preparation.

Strangely apart, yet strangely close together,
Silence between them like a thread to hold
And not wind in. And time itself's a feather
Touching them gently. Do they know they're old,
These two who are my father and my mother
Whose fire from which I came, has now grown cold?

MARIN SORESCU

Getting Matches

We're going out to get matches,
the firs say every morning
when they leave for the mountains
and the wind blows ideas
around their foreheads and

a cloud-mass rises, magma
conglomerations for future planets . . .
Only the resin that weeps from
their trunks knows
that their great migration,
their craving to burn,
has been mourned by us for a long time,
by us who stand
at the chasm's edge,

you at one end of the table,
I at the other.

translated from the Romanian by Michael Hamburger

ANNA ŚWIRSZCZYŃSKA

The Greatest Love

She is sixty. She lives
the greatest love of her life.

She walks arm-in-arm with her dear one,
her hair streams in the wind.
Her dear one says:
'You have hair like pearls.'

Her children say:
'Old fool.'

translated from the Polish by Czesław Miłosz and Leonard Nathan

JOHN MILTON

'Methought I saw ...'

Methought I saw my late espousèd saint
    Brought to me like Alcestis from the grave,
    Whom Jove's great son to her glad husband gave,
    Rescued from death by force, though pale and faint.
Mine, as whom washed from spot of child-bed taint
    Purification in the old Law did save,
    And such as yet once more I trust to have
    Full sight of her in heaven without restraint,
Came vested all in white, pure as her mind.
    Her face was veiled, yet to my fancied sight
    Love, sweetness, goodness in her person shined
So clear as in no face with more delight.
    But O as to embrace me she inclined,
    I waked, she fled, and day brought back my night.

WILLIAM BARNES

The Wife a-Lost

Since I noo mwore do zee your feäce,
    Up steäirs or down below,
I'll zit me in the lwonesome pleäce,
    Where flat-bough'd beech do grow;
Below the beeches' bough, my love,
    Where you did never come,
An' I don't look to meet ye now,
    As I do look at hwome.

Since you noo mwore be at my zide,
    In walks in zummer het,
I'll goo alwone where mist do ride,
    Drough trees a-drippen wet;
Below the raïn-wet bough, my love,
    Where you did never come,

An' I don't grieve to miss ye now,
    As I do grieve at hwome.

Since now bezide my dinner-bwoard
    Your vaïce do never sound,
I'll eat the bit I can avvword,
    A-yield upon the ground;
Below the darksome bough, my love,
    Where you did never dine,
an' I don't grieve to miss ye now,
    As I at hwome do pine.

Since I do miss your vaïce an' feäce
    In praÿer at eventide,
I'll praÿ wi' woone sad vaïce vor greäce
    To goo where you do bide;
Above the tree an' bough, my love,
    Where you be gone avore,
An' be a-waïten vor me now,
    To come vor evermwore.

DOUGLAS DUNN

The Kaleidoscope

To climb these stairs again, bearing a tray,
Might be to find you pillowed with your books,
Your inventories listing gowns and frocks
As if preparing for a holiday.
Or, turning from the landing, I might find
My presence watched through your kaleidoscope,
A symmetry of husbands, each redesigned
In lovely forms of foresight, prayer and hope.
I climb these stairs a dozen times a day
And, by that open door, wait, looking in
At where you died. My hands become a tray
Offering me, my flesh, my soul, my skin.

Grief wrongs us so. I stand, and wait, and cry
For the absurd forgiveness, not knowing why.

HENRY KING

Exequy upon His Wife

Accept, thou shrine of my dead saint,
Instead of dirges this complaint;
And for sweet flowers to crown thy hearse,
Receive a strew of weeping verse
From thy grieved friend, whom thou mightst see
Quite melted into tears for thee.
    Dear loss! since thy untimely fate
My task hath been to meditate
On thee, on thee! Thou art the book,
The library, whereon I look
Though almost blind. For thee, loved clay,
I languish out, not live, the day,
Using no other exercise
But what I practise with mine eyes.
By which wet glasses I find out
How lazily time creeps about
To one that mourns. This, only this,
My exercise and business is:
So I compute the weary hours
With sighs dissolvèd into showers.
    Nor wonder if my time go thus
Backward and most preposterous:
Thou hast benighted me. Thy set
This eve of blackness did beget,
Who wast my day (though overcast
Before thou hadst thy noon-tide past)
And I remember must in tears
Thou scarce hadst seen so many years
As day tells hours. By thy clear sun
My love and fortune first did run;

But thou wilt never more appear
Folded within my hemisphere,
Since both thy light and motion,
Like a fled star, is fallen and gone,
And 'twixt me and my soul's dear wish
The earth now interposèd is.
Which such a strange eclipse doth make
As ne'er was read in almanac.

    I could allow thee for a time
To darken me and my sad clime;
Were it a month, a year, or ten,
I would thy exile live till then;
And all that space my mirth adjourn,
So thou wouldst promise to return
And, putting off thy ashy shroud,
At length disperse this sorrow's cloud.

    But woe is me! the longest date
Too narrow is to calculate
These empty hopes. Never shall I
Be so much blest as to descry
A glimpse of thee, till that day come
Which shall the earth to cinders doom,
And a fierce fever must calcine
The body of this world, like thine,
My little world! That fit of fire
Once off, our bodies shall aspire
to our souls' bliss: then we shall rise,
And view ourselves with clearer eyes
In that calm region where no night
Can hide us from each other's sight.

    Meantime thou hast her, Earth: much good
May my harm do thee. Since it stood
With Heaven's will I might not call
Her longer mine, I give thee all
My short-lived right and interest
In her, whom living I loved best:

With a most free and bounteous grief,
I give thee what I could not keep.
Be kind to her, and prithee look
Thou write into thy Doomsday book
Each parcel of this rarity,
Which in thy casket shrined doth lie.
See that thou make thy reckoning straight,
And yield her back again by weight;
For thou must audit on thy trust
Each grain and atom of this dust,
As thou wilt answer him that lent,
Not gave thee, my dear monument.

    So close the ground, and 'bout her shade
Black curtains draw: my bride is laid.

    Sleep on, my Love, in thy cold bed
Never to be disquieted.
My last good night! Thou wilt not wake
Till I thy fate shall overtake:
Till age, or grief, or sickness must
Marry my body to that dust
It so much loves; and fill the room
My heart keeps empty in thy tomb.
Stay for me there: I will not fail
to meet thee in that hollow vale.
And think not much of my delay;
I am already on the way,
And follow thee with all the speed
Desire can make, or sorrows breed.
Each minute is a short degree
And every hour a step towards thee.
At night when I betake to rest,
Next morn I rise nearer my west
Of life, almost by eight hours sail
Than when sleep breathed his drowsy gale.

    Thus from the sun my bottom steers,
And my day's compass downward bears.

Nor labour I to stem the tide
Through which to thee I swiftly glide.
    'Tis true, with shame and grief I yield;
Thou, like the van, first took'st the field
And gotten hast the victory
In thus adventuring to die
Before me, whose more years might crave
A just precedence in the grave.
But hark! my pulse, like a soft drum,
Beats my approach, tells thee I come;
And slow howe'er my marches be
I shall at last sit down by thee.
    The thought of this bids me go on
And wait my dissolution
With hope and comfort. Dear, (forgive
The crime) I am content to live
Divided, with but half a heart,
Till we shall meet and never part.

ANONYMOUS

Two Epitaphs

Here lies the body of Mary Sexton,
Who pleased many a man, but never vex'd one,
Not like the woman who lies under the next stone.

from Devon

Underneath this stone doth lie,
Back to back, my wife and I.
When the last trump sounds so shrill,
If she gets up I'll lie still.

from Yorkshire

The Unquiet Grave

The wind doth blow today, my love,
    And a few small drops of rain.
I never had but one true-love,
    In cold grave she was lain.

I'll do as much for my true-love
    As any young man may,
I'll sit and mourn all at her grave
    For twelvemonth and a day.

The twelvemonth and a day being up,
    The dead began to speak:
Oh who sits weeping on my grave,
    And will not let me sleep?

'Tis I, my love, sits on your grave,
    And will not let you sleep,
For I crave one kiss of your clay-cold lips,
    And that is all I seek.

You crave one kiss of my clay-cold lips,
    But my breath smells earthy strong.
If you have one kiss of my clay-cold lips,
    Your time will not be long.

'Tis down in yonder garden green,
    Love, where we used to walk,
The finest flower that ere was seen
    Is withered to a stalk.

The stalk is withered dry, my love,
    So will our hearts decay.
So make yourself content, my love,
    Till God calls you away.

Epitaph on the Monument of Sir William Dyer at Colmworth, 1641

My dearest dust, could not thy hasty day
Afford thy drowsy patience leave to stay
One hour longer: so that we might either
Sit up, or gone to bed together?
But since thy finished labour hath possessed
Thy weary limbs with early rest,
Enjoy it sweetly: and thy widow bride
Shall soon repose her by thy slumbering side.
Whose business, now, is only to prepare
My nightly dress, and call to prayer:
Mine eyes wax heavy and the day grows cold.
Draw, draw the closèd curtains: and make room:
My dear, my dearest dust; I come, I come.

Travel

The Road not Taken

Two roads diverged in a yellow wood,
And sorry I could not travel both
And be one traveler, long I stood
And looked down one as far as I could
To where it bent in the undergrowth;

Then took the other, as just as fair,
And having perhaps the better claim,
Because it was grassy and wanted wear;
Though as for that, the passing there
Had worn them really about the same,

And both that morning equally lay
In leaves no step had trodden black.
Oh, I kept the first for another day!
Yet knowing how way leads on to way,
I doubted if I should ever come back.

I shall be telling this with a sigh
Somewhere ages and ages hence:
Two roads diverged in a wood, and I –
I took the one less traveled by,
And that has made all the difference.

ROBERT GRAVES

The Legs

There was this road,
And it led up-hill,
And it led down-hill,
And round and in and out.

And the traffic was legs,
Legs from the knees down,

Coming and going,
Never pausing.

And the gutters gurgled
With the rain's overflow,
And the sticks on the pavement
Blindly tapped and tapped.

What drew the legs along
Was the never-stopping,
And the senseless, frightening
Fate of being legs.

Legs for the road,
The road for legs,
Resolutely nowhere
In both directions.

My legs at least
Were not in that rout:
On grass by the road-side
Entire I stood,

Watching the unstoppable
Legs go by
With never a stumble
Between step and step.

Though my smile was broad
The legs could not see,
Though my laugh was loud
The legs could not hear.

My head dizzied, then:
I wondered suddenly,
Might I too be a walker
From the knees down?

Gently I touched my shins.
The doubt unchained them:

They had run in twenty puddles
Before I regained them.

ELIZABETH BISHOP

Questions of Travel

There are too many waterfalls here; the crowded streams
hurry too rapidly down to the sea,
And the pressure of so many clouds on the mountaintops
makes them spill over the sides in soft slow-motion,
turning to waterfalls under our very eyes.
– For if those streaks, those mile-long, shiny, tearstains,
aren't waterfalls yet,
in a quick age or so, as ages go here,
they probably will be.
But if the streams and clouds keep travelling, travelling,
the mountains look like the hulls of capsized ships,
slime-hung and barnacled.

Think of the long trip home.
Should we have stayed at home and thought of here?
Where should we be today?
Is it right to be watching strangers in a play
in this strangest of theatres?
What childishness is it that while there's a breath of life
in our bodies, we are determined to rush
to see the sun the other way around?
The tiniest green hummingbird in the world?
To stare at some inexplicable old stonework,
inexplicable and impenetrable,
at any view,
instantly seen and always, always delightful?
Oh, must we dream our dreams
and have them, too?
And have we room
for one more folded sunset, still quite warm?

But surely it would have been a pity
not to have seen the trees along this road,
really exaggerated in their beauty,
not to have seen them gesturing
like noble pantomimists, robed in pink.
– Not to have had to stop for gas and heard
the sad, two-noted, wooden tune
of disparate wooden clogs
carelessly clacking over
a grease-stained filling-station floor.
(In another country the clogs would all be tested.
Each pair there would have identical pitch.)
– A pity not to have heard
the other, less primitive music of the fat brown bird
who sings above the broken gasoline pump
in a bamboo church of Jesuit baroque:
three towers, five silver crosses.
– Yes, a pity not to have pondered,
blurr'dly and inconclusively,
on what connection can exist for centuries
between the crudest wooden footwear
and, careful and finicky,
the whittled fantasies of wooden cages.
– Never to have studied history in
the weak calligraphy of songbirds' cages.
– And never to have had to listen to rain
so much like politicians' speeches:
two hours of unrelenting oratory
and then a sudden golden silence
in which the traveller takes a notebook, writes:

'Is it lack of imagination that makes us come
to imagined places, not just stay at home?
Or could Pascal have been not entirely right
about just sitting quietly in one's room?

Continent, city, country, society:
the choice is never wide and never free.
And here, or there . . . No. Should we have stayed at home,
wherever that may be?'

ELIZABETH RIDDELL

Wakeful in the Township

Barks the melancholy dog,
Swims in the stream the shadowy fish.
Who would live in a country town
If they had their wish?

When the sun comes hurrying up
I will take the circus train
That cries, cries once in the night
And then not again.

In the stream the shadowy fish
Sleeps below the sleeping fly.
Many around me straitly sleep
But not I.

Near my window a drowsy bird
Flickers its feathers against the thorn.
Around the township's single light
My people die and are born.

I will join the circus train
For mangy leopard and tinsel girl
And the trotting horses' great white haunches
Whiter than a pearl.

When to the dark blue mountains
My captive pigeons flew
I'd no heart to lure them back
With wheat upon the dew.

When the dog at morning
Whines upon the frost
I shall be in another place.
Lost, lost, lost.

ALLEN CURNOW

A Passion for Travel

Absently the proof-reader corrects
the typesetter. According to copy
the word is exotic. He cancels
the literal r and writes an x.

A word replaces a word. Discrepant
signs, absurd similitudes
touch one another, couple promiscuously.
He doesn't need Schopenhauer

to tell him only exceptional intellects
at exceptional moments ever get any
nearer to that, and when they do
it gives them one hell of a fright.

He's exercised, minding his exes and ars.
If Eros laughs, as the other philosopher
says, and if either word's a world
'offering plentiful material for humour',

that's not in copy. After dark,
that's when the fun starts, there's a room
thick with globes, testers, bell-pulls,
rare fruits, painted and woven pictures,

pakeha thistles in the wrong forest,
at Palermo the palm lily *ti australis*
in the Botanical Gardens, Vincento
in white shorts trimming the red canoe

pulled the octopus inside out
like a sock, *Calamari!* The tall German
blonde wading beside, pudenda awash,
exquisitely shocked by a man's hands

doing so much so quickly,
Calamari! Those 'crystalline'
aeolian shallows lap the anemone
which puckers the bikini, her delicacy.

Short of an exceptional moment, if only
just! In this make-do world a word
replaces a white vapour, the sky
heightens by a stroke of the pen.

WILLIAM WORDSWORTH

Stepping Westward

While my Fellow-traveller and I were walking by the side of Loch Ketterine, one fine evening after sunset, in our road to a hut where, in the course of our Tour, we had been hospitably entertained some weeks before, we met, in one of the loneliest parts of that solitary region, two well-dressed Women, one of whom said to us, by way of greeting, 'What, you are stepping westward?'

'What, you are stepping westward?' – 'Yea.'
– 'Twould be a *wildish* destiny,
If we, who thus together roam
In a strange Land, and far from home,
Were in this place the guests of Chance:
Yet who would stop, or fear to advance,
Though home or shelter he had none,
With such a sky to lead him on?

The dewy ground was dark and cold;
Behind, all gloomy to behold;
And stepping westward seemed to be
A kind of *heavenly* destiny:

I liked the greeting; 'twas a sound
Of something without place or bound;
And seemed to give me spiritual right
To travel through that region bright.

The voice was soft, and she who spake
Was walking by her native lake:
The salutation had to me
The very sound of courtesy:
Its power was felt; and while my eye
Was fixed upon the glowing Sky,
The echo of the voice enwrought
A human sweetness with the thought
Of travelling through the world that lay
Before me in my endless way.

THOM GUNN

On the Move

The blue jay scuffling in the bushes follows
Some hidden purpose, and the gust of birds
That spurts across the field, the wheeling swallows,
Has nested in the trees and undergrowth.
Seeking their instinct, or their poise, or both,
One moves with an uncertain violence
Under the dust thrown by a baffled sense
Or the dull thunder of approximate words.

On motorcycles, up the road, they come:
Small, black, as flies hanging in heat, the Boys,
Until the distance throws them forth, their hum
Bulges to thunder held by calf and thigh.
In goggles, donned impersonality,
In gleaming jackets trophied with the dust,
They strap in doubt – by hiding it, robust –
And almost hear a meaning in their noise.

Exact conclusion of their hardiness
Has no shape yet, but from known whereabouts
They ride, direction where the tyres press.
They scare a flight of birds across the field:
Much that is natural, to the will must yield.
Men manufacture both machine and soul,
And use what they imperfectly control
To dare a future from the taken routes.

It is a part solution, after all.
One is not necessarily discord
On earth; or damned because, half animal,
One lacks direct instinct, because one wakes
Afloat on movement that divides and breaks.
One joins the movement in a valueless world,
Choosing it, till, both hurler and the hurled,
One moves as well, always toward, toward.

A minute holds them, who have come to go:
The self-defined, astride the created will
They burst away; the towns they travel through
Are home for neither bird nor holiness,
For birds and saints complete their purposes.
At worst, one is in motion; and at best,
Reaching no absolute, in which to rest,
One is always nearer by not keeping still.

JOHN ASHBERY

At North Farm

Somewhere someone is traveling furiously toward you,
At incredible speed, traveling day and night,
Through blizzards and desert heat, across torrents,
    through narrow passes.
But will he know where to find you,
Recognize you when he sees you,
Give you the thing he has for you?

Hardly anything grows here,
Yet the granaries are bursting with meal,
The sacks of meal piled to the rafters.
The streams run with sweetness, fattening fish;
Birds darken the sky. Is it enough
That the dish of milk is set out at night,
That we think of him sometimes,
Sometimes and always, with mixed feelings?

BERNARD SPENCER

Boat Poem

I wish there were a touch of these boats about my life;
so to speak, a tarring,
the touch of inspired disorder and something more than
    that,
something more too
than the mobility of sails or a primitive bumpy engine,
under that tiny hot-house window,
which eats up oil and benzine perhaps
but will go on beating in spite of the many strains
not needing with luck to be repaired too often,
with luck lasting years piled on years.

There must be a kind of envy which brings me peering
and nosing at the boats along the island quay
either in the hot morning
with the lace-light shaking up against their hulls from the
    water,
or when their mast-tops
keep on drawling lines between stars.
(I do not speak here of the private yachts from the clubs
which stalk across the harbour like magnificent white cats
but sheer off and keep mostly to themselves.)

Look for example at the Bartolomé; a deck-full
of mineral water and bottles of beer in cases

and great booming barrels of wine from the mainland,
endearing trade;
and lengths of timber and iron rods for building
and, curiously a pig with flying ears
ramming a wet snout into whatever it explores.

Or the Virgen del Pilar, mantled and weavy with drooping
    nets
PM/708/3A
with starfish and pieces of cod drying on the wheel-house
    roof
some wine, the remains of supper on an enamel plate
and trousers and singlets 'passim';
both of these boats stinky and forgivable like some great
    men
both needing paint,
but both, one observes, armoured far better than us
    against jolts
by a belt of old motor-tyres lobbed round their sides for
    buffers.

And having in their swerving planks and in the point of
    their bows
the never-enough-to-be-praised
authority of a great tradition, the sea-shape
simple and true like a vase,
something that stays too in the carved head of an eagle
or that white-eyed wooden hound crying up beneath the
    bowsprit.

Qualities clearly admirable. So is their response to occasion,
how they celebrate such times
and suddenly fountain with bunting and stand like ocean
    maypoles
on a Saint's Day when a gun bangs from the fortifications,
and an echo-gun throws a bang back
and all the old kitchen bells start hammering from the
    churches.

Admirable again
how one of them, perhaps tomorrow, will have gone with
   no hooting or fuss,
simply absent from its place among the others,
occupied, without self-importance, in the thousands-of-
millions-of-sea.

BIDDY CUSSROOEE

'My grief on the sea . . .'

My grief on the sea,
   How the waves of it roll!
For they heave between me
   And the love of my soul!

Abandoned, forsaken,
   To grief and to care,
Will the sea ever waken
   Relief from despair?

My grief, and my trouble!
   Would he and I were
In the province of Leinster,
   Or county of Clare.

Were I and my darling –
   Oh, heart-bitter wound! –
On board of the ship
   For America bound.

On a green bed of rushes
   All last night I lay,
And I flung it abroad
   With the heat of the day.

ETER PORTER

The Last of England

It's quiet here among the haunted tenses:
Dread Swiss germs pass the rabbit's throat,
Chemical rain in its brave green hat
Drinks at a South Coast Bar, the hedgehog
Preens on nylon, we dance in Tyrolean
Drag whose mothers were McGregors,
Exiled seas fill every cubit of the bay.

Sailing away from ourselves, we feel
The gentle tug of water at the quay –
Language of the liberal dead speaks
From the soil of Highgate, tears
Show a great water table is intact.
You cannot leave England, it turns
A planet majestically in the mind.

KATHLEEN JAMIE

Pioneers

It's not long ago. There were,
after all, cameras
to show us these wagons and blurred dogs,
this pox of burnt stump-holes
in a clearing. Pioneers;
their remains now strewn
across the small-town
museums of Ontario:
the axe and plough, the grindstone,
the wife by the cabin door
dead, and another sent for.

TOM PAULIN

Settlers

They cross from Glasgow to a black city
    Of gantries, mills and steeples. They begin to belong.
He manages the Iceworks, is an elder of the Kirk;
    She becomes, briefly, a cook in Carson's Army.
Some mornings, walking through the company gate,
    He touches the bonnet of a brown lorry.
It is warm. The men watch and say nothing.
    'Queer, how it runs off in the night,'
He says to McCullough, then climbs to his office.
    He stores a warm knowledge on his palm.

    Nightlandings on the Antrim coast, the movement of
        guns
Now snug in their oiled paper below the floors
    Of sundry kirks and tabernacles in that county.

T. S. ELIOT

Journey of the Magi

    'A cold coming we had of it,
Just the worst time of the year
For a journey, and such a long journey:
The ways deep and the weather sharp,
The very dead of winter.'
And the camels galled, sore-footed, refractory,
Lying down in the melting snow.
There were times we regretted
The summer palaces on slopes, the terraces,
And the silken girls bringing sherbet.
Then the camel men cursing and grumbling
And running away, and wanting their liquor and women,
And the night-fires going out, and the lack of shelters,
And the cities hostile and the towns unfriendly

And the villages dirty and charging high prices:
A hard time we had of it.
At the end we preferred to travel all night,
Sleeping in snatches,
With the voices singing in our ears, saying
That this was all folly.

Then at dawn we came down to a temperate valley,
Wet, below the snow line, smelling of vegetation,
With a running stream and a water-mill beating the
    darkness,
And three trees on the low sky.
And an old white horse galloped away in the meadow.
Then we came to a tavern with vine-leaves over the lintel,
Six hands at an open door dicing for pieces of silver,
And feet kicking the empty wine-skins.
But there was no information, and so we continued
And arrived at evening, not a moment too soon
Finding the place; it was (you may say) satisfactory.

All this was a long time ago, I remember,
And I would do it again, but set down
This set down
This: were we led all that way for
Birth or Death? There was a Birth, certainly,
We had evidence and no doubt. I had seen birth and death,
But had thought they were different; this Birth was
Hard and bitter agony for us, like Death, our death.
We returned to our places, these Kingdoms,
But no longer at ease here, in the old dispensation,
With an alien people clutching their gods.
I should be glad of another death.

Father in America

When father went off to America
he wore a white suit. Later he shaved his head.
Our ancient town burned white throughout the summer
and white flowers blossomed in the cemetery –
the flowers of course remain though he is dead.

It was everybody's most idyllic picture –
white suits against pale brick or amber corn,
and gentlemen and ladies in such posture
with parasols and petticoats in pastoral
benevolence before his head was shorn.

I fear shorn heads – I touch my own skull now
and feel skin pimpling in between the roots,
with father's skull beneath. I feel it grow
progressively more bulbous under mine,
his brain is still developing new shoots.

I feel, but know that feeling isn't knowledge.
The glass distorts in the amusement park,
your skirt blows high, you cross a swaying bridge,
you hear a scream, you stand before the mirror
and face your masters in the gathering dark.

I wish this train were going elsewhere but
a wish is powerless. The skulls appear,
one on top of another. The doors are shut,
and I'd be lying if the truth were told
on picture postcards, wishing you were here.

The marshalling yard

In the goods yard the tracks are unmarked.
Snow lies, the sky is full of it.
Its hush swells in the dark.

Grasped by black ice on black
a massive noise of breathing
fills the tracks;

cold women, ready for departure
smooth their worn skirts
and ice steals through their hands like children
from whose touch they have already been parted.

Now like a summer
the train comes
beating the platform
with its blue wings.

The women stir. They sigh.
Feet slide
warm on a wooden stairway
then a voice calls and
milk drenched with aniseed
drawls on the walk to school.

At last they leave.
Their breathless neighbours
steal from the woods, the barns,
and tender straw
sticks to their palms.

Tom O'Bedlam's Song

From the hag and hungry goblin
That into rags would rend ye,
And the spirit that stands by the naked man
In the Book of Moons defend ye!
That of your five sound senses
You never be forsaken,
Nor wander from yourselves with Tom.
Abroad to beg your bacon.

While I do sing 'any food, any feeding,
Feeding, drink or clothing',
Come dame or maid, be not afraid,
Poor Tom will injure nothing . . .

With a host of furious fancies,
Whereof I am commander,
With the burning spear, and a horse of air,
To the wilderness I wander.
By a knight of ghosts and shadows
I summoned am to tourney,
Ten leagues beyond the wide world's end:
Methink it is no journey.

GEORGE HERBERT

The Pilgrimage

I travell'd on, seeing the hill, where lay
        My expectation.
    A long it was and weary way
        The gloomy cave of Desperation
I left on th' one, and on the other side
        The rock of Pride.

And so I came to phansies medow strow'd
        With many a flower:
    Fain would I here have made abode,
    But I was quicken'd by my hour.
So to cares cops I came, and there got through
        With much ado.

That led me to the wild of passion, which
        Some call the wold;
    A wasted place, but sometimes rich.
    Here I was robb'd of all my gold,
Save one good Angel, which a friend had ti'd
        Close to my side.

At length I got unto the gladsome hill,
        Where lay my hope,
    Where lay my heart; and climbing still,
    When I had gain'd the brow and top,
A lake of brackish waters on the ground
        Was all I found.

With that abash'd and struck with many a sting
        Of swarming fears,
    I fell, and cry'd, Alas my King;
    Can both the way and end be tears?
Yet taking heart I rose, and then perceiv'd
        I was deceiv'd:

My hill was further: so I flung away,
        Yet heard a cry
    Just as I went, *None goes that way*
    And lives: If that be all, said I,
After so foul a journey death is fair,
        And but a chair.

Why Brownlee Left

Why Brownlee left, and where he went,
Is a mystery even now.
For if a man should have been content
It was him; two acres of barley,
One of potatoes, four bullocks,
A milker, a slated farmhouse.
He was last seen going out to plough
On a March morning, bright and early.

By noon Brownlee was famous;
They had found all abandoned, with
The last rig unbroken, his pair of black
Horses, like man and wife,
Shifting their weight from foot to
Foot, and gazing into the future.

BERTOLT BRECHT

Emigrant's Lament

I earned my bread and ate it just like you.
I am a doctor; or at least I was.
The colour of my hair, shape of my nose
Cost me my home, my bread and butter too.

She who for seven years had slept with me
My hand upon her lap, her face against my face
Took me to court. The cause of my disgrace:
My hair was black. So she got rid of me.

But I escaped at night-time through a wood
(For reasons of my mother's ancestry)
To find a country that would be my host.

Yet when I asked for work it was no good.
You are impertinent, they said to me.
I'm not impertinent, I said: I'm lost.

translated from the German by Edith Roseveane

AMES BERRY

Old Man in New Country

I am both Watutsi and Pygmy.
I have shone the moment's glory.
I have been the total loss.

Both leaf and flesh grinder,
both sucker of milk and narcotics,
I have been full and still;
my knees have rattled without flesh.

My shoulder supporting spear and bag,
I have ambled along tracks,
shoeless and not clothed. With leaves,
with secret eyes, with butterflies,
I have been the sun's painting exhibited.

Needing not one machine,
no sounds marked down,
I grew certain with my skills.
From all streams
the seasons wake in my blood.

But challenges and attacks
have entangled my peace.
My bag has repeated emptiness
to my bed. My hands have attended wounds
of wars undeclared.

Now my world is new
I cannot find a waterhole.

Day of Reckoning

When we drove across America, going West,
I tanned through the sandwich glass windscreen.
Though I was eight, and my legs weren't yet long
in their long pants, I could still sit in front –

your co-driver who couldn't spell you . . .
My jagged elbow stuck out of the right-hand window,
I kept a tough diary, owned a blunt knife,
and my mother sat in the back with the girls.

I can't remember if we talked, or if, even then,
you played the radio, but when I got tired
I huddled in my legroom in the Chevy Belair,
and watched the coloured stars under the dashboard . . .

I learned fractions from you in a single day,
multiplying and dividing. In Kingston, Ontario,
I had a cruel haircut. For you, it was a dry time –
in two years one short play about bankruptcy:

Let Them Down, Gently. There followed the great crash.

C. K. WILLIAMS

Travelers

He drives, she mostly sleeps; when she's awake, they
    quarrel, and now, in a violet dusk,
a rangy, raw-boned, efficient-looking mongrel loping
    toward them down the other shoulder
for no apparent reason swerves out on the roadbed just a
    a battered taxi is going by.
Horrible how it goes under, how it's jammed into the
    asphalt, compressed, abraded, crumpled,
then is ejected out behind, still, a miracle, alive, but
    spinning wildly on itself, tearing,

frenzied, at its broken spine, the mindless taxi never
    slowing, never noticing or caring,
they slowing, only for a moment, though, as, 'Go on,' she
    says, 'go on, go on,' face averted,
she can't look, while he, guilty as usual, fearful, fascinated
    and uncouth, can't not.

AMY CLAMPITT

Witness

An ordinary evening in Wisconsin
seen from a Greyhound bus – mute aisles
of merchandise the sole inhabitants
of the half-darkened Five and Ten,

the tables of the single lit café awash
with unarticulated pathos, the surface membrane
of the inadvertently transparent instant
when no one is looking : outside town

the barns, their red gone dark with sundown,
withhold the shudder of a warped terrain –
the castle rocks above, tree-clogged ravines
already submarine with nightfall, flocks

(like dark sheep) of toehold junipers,
the lucent arms of birches: purity
without a mirror, other than a mind bound
elsewhere, to tell it how it looks.

ANNE STEVENSON

Utah

Somewhere nowhere in Utah, a boy by the roadside,
gun in his hand, and the rare dumb hard tears flowing.
Beside him, the greyheaded man has let one arm slide
awkwardly over his shoulder, is talking and pointing
at whatever it is, dead, in the dust on the ground.

By the old parked Chevy, two women, talking and
    watching.
Their skirts flag forward. Bandannas twist with their hair
Around them some sheep and a fence and the sagebrush
    burning
and burning with its blue flame. In the distance, where
the mountains are clouds, lightning, but no rain.

THOMAS HARDY

Midnight on the Great Western

In the third-class seat sat the journeying boy,
    And the roof-lamp's oily flame
Played down on his listless form and face,
Bewrapt past knowing to what he was going,
        Or whence he came.

In the band of his hat the journeying boy
    Had a ticket stuck; and a string
Around his neck bore the key of his box,
That twinkled gleams of the lamp's sad beams
        Like a living thing.

What past can be yours, O journeying boy
    Towards a world unknown,
Who calmly, as if uncurious quite
On all at stake, can undertake
        This plunge alone?

Knows your soul a sphere, O journeying boy,
    Our rude realms far above,
Whence with spacious vision you mark and mete
This region of sin that you find you in,
        But are not of?

Limited

I am riding on a limited express, one of the crack trains of
    the nation.
Hurtling across the prairie into blue haze and dark air go
    fifteen all-steel coaches holding a thousand people.
(All the coaches shall be scrap and rust and all the men
    and women laughing in the diners and sleepers shall
    pass to ashes.)
I ask a man in the smoker where he is going and he
    answers: 'Omaha.'

DON PATERSON

14:50: Rosekinghall
(*Beecking Memorial Railway, Forfarshire Division*)

The next train on Platform 6 will be the 14:50
Rosekinghall – Gallowshill and Blindwell, calling at:

Fairygreen – Templelands – Stars of Forthneth –
    Silverwells –
Honeyhole – Bee Cott – Pleasance – Sunnyblink –
Butterglen – Heatheryhaugh – St Bride's Ring – Diltie Moss –
Silvie – Leyshade – Bourtreebush – Little Fithie –
Dusty Drum – Spiral Wood – Wandershiell – Windygates –
Red Roofs – Ark Hill – Egypt – Formal –
Letter – Laverockhall – Windyedge – Catchpenny –
Framedrum – Drumtick – Little Fardle – Packhorse –
Carrot – Clatteringbrigs – Smyrna – Bucklerheads –
Outfield – Jericho – Horn – Roughstones –
Loak – Skitchen – Start – Oathlaw –
Wolflaw – Farnought – Drunkendubs – Stronetic –
Ironharrow Well – Goats – Tarbrax – Dameye –
Dummiesholes – Caldhame – Hagmuir – Slug of
    Auchrannie –

Baldragon – Thorn – Wreaths – Spurn Hill –
Drowndubs – The Bloody Inches – Halfway – Groan,
where the train will divide

EDWARD THOMAS

Adlestrop

Yes. I remember Adlestrop –
The name, because one afternoon
Of heat the express-train drew up there
Unwontedly. It was late June.

The steam hissed. Someone cleared his throat.
No one left and no one came
On the bare platform. What I saw
Was Adlestrop – only the name

And willows, willow-herb, and grass,
And meadowsweet, and haycocks dry,
No whit less still and lonely fair
Than the high cloudlets in the sky.

And for that minute a blackbird sang
Close by, and round him, mistier,
Farther and farther, all the birds
Of Oxfordshire and Gloucestershire.

CZESLAW MILOSZ

Encounter

We were riding through frozen fields in a wagon at dawn.
A red wing rose in the darkness.

And suddenly a hare ran across the road.
One of us pointed to it with his hand.

That was long ago. Today neither of them is alive,
Not the hare, nor the man who made the gesture.

O my love, where are they, where are they going
The flash of a hand, streak of movement, rustle of pebbles.
I ask not out of sorrow, but in wonder.

translated from the Polish by the author

GRETE TARTLER

Orient Express

Nearly asleep, I'm reading the Desert Fathers.
There are towns, turquoise plains;
at stations I hear announcements in unknown languages.
A man in my compartment was in the war;
he used to play the trumpet.
The woman next to me is crocheting (knots
between good and bad, between truth and falsehood).
It's as if I'm conducting the rhythmic pulse of the train,
the chorus of those who are staying awake
for fear of the dawn.
Once, on holiday in the mountains,
I heard this train go by,
the one I'm on today;
someone told a story about the snake that sucked from a
    cow:
the men found it asleep among the rocks
and struck it with an axe;
milk flowed from it as if from a cask.
Now over the hills, over the acid waters,
over the Greenpeace ships, over the explosions,
the small publicity, the smog, the dried-up springs,
milk flows in waves.
I feel it taking the form of hills,
the form of the brain:
dawn flows into it without filling it;
dawn leaves it without emptying it.

translated from the Romanian by Fleur Adcock

JOHN BURNSIDE

Out of Exile

When we are driving through the border towns
we talk of houses, empty after years
of tea and conversation;
of afternoons marooned against a clock
and silences elected out of fear,
of lives endured for what we disbelieved.

We recognise the shop fronts and the names,
the rushing trees and streets into the dark;
we recognise a pattern in the sky:
blackness flapping like a broken tent,
shadow foxes running in the stars,
But what we recognise is what we bring.

Driving, early, through the border towns,
the dark stone houses clanging at our wheels,
and we invent things as they might have been:
a light switched on, some night, against the cold,
and children at the door, with bags and coats,
telling stories, laughing, coming home.

SOMHAIRLE MACGILL-EAIN (SORLEY MACLEAN)

Creagan Beaga

I am going through Creagan Beaga
in the darkness alone
and the surf on Camus Alba
in a sough on smooth shingle.

The curlew and the plover
are crying down about the Suil;
and south-east of Sgurr nan Gillean,
Blaven, and the stainless moon.

The light levels the sea flatness
from Rubha na Fainge stretched north,
and the current in Caol na h-Airde
is running south with swift glitter.

GEORGE GORDON, LORD BYRON

from Childe Harold's Pilgrimage

I stood in Venice on the Bridge of Sighs,
A palace and a prison on each hand:
I saw from out the wave her structures rise
As from the stroke of the enchanter's wand;
A thousand years their cloudy wings expand
Around me, and a dying glory smiles
O'er the far times, when many a subject land
Looked to the wingèd Lion's marble piles,
Where Venice sat in state, throned on her hundred isles!

She looks a sea Cybele, fresh from ocean,
Rising with her tiara of proud towers
At airy distance, with majestic motion,
A ruler of the waters and their powers,
And such she was; her daughters had their dowers
From spoils of nations, and the exhaustless East
Poured in her lap all gems in sparkling showers:
In purple she was robed, and of her feast
Monarchs partook, and deemed their dignity increased.

In Venice Tasso's echoes are no more,
And silent rows the songless gondolier;
Her palaces are crumbling to the shore,
And music meets not always now the ear:
Those days are gone, but Beauty still is here;
States fall, arts fade, but Nature doth not die,
Nor yet forget how Venice once was dear,
The pleasant place of all festivity,
The revel of the earth, the masque of Italy!

But unto us she hath a spell beyond
Her name is story, and her long array
Of mighty shadows, whose dim forms despond
Above the Dogeless city's vanished sway:
Ours is a trophy which will not decay
With the Rialto; Shylock and the Moor,
And Pierre, cannot be swept or worn away, –
The keystones of the arch! – though all were o'er,
For us repeopled were the solitary shore.

EARLE BIRNEY

Curaçao

I think I am going to love it here

I ask the man in the telegraph office
the way to the bank
He locks the door and walks with me
insisting he needs the exercise

When I ask the lady at my hotel desk
what bus to take to the beach
she gets me a lift with her beautiful sister
who is just driving by in a sports job

And already I have thought of something
I want to ask the sister

ARTHUR HUGH CLOUGH

from Amours de Voyage

CLAUDE TO EUSTACE

I

Dear Eustatio, I write that you may write me an answer,
Or at the least to put us again *en rapport* with each other.
Rome disappoints me much, – St Peter's, perhaps, in
    especial;

Only the Arch of Titus and view from the Lateran please
  me:
This, however, perhaps is the weather, which truly is
  horrid.
Greece must be better, surely; and yet I am feeling so
  spiteful,
That I could travel to Athens, to Delphi, and Troy, and
  Mount Sinai,
Though but to see with my eyes that these are vanity also.
  Rome disappoints me much; I hardly as yet understand,
  but
Rubbishy seems the word that most exactly would suit it.
All the foolish destructions, and all the sillier savings,
All the incongruous things of past incompatible ages,
Seem to be treasured up here to make fools of present and
  future.
Would to Heaven the old Goths had made a cleaner sweep
  of it!
Would to Heaven some new ones would come and destroy
  these churches!
However, one can live in Rome as also in London.
Rome is better than London, because it is other than
  London.
It is a blessing, no doubt, to be rid, at least for a time, of
All one's friends and relations, – yourself (forgive me!)
  included –
All the *assujettissement* of having been what one has been,
What one thinks one is, or thinks that others suppose one;
Yet, in despite of all, we turn like fools to the English.
Vernon has been my fate; who is here the same that you
  knew him
Making the tour, it seems, with friends of the name of
  Trevellyn.

11

Rome disappoints me still; but I shrink and adapt myself to
 it.
Somehow a tyrannous sense of a superincumbent
 oppression
Still, wherever I go, accompanies ever, and makes me
Feel like a tree (shall I say?) buried under a ruin of
 brickwork.
Rome, believe me, my friend, is like its own Monte
 Testaceo,
Merely a marvellous mass of broken and castaway wine-
 pots.
Ye gods! what do I want with this rubbish of ages departed,
Things that Nature abhors, the experiments that she has
 failed in?
What do I find in the Forum? An archway and two or three
 pillars.
Well, but St Peter's? Alas, Bernini has filled it with
 sculpture!
No one can cavil, I grant, at the size of the great Coliseum.
Doubtless the notion of grand and capacious and massive
 amusement,
This the old Romans had; but tell me, is this an idea?
Yet of solidity much, but of splendour little is extant:
'Brickwork I found thee, and marble I left thee!' their
 Emperor vaunted;
'Marble I thought thee, and brickwork I find thee!' the
 Tourist may answer.

TED HUGHES

You Hated Spain

Spain frightened you. Spain
Where I felt at home. The blood-raw light,
The oiled anchovy faces, the African
Black edges to everything, frightened you.

Your schooling had somehow neglected Spain.
The wrought-iron grille, death and the Arab drum.
You did not know the language, your soul was empty
Of the signs, and the welding light
Made your blood shrivel. Bosch
Held out a spidery hand and you took it
Timidly, a bobby-sox American.
You saw right down to the Goya funeral grin
And recognized it, and recoiled
As your poems winced into chill, as your panic
Clutched back towards college America.
So we sat as tourists at the bullfight
Watching bewildered bulls awkwardly butchered,
Seeing the grey-faced matador, at the barrier
Just below us, straightening his bent sword
And vomiting with fear. And the horn
That hid itself inside the blowfly belly
Of the toppled picador punctured
What was waiting for you. Spain
Was the land of your dreams: the dust-red cadaver
You dared not wake with, the puckering amputations
No literature course had glamorized.
The juju land behind your African lips.
Spain was what you tried to wake up from
And could not. I see you, in moonlight,
Walking the empty wharf at Alicante
Like a soul waiting for the ferry,
A new soul, still not understanding,
Thinking it is still your honeymoon
In the happy world, with your whole life waiting,
Happy, and all your poems still to be found.

CHARLES CAUSLEY

On the Border

By the window-drizzling leaves,
Underneath the rain's shadow,
'What is that land,' you said, 'beyond
Where the river bends the meadow?

'Is it Cornwall? Is it Devon?
Those promised fields, blue as the vine,
Wavering under new-grown hills;
Are they yours, or mine?'

When day, like a crystal, broke
We saw what we could see.
No Man's Land was no man's land.
It was the sea.

GLYN MAXWELL

The Furthest West

You lot got dazzled and burned
All afternoon. We two were last to arrive,
Tipsy and hand in hand
And, if they go, and they do, will be last to leave.

The rocks encroach and the Cornish sand stretches
Where we settle. This
Is the furthest west she says she has gone for ages,
Which isn't true, I think, but I say yes.

Blues emerge and blur, like the promenade sketcher
Couldn't do edges well and thought
A vague, dark and watery picture
The pricier art.

Fine constellations spoil his plan. I
Sweep them up in my right hand.

More grains in here, you know, than stars in the sky.
Yes, she says with a sniff. Other way round.

Now the sea goes quiet, straining to hear
Our shared and differing views.
Then gathers, rolling, breaking clean out of nowhere
Its only news.

MONIZA ALVI

Arrival 1946

The boat docked in at Liverpool.
From the train Tariq stared
at an unbroken line of washing
from the North West to Euston.

These are strange people, he thought –
an Empire, and all this washing,
the underwear, the Englishman's garden.
It was Monday, and very sharp.

MARGARET ATWOOD

Disembarking at Quebec

Is it my clothes, my way of walking,
the things I carry in my hand
– a book, a bag with knitting –
the incongruous pink of my shawl
this space cannot hear

or is it my own lack
of conviction which makes
these vistas of desolation,
long hills, the swamps, the barren sand, the glare
of sun on the bone-white
driftlogs, omens of winter,
the moon alien in day-
time a thin refusal

The others leap, shout

    Freedom!

The moving water will not show me
my reflection.

The rocks ignore.

I am a word
in a foreign language.

ANTHONY THWAITE

At the Frontier Post: Om

Under the one step up into the hut
A toad broods by the sergeant's shabby boots.
A single light bulb, acid and unshaded,
Marks out, inside, a function of the state
As well as marking where one road has ended.

Slogans ('To be on guard is half the battle')
Assure the walls if not the occupants.
Only behind a door do I catch glimpses
Of cruder appetites: a brown thigh, supple
With bourgeois blandishments, coyly entices.

Ripped from some old *Paris Match* or *Playboy*,
This functionary's unofficial decor
Cheers me a little as I sit and wait
While name and date of birth and date of entry
Are slowly copied to a dossier sheet.

Outside, between the frontier posts, the hills
Are black, unpeopled. Hours of restlessness
Seep from the silence, silt across the road.
At last the sergeant puts away his files,
Hands me my papers. And I see the toad

Hop into darkness, neutral and unstopped,
Companion of the brown-thighed cover girl
Hidden behind the door, beyond the frontier,
Where appetite and nature are adept
At moving quietly, or at staying still.

AN PAGIS

Instructions for Crossing the Border

Imaginary man, go. Here is your passport.
You are not allowed to remember.
You have to match the description:
your eyes are already blue.
Don't escape with the sparks
inside the smokestack:
you are a man, you sit in the train.
Sit comfortably.
You've got a decent coat now,
a repaired body, a new name
ready in your throat.
Go. You are not allowed to forget.

translated from the Hebrew by Stephen Mitchell

ADRIENNE RICH

Boundary

What has happened here will do
To bite the living world in two,
Half for me and half for you.
Here at last I fix a line
Severing the world's design
Too small to hold both yours and mine.
There's enormity in a hair
Enough to lead men not to share
Narrow confines of a sphere

But put an ocean or a fence
Between two opposite intents.
A hair would span the difference.

TOMAS TRANSTRÖMER

To Friends behind a Frontier

1

I wrote so meagrely to you. But what I couldn't write
swelled and swelled like an old-fashioned airship
and drifted away at last through the night sky.

2

The letter is now at the censor's. He lights his lamp.
In the glare my words fly up like monkeys on a grille,
rattle it, stop, and bare their teeth.

3

Read between the lines. We'll meet in 200 years
when the microphones in the hotel walls are forgotten
and can at last sleep, become trilobites.

translated from the Swedish by Robin Fulton

LAVINIA GREENLAW

A World Where News Travelled Slowly

It could take from Monday to Thursday
and three horses. The ink was unstable,
the characters cramped, the paper tore where it creased.
Stained with the leather and sweat of its journey,
the envelope absorbed each climatic shift,
as well as the salt and grease of the rider
who handed it over with a four-day chance
that by now things were different and while the head
had to listen, the heart could wait.

Semaphore was invented at a time of revolution;
the judgement of swing in a vertical arm.
News travelled letter by letter, along a chain of towers,
each built within telescopic distance of the next.
The clattering mechanics of the six-shutter telegraph
still took three men with all their variables
added to those of light and weather,
to read, record and pass the message on.

Now words are faster, smaller, harder
... *we're almost talking in one another's arms.*
Coded and squeezed, what chance has my voice
to reach your voice unaltered and to leave no trace?
Nets tighten across the sky and the sea bed.
When London made contact with New York,
there were such fireworks, City Hall caught light.
It could have burned to the ground.

LFRED, LORD TENNYSON

Ulysses

It little profits that an idle king,
By this still hearth, among these barren crags,
Match'd with an aged wife, I mete and dole
Unequal laws unto a savage race,
That hoard, and sleep, and feed, and know not me.
I cannot rest from travel: I will drink
Life to the lees: all times I have enjoy'd
Greatly, have suffer'd greatly, both with those
That loved me, and alone; on shore, and when
Thro' scudding drifts the rainy Hyades
Vext the dim sea: I am become a name;
For always roaming with a hungry heart
Much have I seen and known; cities of men
And manners, climates, councils, governments,
Myself not least, but honour'd of them all;

And drunk delight of battle with my peers,
Far on the ringing plains of windy Troy.
I am a part of all that I have met;
Yet all experience is an arch wherethro'
Gleams that untravell'd world, whose margin fades
For ever and for ever when I move.
How dull it is to pause, to make an end,
To rust unburnish'd, not to shine in use!
As tho' to breathe were life. Life piled on life
Were all too little, and of one to me
Little remains: but every hour is saved
From that eternal silence, something more,
A bringer of new things; and vile it were
For some three suns to store and hoard myself,
And this gray spirit yearning in desire
To follow knowledge like a sinking star,
Beyond the utmost bound of human thought.

    This is my son, mine own Telemachus,
To whom I leave the sceptre and the isle –
Well-loved of me, discerning to fulfil
This labour, by slow prudence to make mild
A rugged people, and thro' soft degrees
Subdue them to the useful and the good.
Most blameless is he, centred in the sphere
Of common duties, decent not to fail
In offices of tenderness, and pay
Meet adoration to my household gods,
When I am gone. He works his work, I mine.

    There lies the port; the vessel puffs her sail:
There gloom the dark broad seas. My mariners,
Souls that have toil'd, and wrought, and thought with
    me –
That ever with a frolic welcome took
The thunder and the sunshine, and opposed
Free hearts, free foreheads – you and I are old;
Old age hath yet his honour and his toil;

Death closes all: but something ere the end,
Some work of noble note, may yet be done,
Not unbecoming men that strove with Gods.
The lights begin to twinkle from the rocks:
The long day wanes: the slow moon climbs: the deep
Moans round with many voices. Come, my friends,
'Tis not too late to seek a newer world.
Push off, and sitting well in order smite
The sounding furrows; for my purpose holds
To sail beyond the sunset, and the baths
Of all the western stars, until I die.
It may be that the gulfs will wash us down:
It may be we shall touch the Happy Isles,
And see the great Achilles, whom we knew.
Tho' much is taken, much abides; and tho'
We are not now that strength which in old days
Moved earth and heaven; that which we are, we are;
One equal temper of heroic hearts,
Made weak by time and fate, but strong in will
To strive, to seek, to find, and not to yield.

LAURA RIDING

The Map of Places

The map of places passes.
The reality of paper tears.
Land and water where they are
Are only where they were
When words read *here* and *here*
Before ships happened there.

Now on naked names feet stand,
No geographies in the hand,
And paper reads anciently,
And ships at sea
Turn round and round.

All is known, all is found.
Death meets itself everywhere.
Holes in maps look through to nowhere.

SYLVIA PLATH

Crossing the Water

Black lake, black boat, two black, cut-paper people.
Where do the black trees go that drink here?
Their shadows must cover Canada.

A little light is filtering from the water flowers.
Their leaves do not wish us to hurry:
They are round and flat and full of dark advice.

Cold worlds shake from the oar.
The spirit of blackness is in us, it is in the fishes.
A snag is lifting a valedictory, pale hand;

Stars open among the lilies.
Are you not blinded by such expressionless sirens?
This is the silence of astounded souls.

ANONYMOUS

For William Harrison, Mariner
(In Hessle Cemetery, Hull)

Long time I ploughed the ocean wide,
    A life of toil I spent;
But now in harbour safe arrived
    From care and discontent.

My anchor's cast, my sails are furled,
    And now I am at rest;
Of all the ports throughout the world,
    Sailors, this is the best.

War

Target Practice

Near Mexico, near April, in the morning.
Desert where the sun casts his circles of power
on acquiescent sand shifting beneath them. Car
speeding among white landscapes;   suddenly
the permanent scene at the dead-center.

Photo, in circles of speed, how at raw barnside
father and son stand, man with his rifle up
levelled at heartpoint of a nailed-up bird
spread, wings against the wood. The boy's arm thrown
up over his eyes, flinching from coming shot.

Bullseye, you bullet! pinning down the scene.
And speed you car over the waste of noon
into the boundaries of distance where
the first ring lessens into memory.
Until, a little lower than the sun,

centered in that last circle, hangs a free
fierce bird down-staring on the target of land,
circle on circle of power spread, and speeding
eyes passing from zone to zone, from war to where
their bullets will never bring him down.

Range-Finding

The battle rent a cobweb diamond-strung
And cut a flower beside a groundbird's nest
Before it stained a single human breast.
The stricken flower bent double and so hung.
And still the bird revisited her young.
A butterfly its fall had dispossessed,
A moment sought in air his flower of rest,

Then lightly stooped to it and fluttering clung.
On the bare upland pasture there had spread
O'ernight 'twixt mullein stalks a wheel of thread
And straining cables wet with silver dew.
A sudden passing bullet shook it dry.
The indwelling spider ran to greet the fly,
But finding nothing, sullenly withdrew.

W. B. YEATS

An Irish Airman Foresees His Death

I know that I shall meet my fate
Somewhere among the clouds above;
Those that I fight I do not hate,
Those that I guard I do not love;
My country is Kiltartan Cross,
My countrymen Kiltartan's poor,
No likely end could bring them loss
Or leave them happier than before.
Nor law, nor duty bade me fight,
Nor public men, nor cheering crowds,
A lonely impulse of delight
Drove to this tumult in the clouds;
I balanced all, brought all to mind,
The years to come seemed waste of breath,
A waste of breath the years behind
In balance with this life, this death.

EDWARD THOMAS

As the team's head brass

As the team's head brass flashed out on the turn
The lovers disappeared into the wood.
I sat among the boughs of the fallen elm
That strewed an angle of the fallow, and
Watched the plough narrowing a yellow square

Of charlock. Every time the horses turned
Instead of treading me down, the ploughman leaned
Upon the handles to say or ask a word,
About the weather, next about the war.
Scraping the share he faced towards the wood,
And screwed along the furrow till the brass flashed
Once more.
        The blizzard felled the elm whose crest
I sat in, by a woodpecker's round hole,
The ploughman said. 'When will they take it away?'
'When the war's over.' So the talk began –
One minute and an interval of ten,
A minute more and the same interval.
'Have you been out?' 'No.' 'And don't want to, perhaps?'
'If I could only come back again, I should.
I could spare an arm. I shouldn't want to lose
A leg. If I should lose my head, why, so,
I should want nothing more. . . . Have many gone
From here?' 'Yes.' 'Many lost?' 'Yes, a good few.
Only two teams work on the farm this year.
One of my mates is dead. The second day
In France they killed him. It was back in March,
The very night of the blizzard, too. Now if
He had stayed here we should have moved the tree.'
'And I should not have sat here. Everything
Would have been different. For it would have been
Another world.' 'Ay, and a better, though
If we could see all all might seem good.' Then
The lovers came out of the wood again:
The horses started and for the last time
I watched the clods crumble and topple over
After the ploughshare and the stumbling team.

HENRY REED

from Lessons of the War

NAMING OF PARTS

To-day we have naming of parts. Yesterday,
We had daily cleaning. And to-morrow morning,
We shall have what to do after firing. But to-day,
To-day we have naming of parts. Japonica
Glistens like coral in all of the neighbouring gardens,
    And to-day we have naming of parts.

This is the lower sling swivel. And this
Is the upper sling swivel, whose use you will see,
    When you are given your slings. And this is the piling
      swivel,
Which in your case you have not got. The branches
Hold in the gardens their silent, eloquent gestures,
    Which in our case we have not got.

This is the safety-catch, which is always released
With an easy flick of the thumb. And please do not let me
See anyone using his finger. You can do it quite easy
If you have any strength in your thumb. The blossoms
Are fragile and motionless, never letting anyone see
    Any of them using their finger.

And this you can see is the bolt. The purpose of this
Is to open the breech, as you see. We can slide it
Rapidly backwards and forwards: we call this
Easing the spring. And rapidly backwards and forwards
The early bees are assaulting and fumbling the flowers:
    They call it easing the Spring.

They call it easing the Spring: it is perfectly easy
If you have any strength in your thumb: like the bolt,
And the breech, and the cocking-piece, and the point of
    balance,

Which in our case we have not got; and the almond-
    blossom
Silent in all of the gardens and the bees going backwards
    and forwards,
        For to-day we have naming of parts.

JAMIE MCKENDRICK

In the Hold

Route-marching, field-postcards, tents hung with scrim
– we waited in those Domesday parishes
for D-Day to begin.

Beyond the wood there was a flint-harled church
and a watertower like a missile in plainclothes
– a tall tube with a concrete hat on top.

I can still feel the pink rim the beret left
embossed on my receded hairline
and the veins in my forehead swelling

with the notes of the birds I couldn't see
bubbling like water through a sea-vent
while darkness linked the leaves and thickened.

From Suffolk they drove us down by night
to the New Forest where we were nearer still
the zero-hour

that months of training had prepared us for
not thinking too far ahead of or about
by filling the days with strict inspections.

And then the lorry drive in convoy
to the blunt-hulled landing ships,
the gangplank a small step from the footboard.

Once in the hold I heard the air compress
as the round steel hatch was clamped down shut
and tightened by a half-turn on the hand-grips

and there we all were in the dim light that came on
stowed in the hollow belly of the war
– a box that clanged and stank of diesel –

till daylight heaped us on the other shore.

JOHN DRYDEN

from Annus Mirabilis:
The Year of Wonders, 1666

The warlike Prince had severed from the rest
   Two giant ships, the pride of all the main,
Which with his one so vigorously he pressed
   And flew so home they could not rise again.

Already battered, by his lee they lay,
   In vain upon the passing winds they call:
The passing winds through their torn canvas play,
   And flagging sails on heartless sailors fall.

Their opened sides receive a gloomy light,
   Dreadful as day let in to shades below;
Without, grim Death rides bare-faced in their sight,
   And urges entering billows as they flow.

When one dire shot, the last they could supply,
   Close by the board the Prince's mainmast bore,
All three now helpless by each other lie,
   And this offends not, and those fear no more.

So have I seen some fearful hare maintain
   A course, till tired before the dog she lay,
Who, stretched behind her, pants upon the plain,
   Past power to kill as she to get away:

And now no longer letted of his prey
   He leaps up at it with enraged desire,
O'erlooks the neighbours with a wide survey,
   And nods at every house his threatening fire.

from War Music (Homer; The Iliad)

   Swarming up and off the beach
Patroclus swung Achilles' Myrmidons
Left at the ditch.
   Keeping it on their right they streamed
Along the camp's main track; one side, the rampart;
On the other, ships.
   Things were so close you could not see your front;
And from the footplate of his wheels, Patroclus cried:
   'For Achilles!'
As the enemies closed.

   The Trojans lay across the ship,
Most of them busy seeing that it burned.
Others slid underneath and were so occupied
Knocking away the chocks that kept it upright,
They did not see Patroclus stoop.
   But those above did.
In less time than it takes to dip and light a match
Achilles' helmet loomed above their cheeks
With Myrmidons splayed out on either side
Like iron wings.
   Dropping the pitch
They reached for javelins, keelspikes, boat-hooks, Oh,
Anything to keep Achilles off –
Have he and Agamemnon patched things up?

   Patroclus aimed his spear where they were thickest.
That is to say, around
The chariot commander, Akafact.
But as Patroclus threw
The ship's mast flamed from stem to peak, and fell
Lengthwise across the incident.
   Its fat waist clubbed the hull's top deck
And the ship flopped sideways.

Those underneath got crunched.
And howling Greeks ran up
To pike the others as they slithered off.
    This fate was not for Akafact:
Because the mast's peak hit the sand no more than six
Feet from Patroclus' car, the horses shied,
Spoiling his cast. Nothing was lost.
    As he fell back, back arched,
God blew the javelin straight; and thus
Mid-air, the cold bronze apex sank
Between his teeth and tongue, parted his brain,
Pressed on, and stapled him against the upturned hull.
His dead jaw gaped. His soul
Crawled off his tongue and vanished into sunlight.

JOHN DONNE

A Burnt Ship

Out of a fired ship, which, by no way
But drowning, could be rescued from the flame,
Some men leaped forth, and ever as they came
Near the foe's ships, did by their shot decay;
So all were lost, which in the ship were found,
    They in the sea being burnt, they in the burnt ship
    drowned.

MOLLY HOLDEN

Seaman, 1941

This was not to be expected.

Waves, wind, and tide brought him again
to Barra. Clinging to driftwood many hours
the night before, he had not recognised
the current far off-shore his own nor
known he drifted home. He gave up, anyway,

some time before the smell of land reached out
or dawn outlined the morning gulls.

                              They found him
on the white sand southward of the ness,
not long enough in the sea to be
disfigured, cheek sideways as in sleep,
old men who had fished with his father
and grandfather and knew him at once,
before they even turned him on his back, by the set
of the dead shoulders, and were shocked.

This was not to be expected.

His mother, with hot eyes, preparing the parlour
for his corpse, would have preferred, she thought,
to have been told by telegram rather
than so to know that convoy, ship, and son
had only been a hundred miles north-west
of home when the torpedoes struck.
She could have gone on thinking that
he'd had no chance; but to die offshore,
in Hebridean tides, as if he'd stayed
a fisherman for life and never gone to war
was not to be expected.

CHARLES CAUSLEY

Rattler Morgan

Now his eyes are bright farthings
   And he spindles
In seas deeper than death.
   His lips are no longer wet with wine
But gleam with green salt
   And the Gulf Stream is his breath.

Now he is fumbled by ancient tides
   Among decks flagged with seaweed

But no flags sees he there.
   His fingers are washed to stone
And to phosphor
   And there are starfish in his hair.

[HMS *Cabbala*]

RICHARD EBERHART

The Fury of Aerial Bombardment

You would think the fury of aerial bombardment
Would rouse God to relent; the infinite spaces
Are still silent. He looks on shock-pried faces.
History, even, does not know what is meant.

You would feel that after so many centuries
God would give man to repent; yet he can kill
As Cain could, but with multitudinous will,
No farther advanced than in his ancient furies.

Was man made stupid to see his own stupidity?
Is God by definition indifferent, beyond us all?
Is the eternal truth man's fighting soul
Wherein the Beast ravens in its own avidity?

Of Van Wettering I speak, and Averill,
Names on a list, whose faces I do not recall
But they are gone to early death, who late in school
Distinguished the belt feed lever from the belt holding
   pawl.

RANDALL JARRELL

The Death of the Ball Turret Gunner

From my mother's sleep I fell into the State,
And I hunched in its belly till my wet fur froze.
Six miles from earth, loosed from its dream of life,

I woke to black flak and the nightmare fighters.
When I died they washed me out of the turret with a hose.

MIROSLAV HOLUB

Five minutes after the air raid

In Pilsen,
twenty-six Station Road,
she climbed to the third floor
up stairs which were all that was left
of the whole house,
she opened her door
full on to the sky,
stood gaping over the edge.

For this was the place
the world ended.

Then
she locked up carefully
lest someone steal
Sirius
or Aldebaran
from her kitchen,
went back downstairs
and settled herself
to wait
for the house to rise again
and for her husband to rise from the ashes
and for her children's hands and feet to be stuck back in
    place.

In the morning they found her
still as stone,
sparrows pecking her hands.

> translated from the Czech by Ewald Osers

from The Battle of Maldon

Then the wolvish Vikings, avid for slaughter,
Waded to the west across the River Panta;
The seafarers hoisted their shields on high
And carried them over the gleaming water.
Byrhtnoth and his warriors awaited them,
Ready for battle: he ordered his men
To form a phalanx with their shields, and to stand firm
Against the onslaught of the enemy. Then was the battle,
With its chance of glory, about to begin. The time had
    come
For all the doomed men to fall in the fight.
The clamour began; the ravens wheeled and the eagle
Circled overhead, craving for carrion; there was shouting
    on earth.
They hurled their spears, hard as files,
And sent sharp darts flying from their hands.
Bow strings were busy, shield parried point,
Bitter was the battle. Brave men fell
On both sides, youths choking in the dust.
Byrhtnoth's sister's son, *Wulfmær*, was wounded;
Slashed by the sword, he decided
To sleep on the bed of death.
This was violently requited, the Vikings were repaid in
    kind.
I was told that *Eadweard* swung his sword
So savagely – a full-blooded blow –
That a fated warrior fell lifeless at his feet.
Byrhtnoth shouted out his thanks to him,
His chamberlain, as soon as he had a chance to do so.
The brave men stood resolute, rock firm.
Each of them eagerly hunted for a way
To be first in with his spear,
Winning with his weapons the life

Of a doomed warrior; the dead sank down to the earth.
But the rest stood unshaken and *Byrhtnoth* spurred them
 on,
Inciting each man to fight ferociously
Who wished to gain glory against the Danes.
Then a brave seafarer raised up his spear,
Gripped his shield and advanced towards *Byrhtnoth*.
The resolute earl advanced towards the churl;
Each had evil designs on the other.
The Viking was the quicker – he hurled his foreign spear
Wounding the lord of the warriors.
Byrhtnoth broke the shaft with the edge of his shield;
The imbedded spear-head sprang out of his wound.
Then he flung his spear in fury
At the proud Viking who dared inflict such pain.
His aim was skilful. The spear
Slit open the warrior's neck.
Thus *Byrhtnoth* put paid to his enemy's life.
Then, for safety's sake, he swiftly hurled another
Which burst the Viking's breastplate, cruelly wounding
 him
In the chest; the deadly spear pierced his heart.

translated from the Anglo-Saxon by Kevin Crossley-Holland and
Bruce Mitchell

EAVAN BOLAND

The War Horse

This dry night, nothing unusual
About the clip, clop, casual

Iron of his shoes as he stamps death
Like a mint on the innocent coinage of earth.

I lift the window, watch the ambling feather
Of hock and fetlock, loosed from its daily tether

In the tinker camp on the Enniskerry Road,
Pass, his breath hissing, his snuffling head

Down. He is gone. No great harm is done.
Only a leaf of our laurel hedge is torn –

Of distant interest like a maimed limb,
Only a rose which now will never climb

The stone of our house, expendable, a mere
Line of defence against him, a volunteer

You might say, only a crocus its bulbous head
Blown from growth, one of the screamless dead.

But we, we are safe, our unformed fear
Of fierce commitment gone; why should we care

If a rose, a hedge, a crocus are uprooted
Like corpses, remote, crushed, mutilated?

He stumbles on like a rumour of war, huge,
Threatening; neighbours use the subterfuge

Of curtains; he stumbles down our short street
Thankfully passing us. I pause, wait.

Then to breathe relief lean on the sill
And for a second only my blood is still

With atavism. That rose he smashed frays
Ribboned across our hedge, recalling days

Of burned countryside, illicit braid:
A cause ruined before, a world betrayed.

ISAAC ROSENBERG

Break of Day in the Trenches

The darkness crumbles away.
It is the same old druid Time as ever,

Only a live thing leaps my hand,
A queer sardonic rat,
As I pull the parapet's poppy
To stick behind my ear.
Droll rat, they would shoot you if they knew
Your cosmopolitan sympathies.
Now you have touched this English hand
You will do the same to a German
Soon, no doubt, if it be your pleasure
To cross the sleeping green between.
It seems you inwardly grin as you pass
Strong eyes, fine limbs, haughty athletes,
Less chanced than you for life,
Bonds to the whims of murder,
Sprawled in the bowels of the earth,
The torn fields of France.
What do you see in our eyes
At the shrieking iron and flame
Hurled through still heavens?
What quaver – what heart aghast?
Poppies whose roots are in man's veins
Drop, and are ever dropping;
But mine in my ear is safe –
Just a little white with the dust.

SIEGFRIED SASSOON

The Rear-Guard

(Hindenberg Line, April 1917)

Groping along the tunnel, step by step,
He winked his prying torch with patching glare
From side to side, and sniffed the unwholesome air.

Tins, boxes, bottles, shapes too vague to know;
A mirror smashed, the mattress from a bed;
And he, exploring fifty feet below
The rosy gloom of battle overhead.

Tripping, he grabbed the wall; saw someone lie
Humped at his feet, half-hidden by a rug,
And stooped to give the sleeper's arm a tug.
'I'm looking for headquarters.' No reply.
'God blast your neck!' (For days he'd had no sleep,)
'Get up and guide me through this stinking place.'

Savage, he kicked a soft, unanswering heap,
And flashed his beam across the livid face
Terribly glaring up, whose eyes yet wore
Agony dying hard ten days before;
And fists of fingers clutched a blackening wound.

Alone he staggered on until he found
Dawn's ghost that filtered down a shafted stair
To the dazed, muttering creatures underground
Who hear the boom of shells in muffled sound.
At last, with sweat of horror in his hair,
He climbed through darkness to the twilight air,
Unloading hell behind him step by step.

PAUL MULDOON

Truce

It begins with one or two soldiers
And one or two following
With hampers over their shoulders.
They might be off wildfowling

As they would another Christmas Day,
So gingerly they pick their steps.
No one seems sure of what to do.
All stop when one stops.

A fire gets lit. Some spread
Their greatcoats on the frozen ground.
Polish vodka, fruit and bread
Are broken out and passed round.

The air of an old German song,
The rules of Patience, are the secrets
They'll share before long.
They draw on their last cigarettes

As Friday-night lovers, when it's over,
Might get up from their mattresses
To congratulate each other
And exchange names and addresses.

DAVID JONES

from In Parenthesis, Part 7

And now all the wood-ways live with familiar faces and
your mate moves like Jack o' the Green: for this season's
fertility gone unpruned, & this year's renewing sap shot
up fresh tendrils to cumber greenly the heaped decay of
last fall, and no forester to tend the paths, nor strike with
axes to the root of selected boles, nor had come Jacqueline
to fill a pinafore with may-thorn.

But keepers who engineer new and powerful devices,
forewarned against this morning
prepared with booby-trap beneath
and platforms in the stronger branches
like main-top for an arbalestier,
precisely and competently advised and all in the know,
as to this hour
        when unicorns break cover
and come down
and foxes flee, whose warrens know the shock,
and birds complain in flight – for their nests fall like stars
        and all their airy world gone crazed
and the whole woodland rocks where these break their
    horns.

It was largely his machine guns in Acid Copse that did it and our own heavies firing by map reference, with all lines phut and no reliable liaison.

So you just lay where you were and shielded what you could of your body.

It slackened a little and they try short rushes and you find yourself alone in a denseness of hazel-brush and body high bramble and between the bright interstices and multifarious green-stuff, grey textile, scarlet-edged goes and comes – and there is another withdrawing-heel from the thicket.

His light stick-bomb winged above your thorn-bush, and aged oak-timbers shiver and leaves shower like thrown blossom for a conqueror.
You tug at rusted pin –
it gives unexpectedly and your fingers pressed to released flange.
You loose the thing into the underbrush.

Dark-faceted iron oval lobs heavily to fungus-cushioned dank, wobbles under low leaf to lie, near where the heel drew out just now; and tough root-fibres boomerang to top-most green filigree and earth clods flung disturb fresh fragile shoots that brush the sky.

You huddle closer to your mossy bed
you make yourself scarce
you scramble forward and pretend not to see,
but ruby drops from young beech-sprigs –
are bright your hands and face.

And the other one cries from the breaking-buckthorn.

He calls for Elsa, for Manuela
for the parish priest of Burkersdorf in Saxe Altenburg.

You grab his dropt stick-bomb as you go, but somehow you don't fancy it and anyway you forget how it works. You definitely like the coloured label on the handle, you throw it to the tall wood-weeds.

So double detonations, back and fro like well-played-
up-to service at a net, mark left and right the forcing of
the groves.

WILFRED OWEN

Dulce Et Decorum Est

Bent double, like old beggars under sacks,
Knock-kneed, coughing like hags, we cursed through
    sludge,
Till on the haunting flares we turned our backs
And towards our distant rest began to trudge.
Men marched asleep. Many had lost their boots
But limped on, blood-shod. All went lame; all blind;
Drunk with fatigue; deaf even to the hoots
Of tired, outstripped Five-Nines that dropped behind.

Gas! GAS! Quick, boys – An ecstasy of fumbling,
Fitting the clumsy helmets just in time;
But someone still was yelling out and stumbling,
And flound'ring like a man in fire or lime . . .
Dim, through the misty panes and thick green light,
As under a green sea, I saw him drowning.
In all my dreams, before my helpless sight,
He plunges at me, guttering, choking, drowning.

If in some smothering dreams you too could pace
Behind the wagon that we flung him in,
And watch the white eyes writhing in his face,
His hanging face, like a devil's sick of sin;
If you could hear, at every jolt, the blood
Come gargling from the froth-corrupted lungs,
Obscene as cancer, bitter as the cud
Of vile, incurable sores on innocent tongues, –
My friend, you would not tell with such high zest
To children ardent for some desperate glory,

The old Lie: Dulce et decorum est
Pro patria mori.

RUDYARD KIPLING

from Epitaphs of the War 1914–18

'EQUALITY OF SACRIFICE'

A. 'I was a Have.' B. 'I was a "have-not."'
   (*Together.*) 'What hast thou given which I gave not?'

A SON

My son was killed while laughing at some jest. I would I
   knew
What it was, and it might serve me in a time when jests are
   few.

AN ONLY SON

I have slain none except my Mother. She
(Blessing her slayer) died of grief for me.

THE COWARD

I could not look on Death, which being known,
Men led me to him, blindfold and alone.

A GRAVE NEAR CAIRO

Gods of the Nile, should this stout fellow here
Get out – get out! He knows not shame nor fear.

THE FAVOUR

Death favoured me from the first, well knowing I could not
   endure
   To wait on him day by day. He quitted my betters and
     came
Whistling over the fields, and, when he had made all sure,
   'Thy line is at end,' he said, 'but at least I have saved its
     name.'

THE BEGINNER

On the first hour of my first day
   In the front trench I fell.
(Children in boxes at a play
   Stand up to watch it well.)

THE SLEEPY SENTINEL

Faithless the watch that I kept: now I have none to keep.
I was slain because I slept: now I am slain I sleep.
Let no man reproach me again, whatever watch is
     unkept –
I sleep because I am slain. They slew me because I slept.

COMMON FORM

If any question why we died,
Tell them, because our fathers lied.

SYLVIA TOWNSEND WARNER

Road 1940

Why do I carry, she said,
This child that is no child of mine?
Through the heat of the day it did nothing but fidget and
   whine,
Now it snuffles under the dew and the cold star-shine,
And lies across my heart heavy as lead,
Heavy as the dead.

Why did I lift it, she said,
Out of its cradle in the wheel-tracks?
On the dusty road burdens have melted like wax,
Soldiers have thrown down their rifles, misers slipped
   their packs:
Yes, and the woman who left it there has sped
With a lighter tread.

Though I should save it, she said,
What have I saved for the world's use?

If it grow to hero it will die or let loose
Death, or to hireling, nature already is too profuse
Of such, who hope and are disinherited,
Plough, and are not fed.

But since I've carried it, she said,
So far I might as well carry it still.
If we ever should come to kindness someone will
Pity me perhaps as the mother of a child so ill,
Grant me even to lie down on a bed;
Give me at least bread.

ANNA ŚWIRSZCZYŃSKA

Building the Barricade

We were afraid as we built the barricade
under fire.

The tavern-keeper, the jeweller's mistress, the barber,
all of us cowards.

The servant-girl fell to the ground
as she lugged a paving stone, we were terribly afraid
all of us cowards –
the janitor, the market-woman, the pensioner.

The pharmacist fell to the ground
as he dragged the door of a toilet,
we were even more afraid, the smuggler-woman,
the dressmaker, the streetcar driver,
all of us cowards.

A kid from reform school fell
as he dragged a sandbag,
you see we were really
afraid.

Though no one forced us,
we did build the barricade
under fire.

translated from the Polish by Magnus Jan Krynski and
Robert Maguire

ANTHONY HECHT

'More Light! More Light!'
for Heinrich Blücher and Hannah Arendt

Composed in the Tower before his execution
These moving verses, and being brought at that time
Painfully to the stake, submitted, declaring thus:
'I implore my God to witness that I have made no crime.'

Nor was he forsaken of courage, but the death was
   horrible
The sack of gunpowder failing to ignite.
His legs were blistered sticks on which the black sap
Bubbled and burst as he howled for the Kindly Light.

And that was but one, and by no means one of the worst:
Permitted at least his pitiful dignity;
And such as were by made prayers in the name of Christ,
That shall judge all men, for his soul's tranquillity.

We move now to outside a German wood.
Three men are there commanded to dig a hole
In which the two Jews are ordered to lie down
And be buried alive by the third, who is a Pole.

Not light from the shrine at Weimar beyond the hill
Nor light from heaven appeared. But he did refuse.
A Lüger settled back deeply in its glove.
He was ordered to change places with the Jews.

Much casual death had drained away their souls.
The thick dirt mounted toward the quivering chin.

When only the head was exposed the order came
To dig him out again and to get back in.

No light, no light in the blue Polish eye.
When he finished a riding boot packed down the earth.
The Lüger hovered lightly in its glove.
He was shot in the belly and in three hours bled to death.

No prayers or incense rose up in those hours
Which grew to be years, and every day came mute
Ghosts from the ovens, sifting through crisp air,
And settled upon his eyes in a black soot.

CIARAN CARSON

Army

The duck patrol is waddling down the odd-numbers side of
     Raglan Street,
The bass-ackwards private at the rear trying not to think
     of a third eye
Being drilled in the back of his head. Fifty-five. They stop.
     The head
Peers round, then leaps the gap of Balaclava Street. He
     waves the body over
One by one. Forty-nine. Cape Street. A gable wall. Garnet
     Street. A gable wall.

Frere Street. Forty-seven. Forty-five-and-a-half. Milan
     Street. A grocer's shop.
They stop. They check their guns. Thirteen. Milton Street.
     An iron lamp-post.
Number one. Ormond Street. *Two ducks in front of a duck and*
     two ducks
Behind a duck, how many ducks? Five? *No. Three.* This is not
     the end.

To His Love

He's gone, and all our plans
    Are useless indeed.
We'll walk no more on Cotswold
    Where the sheep feed
    Quietly and take no heed.

His body that was so quick
    Is not as you
Knew it, on Severn river
    Under the blue
    Driving our small boat through.

You would not know him now . . .
    But still he died
Nobly, so cover him over
    With violets of pride
    Purple from Severn side.

Cover him, cover him soon!
    And with thick-set
Masses of memoried flowers –
    Hide that red wet
    Thing I must somehow forget.

RICHARD WILBUR

Tywater

Death of Sir Nihil, book the *nth*,
Upon the charred and clotted sward,
Lacking the lily of our Lord,
Alases of the hyacinth.

Could flicker from behind his ear
A whistling silver throwing knife

And with a holler punch the life
Out of a swallow in the air.

Behind the lariat's butterfly
Shuttled his white and gritted grin,
And cuts of sky would roll within
The noose-hole, when he spun it high.

The violent, neat and practised skill
Was all he loved and all he learned;
When he was hit, his body turned
To clumsy dirt before it fell.

And what to say of him, God knows.
Such violence. And such repose.

MARTIN BELL

David Guest

Well O.K., he was wrong
Getting killed in Spain
Like that. Wal Hannington
Sat and tried to argue him out of going.
He was wrong, he was wrong,
The angel has not descended, the state
Hasn't the faintest chance of withering away,
And nobody is sure which way Hegel is up any more.
He was the greatest hero I've met because he was brave,
And would argue with anybody,
And could interest people because he was interested –
If he was so bloody interested he should have gone on
    talking, gone on talking,
Something might have been talked out.
Near to a saint, he should not have got himself killed,
Thereby making himself an ineffectual angel, a moth.
The Professor of economics was right:
He just couldn't keep still at a public meeting,

He would keep turning round and standing up to see what
    was happening and who was talking,
And this was probably how the bullet got him in the
    trenches at Jarama.

TAMIKI HARA

Glittering Fragments

Glittering fragments
Ashen embers
Like a rippling panorama,
Burning red then dulled.
Strange rhythm of human corpses.
All existence, all that could exist
Laid bare in a flash. The rest of the world
The swelling of a horse's corpse
At the side of an upturned train,
The smell of smouldering electric wires.

    translated from the Japanese by Geoffrey Bownas and
    Anthony Thwaite

KEITH DOUGLAS

Vergissmeinicht

Three weeks gone and the combatants gone,
returning over the nightmare ground
we found the place again, and found
the soldier sprawling in the sun.

The frowning barrel of his gun
overshadowing. As we came on
that day, he hit my tank with one
like the entry of a demon.

Look. Here in the gunpit spoil
the dishonoured picture of his girl

who has put: *Steffi. Vergissmeinicht*
in a copybook gothic script.

We see him almost with content
abased, and seeming to have paid
and mocked at by his own equipment
that's hard and good when he's decayed.

But she would weep to see today
how on his skin the swart flies move;
the dust upon the paper eye
and the burst stomach like a cave.

For here the lover and killer are mingled
who had one body and one heart.
And death who had the soldier singled
has done the lover mortal hurt.

MIKLÓS RADNOTI

Fragment

I lived on this earth in an age
when man became so debased
that he killed on his own, with lust, not just on orders,
and while holding false beliefs and foaming raving, lost,
wild obsessions braided, choked off his lot.

I lived on this earth in an age
when in informing lay merit and murderers,
backstabbers and muggers were your heroes –
and the man who kept silent and was loath to applaud,
they hated even him, as if he carried the plague.

I lived on this earth in an age
when the man who spoke up could go into hiding
and could there gnaw on his clenched fists in shame –
the country went wild and at a terrible fate
gloated, reeling drunk from blood and from filth.

I lived on this earth in an age
when a mother was a curse to her child
and the woman was happy to miscarry,
the living envied the worm-eaten dead their prison,
and on the table there foamed a thick drink of poison.

. . . .

. . . .

I lived on this earth in an age
when the poet too just kept his silence
and waited, maybe to find his voice again –
for, surely, no one else could utter a worthy curse
but Isaiah, learned master of terrible words.

. . . .

translated from the Hungarian by Emery George

ANONYMOUS

The Twa Corbies

As I was walking all alane
I heard twa corbies making a mane;
The tane unto the t'other say,
'Where sall we gang and dine today?'

'– In behint yon auld fail dyke,
I wot there lies a new-slain Knight;
And naebody kens that he lies there,
But his hawk, his hound, and lady fair.

'His hound is to the hunting gane,
His hawk to fetch the wild-fowl hame,
His lady's ta'en another mate,
So we may mak our dinner sweet.

'Ye'll sit on his white hause-bane,
And I'll pick out his bonnie blue een;
Wi' ae lock o' his gowden hair
We'll theek our nest when it grows bare.

'Mony a one for him makes mane,
But nane sall ken where he is gane;
O'er his white banes, when they are bare,
The wind sall blaw for evermair.'

GEOFFREY HILL

from Funeral Music

They bespoke doomsday and they meant it by
God, their curved metal rimming the low ridge.
But few appearances are like this. Once
Every five hundred years a comet's
Over-riding stillness might reveal men
In such array, livid and featureless,
With England crouched beastwise beneath it all.
'Oh, that old northern business . . .' A field
After battle utters its own sound
Which is like nothing on earth, but is earth.
Blindly the questing snail, vulnerable
Mole emerge, blindly we lie down, blindly
Among carnage the most delicate souls
Tup in their marriage-blood, gasping 'Jesus'.

ROBERT BURNS

Lament for Culloden

The lovely lass o' Inverness,
Nae joy nor pleasure can she see;
For e'en and morn she cries, Alas!
And aye the saut tear blins her ee:
Drumossie moor – Drumossie day –
A waefu' day it was to me!
For there I lost my father dear,
My father dear, and brethren three.

Their winding-sheet the bluidy clay,
Their graves are growing green to see:
And by them lies the dearest lad
That ever blest a woman's ee!
Now wae to thee, thou cruel lord,
A bluidy man I trow thou be;
For mony a heart thou hast made sair
That ne'er did wrang to thine or thee.

MARINA TSVETAYEVA

from Poems to Czechoslovakia

They took   quickly, they took   hugely,
   took the mountains and their entrails.
They took our coal, and took our steel
   from us, lead they took also and crystal.

They took the sugar, and they took the clover
   they took the North and took the West.
They took the hive, and took the haystack
   they took the South from us, and took the East.

Vary   they took and Tatras   they took,
   they took the near at hand and far away.
But   worse than taking paradise on earth from us
   they won the battle for our native land.

Bullets they took from us, they took our rifles
   minerals they took, and comrades too:
But while our mouths have spittle in them
   The whole country   is still armed.

translated from the Russian by Elaine Feinstein

ROBERT LOWELL

Fall 1961

Back and forth, back and forth
goes the tock, tock, tock
of the orange, bland, ambassadorial
face of the moon
on the grandfather clock.

All autumn, the chafe and jar
of nuclear war;
we have talked our extinction to death.
I swim like a minnow
Behind my studio window.

Our end drifts nearer,
the moon lifts,
radiant with terror.
The state
is a diver under a glass bell.

A father's no shield
for his child.
We are like a lot of wild
spiders crying together,
but without tears.

Nature holds up a mirror.
One swallow makes a summer.
It's easy to tick
off the minutes,
but the clockhands stick.

Back and forth!
Back and forth, back and forth –
my one point of rest
is the orange and black
oriole's swinging nest!

MARGARET ATWOOD

It is Dangerous to Read Newspapers

While I was building neat
castles in the sandbox,
the hasty pits were
filling with bulldozed corpses

and as I walked to the school
washed and combed, my feet
stepping on the cracks in the cement
detonated red bombs.

Now I am grownup
and literate, and I sit in my chair
as quietly as a fuse

and the jungles are flaming, the under-
brush is charged with soldiers,
the names on the difficult
maps go up in smoke.

I am the cause, I am a stockpile of chemical
toys, my body
is a deadly gadget,
I reach out in love, my hands are guns,
my good intentions are completely lethal.

Even my
passive eyes transmute
everything I look at to the pocked
black and white of a war photo,
how
can I stop myself

It is dangerous to read newspapers.

Each time I hit a key
on my electric typewriter,
speaking of peaceful trees

another village explodes.

MICHAEL LONGLEY

Wounds

Here are two pictures from my father's head –
I have kept them like secrets until now:
First, the Ulster Division at the Somme
Going over the top with 'Fuck the Pope!'
'No Surrender!': a boy about to die,
Screaming 'Give 'em one for the Shankill!'
'Wilder than Gurkhas' were my father's words
Of admiration and bewilderment.
Next comes the London–Scottish padre
Resettling kilts with his swagger-stick,
With a stylish backhand and a prayer.
Over a landscape of dead buttocks
My father followed him for fifty years.
At last, a belated casualty,
He said – lead traces flaring till they hurt –
'I am dying for King and Country, slowly.'
I touched his hand, his thin head I touched.

Now, with military honours of a kind,
With his badges, his medals like rainbows,
His spinning compass, I bury beside him
Three teenage soldiers, bellies full of
Bullets and Irish beer, their flies undone.
A packet of Woodbines I throw in,
A lucifer, the Sacred Heart of Jesus
Paralysed as heavy guns put out
The night-light in a nursery for ever;
Also a bus-conductor's uniform –

He collapsed beside his carpet-slippers
Without a murmur, shot through the head
By a shivering boy who wandered in
Before they could turn the television down
Or tidy away the supper dishes.
To the children, to a bewildered wife,
I think 'Sorry Missus' was what he said.

JAMES FENTON

In a Notebook

There was a river overhung with trees
With wooden houses built along its shallows
From which the morning sun drew up a haze
And the gyrations of the early swallows
Paid no attention to the gentle breeze
Which spoke discreetly from the weeping willows.
There was a jetty by the forest clearing
Where a small boat was tugging at its mooring.

And night still lingered underneath the eaves.
In the dark houseboats families were stirring
And Chinese soup was cooked on charcoal stoves.
Then one by one there came into the clearing
Mothers and daughters bowed beneath their sheaves.
The silent children gathered round me staring
And the shy soldiers setting out for battle
Asked for a cigarette and laughed a little.

From low canoes old men laid out their nets
While on the bank young boys with lines were fishing.
The wicker traps were drawn up by their floats.
The girls stood waist-deep in the river washing
Or tossed the day's rice on enamel plates
And I sat drinking bitter coffee wishing
The tide would turn to bring me to my senses
After the pleasant war and the evasive answers.

There was a river overhung with trees.
The girls stood waist-deep in the river washing,
And night still lingered underneath the eaves
While on the bank young boys with lines were fishing.
Mothers and daughters bowed beneath their sheaves
While I sat drinking bitter coffee wishing –
And the tide turned and brought me to my senses.
The pleasant war brought the unpleasant answers.

The villages are burnt, the cities void;
The morning light has left the river view;
The distant followers have been dismayed;
And I'm afraid, reading this passage now,
That everything I knew has been destroyed
By those whom I admired but never knew;
The laughing soldiers fought to their defeat
And I'm afraid most of my friends are dead.

SEAMUS HEANEY

Punishment

I can feel the tug
of the halter at the nape
of her neck, the wind
on her naked front.

It blows her nipples
to amber beads,
it shakes the frail rigging
of her ribs.

I can see her drowned
body in the bog,
the weighing stone,
the floating rods and boughs.

Under which at first
she was a barked sapling

that is dug up
oak-bone, brain-firkin:

her shaved head
like a stubble of black corn,
her blindfold a soiled bandage,
her noose a ring

to store
the memories of love.
Little adulteress,
before they punished you

you were flaxen-haired,
undernourished, and your
tar-black face was beautiful.
My poor scapegoat,

I almost love you
but would have cast, I know,
the stones of silence.
I am the artful voyeur

of your brain's exposed
and darkened combs,
your muscles' webbing
and all your numbered bones:

I who have stood dumb
when your betraying sisters,
cauled in tar,
wept by the railings,

who would connive
in civilized outrage
yet understand the exact
and tribal, intimate revenge.

DENISE LEVERTOV

What Were They Like?

1 Did the people of Vietnam
    use lanterns of stone?

2 Did they hold ceremonies
    to reverence the opening of buds?

3 Were they inclined to quiet laughter?

4 Did they use bone and ivory,
    jade and silver, for ornament?

5 Had they an epic poem?

6 Did they distinguish between speech and singing?

1 Sir, their light hearts turned to stone.
    It is not remembered whether in gardens
    stone lanterns illumined pleasant ways.

2 Perhaps they gathered once to delight in blossom,
    but after the children were killed there were no more
    buds.

3 Sir, laughter is bitter to the burned mouth.

4 A dream ago, perhaps. Ornament is for joy.
    All the bones were charred.

5 It is not remembered. Remember
    most were peasants; their life
    was in rice and bamboo.
    When peaceful clouds were reflected in the paddies
    and the water buffalo stepped surely along terraces,
    maybe fathers told their sons old tales.
    When bombs smashed those mirrors
    there was time only to scream.

6 There is an echo yet
    of their speech which was like a song.
    It was reported their singing resembled
    the flight of moths in moonlight.
    Who can say? It is silent now.

On the Late Massacre in Piedmont

Avenge, O Lord, thy slaughtered saints, whose bones
   Lie scattered on the Alpine mountains cold,
   Even them who kept thy truth so pure of old
   When all our fathers worshipped stocks and stones,
Forget not; in thy book record their groans
   Who were thy sheep and in their ancient fold
   Slain by the bloody Piedmontese that rolled

Mother with infant down the rocks. Their moans
   The vales redoubled to the hills, and they
   To Heaven. Their martyred blood and ashes sow
   O'er all th' Italian fields where still doth sway
The triple tyrant, that from these may grow
   A hundredfold, who having learnt thy way,
   Early may fly the Babylonian woe.

In Time of 'The Breaking of Nations'

I

Only a man harrowing clods
   In a slow silent walk
With an old horse that stumbles and nods
   Half asleep as they stalk.

II

Only thin smoke without flame
   From the heaps of couch-grass;
Yet this will go onward the same
   Though Dynasties pass.

Yonder a maid and her wight
    Come whispering by:
War's annals will cloud into night
    Ere their story die.

JAMES K. BAXTER

Returned Soldier

The boy who volunteered at seventeen
At twenty-three is heavy on the booze.
Strafed in the desert and bombed out in Crete –
With sore dark eyes and hardened by the heat
Entitled now to call himself a man
And in the doll's-house walk with death at ease:
The Cairo women, cobbers under sand
A death too great for dolls to understand.

Back to a city bed or station hut
At maelstrom centre falling through the night
To dreams where deeper than El Alamein
A buried childhood stirs with leaves and flowers
Remembered girls, the blurred and bitter waters.
Wakes to the midnight rafters and the rain.

JUDITH WRIGHT

Soldier's Farm

This ploughland vapoured with the dust of dreams,
these delicate gatherings of dancing trees,
answered the question of his searching eyes
as his wife's body answered to his arms.

He let the whole gold day pass in a stare,
walking the turning furrow. The horses drew
his line straight where the shakesword corn should grow.
He, lurching mooncalf, let his eyes stride far.

They stooped across the swell and sink of hill;
made record of the leaves that played with light.
The mist was early and the moon was late,
and in between he stared his whole day full.

He asked for nothing but the luck to live,
so now his willing blood moves in these trees
that hold his heart up sunwards with their arms.
The mists dissolve at morning like his dreams
and the creek answers light as once his eyes;
and yet he left here nothing but his love.

MEDBH MCGUCKIAN

The War Degree

You smell of time as a Bible smells of thumbs,
a bank of earth alive with mahogany-coloured
flowers – not time elaborately thrown away,
(you wound yourself so thoroughly into life),
but time outside of time, new pain, new secret,
that I must re-fall in love with the shadow
of your soul, drumming at the back of my skull.

Tonight, when the treaty moves all tongues,
I want to take the night out of you,
the sweet Irish tongue in which
death spoke and happiness wrote:

a wartime, heart-stained autumn drove
fierce half-bricks into the hedges; tree-muffled
streets vanished in the lack of news.
Like a transfusion made direct from arm
to arm, birds call uselessly to each other
in the sub-acid, wintry present. The pursed-up
fragrances of self-fertile herbs
hug defeat like a very future lover.

Now it is my name and not my number
that is nobody now, walking on a demolished
floor, where dreams have no moral.
And the door-kiss is night meeting night.

EMILY DICKINSON

'My Triumph lasted . . .'

My Triumph lasted till the Drums
Had left the Dead alone
And then I dropped my Victory
And chastened stole along
To where the finished Faces
Conclusion turned on me
And then I hated Glory
And wished myself were They.

What is to be is best descried
When it has also been –
Could Prospect taste of Retrospect
The tyrannies of Men
Were Tenderer – diviner
The Transitive toward.
A Bayonet's contrition
Is nothing to the Dead.

WILLIAM SHAKESPEARE

from Othello, Act 1, Scene 3

Othello Her father lov'd me, oft invited me,
Still question'd me the story of my life,
From year to year; the battles, sieges, fortunes,
That I have pass'd:
I ran it through, even from my boyish days,
To the very moment that he bade me tell it.
Wherein I spake of most disastrous chances,
Of moving accidents by flood and field;

Of hair-breadth scapes i' th' imminent deadly breach;
Of being taken by the insolent foe;
And sold to slavery, and my redemption thence,
And with it all my travel's history;
Wherein of antres vast, and deserts idle,
Rough quarries, rocks and hills, whose heads touch
  heaven,
It was my hint to speak, such was the process:
And of the Cannibals, that each other eat;
The Anthropophagi, and men whose heads
Do grow beneath their shoulders: this to hear
Would Desdemona seriously incline;
But still the house-affairs would draw her thence,
And ever as she could with haste dispatch,
She'ld come again, and with a greedy ear
Devour up my discourse; which I observing,
Took once a pliant hour, and found good means
To draw from her a prayer of earnest heart,
That I would all my pilgrimage dilate,
Whereof by parcel she had something heard,
But not intentively: I did consent,
And often did I beguile her of her tears,
When I did speak of some distressèd stroke
That my youth suffer'd: my story being done,
She gave me for my pains a world of sighs;
She swore i' faith 'twas strange, 'twas passing strange;
'Twas pitiful, 'twas wondrous pitiful;
She wish'd she had not heard it, yet she wish'd
That heaven had made her such a man: she thank'd me,
And bade me, if I had a friend that lov'd her,
I should but teach him how to tell my story,
And that would woo her. Upon this hint I spake:
She lov'd me for the dangers I had pass'd,
And I lov'd her that she did pity them.
This only is the witchcraft I have us'd:
Here comes the lady, let her witness it.

RENÉ CHAR

Freedom

It came along this white line that might signify dawn's emergence as well as death's candlestick.

    It passed beyond the unconscious strands; it passed beyond the eviscerated summits.

    They were ending: the cowardly-countenanced renunciation, the holiness of lying, the raw spirits of the executioner.

    Its word was not a blind battering-ram but rather the canvas where my breath was inscribed.

    With a pace unsure only behind absence, it came, a swan on the wound, along this white line.

                translated from the French by Denis Devlin and Jackson Mathews

TADEUSZ RÓŻEWICZ

The Survivor

I am twenty-four
led to slaughter
I survived.

The following are empty synonyms:
man and beast
love and hate
friend and foe
darkness and light.

The way of killing men and beasts is the same
I've seen it:
truckfuls of chopped-up men
who will not be saved.

Ideas are mere words:
virtue and crime
truth and lies

beauty and ugliness
courage and cowardice.

Virtue and crime weigh the same
I've seen it:
in a man who was both
criminal and virtuous.

I seek a teacher and a master
may he restore my sight hearing and speech
may he again name objects and ideas
may he separate darkness from light.

I am twenty-four
led to slaughter
I survived.

   translated from the Polish by Adam Czerniawski

Belief

The Innumerable Christ

Other stars may have their Bethlehem, and their Calvary too.
PROFESSOR J. Y. SIMPSON

Wha kens on whatna Bethlehems
Earth twinkles like a star the nicht,
An' whatna shepherds lift their heids
   In its unearthly licht?

'Yont a' the stars oor een can see
An' farther than their lichts can fly,
I' mony an unco warl' the nicht
   The fatefu' bairnies cry.

I' mony an unco warl' the nicht
The lift gaes black as pitch at noon,
An' sideways on their chests the heids
   O' endless Christs roll doon.

An' when the earth's as cauld's the mune
An' a' its folk are lang syne deid,
On coontless stars the Babe maun cry
   An' the Crucified maun bleed.

Fetish

The objects of wood thatch and stone
decayed relics splinters shell
are a journey

contemplation restores them to our time
makes once more the oar, fossil's bone,
the fetish of our worship

now shard
now pebble
shingle

sand
the sea's useless tune
and wrangle

there was a struggle here
which the spiked fist grass still guesses
the mailed horn of the crab

was our earliest conqueror
its cracked back
now scuttles on tin

torn up roots
broken box-
es, ruins:

old harbour
cartagena
tenochtitlan

ravages.

but out of the ruins
grass
still presses

out of the cracks
crawls
green

out of the silence
harbours
time

Answers

I kept my answers small and kept them near;
Big questions bruised my mind but still I let
Small answers be a bulwark to my fear.

The huge abstractions I kept from the light;
Small things I handled and caressed and loved.
I let the stars assume the whole of night.

But the big answers clamoured to be moved
Into my life. Their great audacity
Shouted to be acknowledged and believed

Even when all small answers build up to
Protection of my spirit, still I hear
Big answers striving for their overthrow

And all the great conclusions coming near.

DEREK MAHON

A Disused Shed in Co. Wexford

Let them not forget us, the weak souls among the asphodels.
SEFERIS, *Mythistorema*
for J. G. Farrell

Even now there are places where a thought might grow –
Peruvian mines, worked out and abandoned
To a slow clock of condensation,
An echo trapped for ever, and a flutter
Of wildflowers in the lift-shaft,
Indian compounds where the wind dances
And a door bangs with diminished confidence,
Lime crevices behind rippling rainbarrels,
Dog corners for bone burials;
And in a disused shed in Co. Wexford,

Deep in the grounds of a burnt-out hotel,
Among the bathtubs and the washbasins
A thousand mushrooms crowd to a keyhole.
This is the one star in their firmament
Or frames a star within a star.
What should they do there but desire?
So many days beyond the rhododendrons
With the world waltzing in its bowl of cloud,
They have learnt patience and silence
Listening to the rooks querulous in the high wood.

They have been waiting for us in a foetor
Of vegetable sweat since civil war days,
Since the gravel-crunching, interminable departure
Of the expropriated mycologist.
He never came back, and light since then
Is a keyhole rusting gently after rain.
Spiders have spun, flies dusted to mildew
And once a day, perhaps, they have heard something –
A trickle of masonry, a shout from the blue
Or a lorry changing gear at the end of the lane.

There have been deaths, the pale flesh flaking
Into the earth that nourished it;
And nightmares, born of these and the grim
Dominion of stale air and rank moisture.
Those nearest the door grow strong –
'Elbow room! Elbow room!'
The rest, dim in a twilight of crumbling
Utensils and broken flower-pots, groaning
For their deliverance, have been so long
Expectant that there is left only the posture.

A half century, without visitors, in the dark –
Poor preparation for the cracking lock
And creak of hinges. Magi, moonmen,
Powdery prisoners of the old regime,

Web-throated, stalked like triffids, racked by drought
And insomnia, only the ghost of a scream
At the flash-bulb firing squad we wake them with
Shows there is life yet in their feverish forms.
Grown beyond nature now, soft food for worms,
They lift frail heads in gravity and good faith.

They are begging us, you see, in their wordless way,
To do something, to speak on their behalf
Or at least not to close the door again.
Lost people of Treblinka and Pompeii!
'Save us, save us,' they seem to say,
'Let the god not abandon us
Who have come so far in darkness and in pain.
We too had our lives to live.
You with your light meter and relaxed itinerary,
Let not our naive labours have been in vain!'

FULKE GREVILLE

from Mustapha: Chorus Sacerdotum

Oh wearisome condition of humanity!
Born under one law, to another bound:
Vainly begot, and yet forbidden vanity,
Created sick, commanded to be sound:
What meaneth Nature by these diverse laws?
Passion and reason, self-division cause:
Is it the mark, or majesty of power
To make offences that it may forgive?
Nature herself, doth her own self deflower,
To hate those errors she herself doth give.
For how should man think that, he may not do
If Nature did not fail, and punish too?
Tyrant to others, to herself unjust,
Only commands things difficult and hard.
Forbids us all things, which it knows is lust,

Makes easy pains, unpossible reward.
If Nature did not take delight in blood,
She would have made more easy ways to good.
We that are bound by vows, and by promotion,
With pomp of holy sacrifice and rites,
To teach belief in good and still devotion,
To preach of Heaven's wonders, and delights:
Yet when each of us, in his own heart looks,
He finds the God there, far unlike his books.

R. S. THOMAS

Kneeling

Moments of great calm,
Kneeling before an altar
Of wood in a stone church
In summer, waiting for the God
To speak; the air a staircase
For silence; the sun's light
Ringing me, as though I acted
A great rôle. And the audiences
Still; all that close throng
Of spirits waiting, as I,
For the message.
      Prompt me, God;
But not yet. When I speak,
Though it be you who speak
Through me, something is lost.
The meaning is in the waiting.

PAUL CELAN

Tenebrae

We are near, Lord,
near and at hand.

Handled already, Lord,
clawed and clawing as though
the body of each of us were
your body, Lord.

Pray, Lord,
pray to us,
we are near.

Wind-awry we went there,
went there to bend
over hollow and ditch.

To be watered we went there, Lord.

It was blood, it was
what you shed, Lord.

It gleamed.

It cast your image into our eyes, Lord.
Our eyes and our mouths are so open and empty, Lord.
We have drunk, Lord.
The blood and the image that was in the blood, Lord.

Pray, Lord.
We are near.

translated from the German by Michael Hamburger

ARTHUR HUGH CLOUGH

There is No God

'There is no God,' the wicked saith,
    'And truly it's a blessing,
For what he might have done with us
    It's better only guessing.'

'There is no God,' a youngster thinks,
    'Or really, if there may be,

He surely didn't mean a man
    Always to be a baby.'

'There is no God, or if there is,'
    The tradesman thinks, ''twere funny
If he should take it ill in me
    To make a little money.'

'Whether there be,' the rich man says,
    'It matters very little,
For I and mine, thank somebody,
    Are not in want of victual.'

Some others, also, to themselves
    Who scarce so much as doubt it,
Think there is none, when they are well,
    And do not think about it.

But country folks who live beneath
    The shadow of the steeple;
The parson and the parson's wife,
    And mostly married people;

Youths green and happy in first love,
    So thankful for illusion;
And men caught out in what the world
    Calls guilt, in first confusion;

And almost everyone when age,
    Disease, or sorrows strike him,
Inclines to think there is a God,
    Or something very like him.

JOHN DONNE

'Batter my heart . . .'

Batter my heart, three person'd God; for, you
As yet but knock, breathe, shine, and seek to mend;
That I may rise, and stand, o'erthrow me, and bend

Your force, to break, blow, burn and make me new.
I, like an usurpt town, to another due,
Labour to admit you, but Oh, to no end,
Reason your viceroy in me, me should defend,
But is captiv'd, and proves weak or untrue.
Yet dearly I love you, and would be loved fain,
But am betroth'd unto your enemy:
Divorce me, untie, or break that knot again,
Take me to you, imprison me, for I
Except you enthrall me, never shall be free,
Nor ever chast, except you ravish me.

ALFRED, LORD TENNYSON

from In Memoriam

Be near me when my light is low,
    When the blood creeps, and the nerves prick
    And tingle; and the heart is sick,
And all the wheels of Being slow.

Be near me when the sensuous frame
    Is rack'd with pangs that conquer trust;
    And Time, a maniac scattering dust,
And Life, a Fury slinging flame.

Be near me when my faith is dry,
    And men the flies of latter spring,
    That lay their eggs, and sting and sing
And weave their petty cells and die.

Be near me when I fade away,
    To point the term of human strife,
    And on the low dark verge of life
The twilight of eternal day.

WILLIAM EMPSON

Homage to the British Museum

There is a Supreme God in the ethnological section;
A hollow toad shape, faced with a blank shield.
He needs his belly to include the Pantheon,
Which is inserted through a hole behind.
At the navel, at the points formally stressed, at the organs
    of sense,
Lice glue themselves, dolls, local deities,
His smooth wood creeps with all the creeds of the world.

Attending there let us absorb the cultures of nations
And dissolve into our judgement all their codes.
Then, being clogged with a natural hesitation
(People are continually asking one the way out),
Let us stand here and admit that we have no road.
Being everything, let us admit that is to be something,
Or give ourselves the benefit of the doubt;
Let us offer our pinch of dust all to this God,
And grant his reign over the entire building.

MICHAEL DONAGHY

A Miracle

This will never do. Get the bird
Of gold enamelling out of the den.
I'm *reading*. Gin, white as winter sun
Is blending juniper with oxygen.

Divinity is imminent. In the parlour
The crystal tinkling into words
Announces the arrival, through the mirror,
Of the host of stars and hummingbirds.

The angels have come early for the miracle.
They've gotten into the bar and drunk it dry.

Grinning, staggering, shedding feathers,
They can barely stand up, let alone fly.

One armoured, peacock feathered cherub
Holds my copy of the future to the glass
And reads backwards (as they do in heaven)
Of how this evening will come to pass.

The seraphim are fencing on the lawn.
Thrust and parry, tipsy physical chess.
'The Conversation of the Blades', they call it,
The actual clink and whirr, the holiness.

JOHN KEATS

from The Fall of Hyperion, Canto One

There was a silence while the altar's blaze
Was fainting for sweet food: I look'd thereon
And on the paved floor, where nigh were pil'd
Faggots of cinnamon, and many heaps
Of other crisped spice-wood – then again
I look'd upon the altar and its horns
Whiten'd with ashes, and its lang'rous flame,
And then upon the offerings again;
And so by turns – till sad Moneta cried,
'The sacrifice is done, but not the less
Will I be kind to thee for thy good will.
My power, which to me is still a curse,
Shall be to thee a wonder; for the scenes
Still swooning vivid through my globèd brain
With an electral changing misery
Thou shalt with those dull mortal eyes behold,
Free from all pain, if wonder pain thee not.'
As near as an immortal's spherèd words
Could to a mother's soften, were these last:
But yet I had a terror of her robes,
And chiefly of the veils, that from her brow

Hung pale, and curtain'd her in mysteries
That made my heart too small to hold its blood.
This saw that Goddess, and with sacred hand
Parted the veils. Then saw I a wan face,
Not pin'd by human sorrows, but bright blanch'd
By an immortal sickness which kills not;
It works a constant change, which happy death
Can put no end to; deathwards progressing
To no death was that visage; it had pass'd
The lily and the snow; and beyond these
I must not think now, though I saw that face –
But for her eyes I should have fled away.
They held me back, with a benignant light,
Soft mitigated by divinest lids
Half closed, and visionless entire they seem'd
Of all external things – they saw me not,
But in blank splendor beam'd like the mild moon,
Who comforts those she sees not, who knows not
What eyes are upward cast.

DEREK WALCOTT

from Tales of the islands

CHAPTER V '*moeurs anciennes*'

The fête took place one morning in the heights
For the approval of some anthropologist.
The priests objected to such savage rites
In a Catholic country; but there was a twist
As one of the fathers was himself a student
Of black customs; it was quite ironic.
They lead sheep to the rivulet with a drum,
Dancing with absolutely natural grace
Remembered from the dark past whence we come.
The whole thing was more like a bloody picnic.
Bottles of white rum and a brawling booth.
They tie the lamb up, then chop off the head,

And ritualists take turns drinking the blood.
Great stuff, old boy; sacrifice, moments of truth.

NORMAN MACCAIG

Celtic cross

The implicated generations made
This symbol of their lives, a stone made light
By what is carved on it.
                    The plaiting masks,
But not with involutions of a shade,
What a stone says and what a stone cross asks.

Something that is not mirrored by nor trapped
In webs of water or bag-nets of cloud;
The tangled mesh of weed
                    lets it go by.
Only men's minds could ever have unmapped
Into abstraction such a territory.

No green bay going yellow over sand
Is written on by winds to tell a tale
Of death-dishevelled gull
                    or heron, stiff
As a cruel clerk with gaunt writs in his hand
– Or even of light, that makes its depths a cliff.

Singing responses order otherwise.
The tangled generations ravelled out
In links of song whose sweet
                    strong choruses
Are these stone involutions to the eyes
Given to the ear in abstract vocables.

The stone remains, and the cross, to let us know
Their unjust, hard demands, as symbols do.
But on them twine and grow

        beneath the dove
Serpents of wisdom whose cool statements show
Such understanding that it seems like love.

WISLAWA SZYMBORSKA

Utopia

An island where everything becomes clear.

Here one can stand on the ground of proofs.

The only road has its destination.

Shrubs are burdened with answers.

Here grows the tree of Proper Conjecture,
its branches eternally untangled.

The dazzlingly straight tree of Understanding
is next to a spring called Ah So That's How It is.

The deeper you're in the wood, the wider grows
the Valley of Obviousness.

Whatever the doubt, the wind blows it away.

Echo speaks uncalled
and readily solves the mysteries of worlds.

On the right a cave where sense reclines.

To the left a lake of Deep Conviction.
Truth stirs from the bottom and lightly breaks the surface.

Unshakeable Certainty dominates the vale
and Essence of Things spreads from its head.

Despite these attractions, the island is deserted,
and the tiny footmarks seen along the shores
all point towards the sea.

As though people always went away from here
and irreversibly plunged into the deep.

In life that's inconceivable.

translated from the Polish by Adam Czerniawski

W. B. YEATS

Byzantium

The unpurged images of day recede;
The Emperor's drunken soldiery are abed;
Night resonance recedes, night-walkers' song
After great cathedral gong;
A starlit or a moonlit dome disdains
All that man is,
All mere complexities,
The fury and the mire of human veins.

Before me floats an image, man or shade,
Shade more than man, more image than a shade;
For Hades' bobbin bound in mummy-cloth
May unwind the winding path;
A mouth that has no moisture and no breath
Breathless mouths may summon;
I hail the superhuman;
I call it death-in-life and life-in-death.

Miracle, bird or golden handiwork,
More miracle than bird or handiwork,
Planted on the star-lit golden bough,
Can like the cocks of Hades crow,
Or, by the moon embittered, scorn aloud
In glory of changeless metal
Common bird or petal
And all complexities of mire or blood.

At midnight on the Emperor's pavement flit
Flames that no faggot feeds, nor steel has lit,
Nor storm disturbs, flames begotten of flame,
Where blood-begotten spirits come
And all complexities of fury leave,
Dying into a dance,
An agony of trance,
An agony of flame that cannot singe a sleeve.

Astraddle on the dolphin's mire and blood,
Spirit after spirit! The smithies break the flood,
The golden smithies of the Emperor!
Marbles of the dancing floor
Break bitter furies of complexity,
Those images that yet
Fresh images beget,
That dolphin-torn, that gong-tormented sea.

SELIMA HILL

The Fowlers of the Marshes

Three thousand years ago
they were fowling in the marshes
around Thebes – men in knotted skirts
and tiered faience collars,
who avoided the brown crocodile,
and loved the ibis, which they stalked
with long striped cats on strings,
under the eye of Nut, the goddess of the sky.

My mother's hushed peculiar world's the same:
she haunts it like the fowlers of the marshes,
tiptoeing gaily into history, sustained by gods
as strange to me as Lady Nut, and Anubis,
the oracular, the jackal-masked.
When I meet her at the station, I say

Hello, Mum! and think *Hello, Thoth,*
This is the Weighing of the Heart.

PERCY BYSSHE SHELLEY

from Adonais

Peace, peace! he is not dead, he doth not sleep –
He hath awakened from the dream of life –
'Tis we, who lost in stormy visions, keep
With phantoms an unprofitable strife,
And in mad trance, strike with our spirit's knife
Invulnerable nothings. – *We* decay
Like corpses in a charnel; fear and grief
Convulse us and consume us day by day,
And cold hopes swarm like worms within our living clay.

He has outsoared the shadow of our night;
Envy and calumny and hate and pain,
And that unrest which men miscall delight,
Can touch him not and torture not again;
From the contagion of the world's slow stain
He is secure, and now can never mourn
A heart grown cold, a head grown gray in vain;
Nor, when the spirit's self has ceased to burn,
With sparkless ashes load an unlamented urn.

He lives, he wakes – 'tis Death is dead, not he;
Mourn not for Adonais. – Thou young Dawn,
Turn all thy dew to splendour, for from thee
The spirit thou lamentest is not gone;
Ye caverns and ye forests, cease to moan!
Cease, ye faint flowers and fountains, and thou Air,
Which like a mourning veil thy scarf hadst thrown
O'er the abandoned Earth, now leave it bare
Even to the joyous stars which smile on its despair!

He is made one with Nature: there is heard
His voice in all her music, from the moan
Of thunder, to the song of night's sweet bird;
He is a presence to be felt and known
In darkness and in light, from herb and stone,
Spreading itself where'er that Power may move
Which has withdrawn his being to its own;
Which wields the world with never-wearied love,
Sustains it from beneath, and kindles it above.

He is a portion of the loveliness
Which once he made more lovely: he doth bear
His part, while the one Spirit's plastic stress
Sweeps through the dull dense world, compelling there,
All new successions to the forms they wear;
Torturing th' unwilling dross that checks its flight
To its own likeness, as each mass may bear;
And bursting in its beauty and its might
From trees and beasts and men into the Heaven's light.

ALLEN GINSBERG

In back of the real

railroad yard in San Jose
  I wandered desolate
in front of a tank factory
  and sat on a bench
near the switchman's shack.

A flower lay on the hay on
  the asphalt highway
– the dread hay flower
  I thought – It had a
brittle black stem and
  corolla of yellowish dirty
spikes like Jesus' inchlong
  crown, and a soiled

dry center cotton tuft
    like a used shaving brush
that's been lying under
    the garage for a year.

Yellow, yellow flower, and
    flower of industry,
tough spiky ugly flower,
    flower nonetheless,
with the form of the great yellow
    Rose in your brain!
This is the flower of the World.

JOHN AGARD

Rainbow

When you see
de rainbow
you know
God know
wha he doing –
one big smile
across the sky –
I tell you
God got style
the man got style

When you see
raincloud pass
and de rainbow
make a show
I tell you
is God doing
limbo
the man doing
limbo

But sometimes
you know
when I see
de rainbow
so full of glow
& curving
like she bearing child
I does want know
if God
ain't a woman

If that is so
the woman got style
man she got style

CHARLES CAUSLEY

I am the Song

I am the song that sings the bird.
I am the leaf that grows the land.
I am the tide that moves the moon.
I am the stream that halts the sand.
I am the cloud that drives the storm.
I am the earth that lights the sun.
I am the fire that strikes the stone.
I am the clay that shapes the hand.
I am the word that speaks the man.

SEAMUS HEANEY

Postscript

And some time make the time to drive out west
Into County Clare, along the Flaggy Shore,
In September or October, when the wind
And the light are working off each other.
So that the ocean on one side is wild
With foam and glitter, and inland among stones

The surface of a slate-grey lake is lit
By the earthed lightning of a flock of swans,
Their feathers roughed and ruffling, white on white
Their fully grown headstrong-looking heads
Tucked or cresting or busy underwater.
Useless to think you'll park and capture it
More thoroughly. You are neither here nor there,
A hurry through which known and strange things past
As big soft buffetings come at the car sideways
And catch the heart off guard and blow it open.

ANONYMOUS

'I Sing of a Maiden ...'

I sing of a maiden
   That is makéless:
King of all kingès
   To her son she ches.

He came all so stillè
   There his mother was
As dew in Apríllè
   That falleth on the grass.

He came all so stillè
   To his mother's bower
As dew in Apríllè
   That falleth on the flower.

He came all so stillè
   There his mother lay
As dew in Apríllè
   That falleth on the spray.

Mother and maiden
   Was never none but she;
Well may such a lady
   Goddès mother be.

JOHN MILTON

At a Solemn Music

Blest pair of Sirens, pledges of Heaven's joy,
Sphere-born harmonious Sisters, Voice and Verse!
Wed your divine sounds, and mixt power employ,
Dead things with inbreathed sense able to pierce;
And to our high-raised phantasy present
That undisturbéd Song of pure concent
Aye sung before the sapphire-colour'd throne
      To Him that sits thereon,
With saintly shout and solemn jubilee;
Where the bright Seraphim in burning row
Their loud uplifted angel-trumpets blow;
And the Cherubic host in thousand quires
Touch their immortal harps of golden wires,
With those just Spirits that wear victorious palms,
      Hymns devout and holy psalms
      Singing everlastingly:
That we on Earth, with undiscording voice
May rightly answer that melodious noise;
As once we did, till disproportion'd sin
Jarr'd against nature's chime, and with harsh din
Broke the fair music that all creatures made
To their great Lord, whose love their motion sway'd
In perfect diapason, whilst they stood
In first obedience, and their state of good.
O may we soon again renew that Song,
And keep in tune with Heaven, till God ere long
To His celestial consort us unite,
To live with Him, and sing in endless morn of light!

The Sparrow's Skull

Memento Mori. Written at the Fall of France.

The kingdoms fall in sequence, like the waves on the
   shore.
All save divine and desperate hopes go down, they are no
   more.
Solitary is our place, the castle in the sea,
And I muse on those I have loved, and on those who have
   loved me.

I gather up my loves, and keep them all warm,
While above our heads blows the bitter storm:
The blessed natural loves, of life-supporting flame,
And those whose name is Wonder, which have no other
   name.

The skull is in my hand, the minute cup of bone,
And I remember her, the tame, the loving one,
Who came in at the window, and seemed to have a mind
More towards sorrowful man than to those of her own kind.

She came for a long time, but at length she grew old;
And on her death-day she came, so feeble and so bold;
And all day, as if knowing what the day would bring,
She waited by the window, with her head beneath her
   wing.

And I will keep the skull, for in the hollow here
Lodged the minute brain that had outgrown a fear;
Transcended an old terror, and found a new love,
And entered a strange life, a world it was not of.

Even so, dread God! even so, my Lord!
The fire is at my feet, and at my breast the sword:
And I must gather up my soul, and clap my wings, and flee
Into the heart of terror, to find myself in thee.

The Collar

I struck the board, and cried, 'No more!
     I will abroad.
What? shall I ever sigh and pine?
My lines and life are free; free as the road,
  Loose as the wind, as large as store.
   Shall I be still in suit?
Have I no harvest but a thorn
To let me blood, and not restore
What I have lost with cordial fruit?
     Sure there was wine
Before my sighs did dry it: there was corn
  Before my tears did drown it.
Is the year only lost to me?
  Have I no bays to crown it?
No flowers, no garlands gay? all blasted?
    All wasted?
Not so, my heart: but there is fruit,
   And thou hast hands.
  Recover all thy sigh-blown age
On double pleasures: leave thy cold dispute
Of what is fit, and not. Forsake thy cage,
    Thy rope of sands,
Which petty thoughts have made, and made to thee
  Good cable, to enforce and draw,
    And be thy law,
While thou didst wink and wouldst not see.
    Away; take heed :
    I will abroad.
Call in thy deaths head there: tie up thy fears.
   He that forbears
  To suit and serve his need,
   Deserves his load.'

But as I raved and grew more fierce and wild
      At every word,
   Me thoughts I heard one calling, 'Child'
      And I reply'd, 'My Lord'.

GEOFFREY HILL

from Lachrimae

LACHRIMAE ANTIQUAE NOVAE

Crucified Lord, so naked to the world,
you live unseen within that nakedness,
consigned by proxy to the judas-kiss
of our devotion, bowed beneath the gold,

with re-enactments, penances foretold:
scentings of love across a wilderness
of retrospection, wild and objectless
longings incarnate in the carnal child.

Beautiful for themselves the icons fade;
the lions and the hermits disappear.
Triumphalism feasts on empty dread,

fulfilling triumphs of the festal year.
We find you wounded by the token spear.
Dominion is swallowed with your blood.

PETER READING

Aeschylus

There was a reason, though it now evades me,
why I should nervously wink at the sky.
Its bland crepuscularity pervades me,
though that can hardly be the reason why.

I read once as a child how a tragedian,
with tragic irony or will of fate,

met death by tortoise and short-sighted eagle
which mis-identified as rock his pate.

Who but perhaps an avant-garde comedian,
or Darwin postulating on board *Beagle*
on how the turtle's flippers were evolved,
could visualise the tortoise so insidious
as, first to take wing, then to get involved
with poets quietly in pursuit of grief.

I view all life now with grave disbelief,
find all on earth reptilian and hideous,
and Heaven sly, potentially perfidious.

GERARD MANLEY HOPKINS

Carrion Comfort

Not, I'll not, carrion comfort, Despair, not feast on thee;
Not untwist – slack they may be – these last strands of man
In me ór, most weary, cry *I can no more*. I can;
Can something, hope, wish day come, not choose not to be
But ah, but O thou terrible, why wouldst thou rude on me
Thy wring-world right foot rock? lay a lionlimb against
    me? scan
With darksome devouring eyes my bruisèd bones? and fan
O in turns of tempest, me heaped there; me frantic to avoid
    thee and flee?

Why? That my chaff might fly; my grain lie, sheer and
    clear.
Nay in all that toil, that coil, since (seems) I kissed the rod,
Hand rather, my heart lo! lapped strength, stole joy, would
    laugh, chéer.
Cheer whom though? the hero whose heaven-handling
    flung me, fóot tród

Me? or me that fought him? O which one? is it each one?
    That night, that year
Of now done darkness I wretch lay wrestling with (my
    God!) my God.

EMILY DICKINSON

'The Soul selects . . .'

The Soul selects her own Society—
Then—shuts the Door—
To her divine Majority—
Present no more—

Unmoved—she notes the Chariots—pausing
At her low Gate—
Unmoved—an Emperor be kneeling
Upon her Mat—

I've known her—from an ample nation—
Choose One—
Then—close the Valves of her attention—
Like Stone—

WILLIAM BLAKE

To God

If you have form'd a Circle to go into,
Go into it yourself & see how you would do.

I am no Homer's Hero, you all know;
I profess not Generosity to a Foe.
My Generosity is to my Friends,
That for their Friendship I may make amends.
The Generous to Enemies promotes their Ends
And becomes the Enemy & Betrayer of his Friends.

WILLIAM COWPER

Lines Written During a Period of Insanity (1774)

Hatred and vengeance, my eternal portion,
Scarce can endure delay of execution,
Wait, with impatient readiness, to seize my
       Soul in a moment.

Damn'd below Judas: more abhorr'd than he was,
Who for a few pence sold his holy Master.
Twice betrayed Jesus me, the last delinquent.
       Deems the profanest.

Man disavows, and Deity disowns me:
Hell might afford my miseries a shelter;
Therefore hell keeps her ever hungry mouths all
       Bolted against me.

Hard lot! encompass'd with a thousand dangers;
Weary, faint, trembling with a thousand terrors;
I'm called, if vanquish'd, to receive a sentence
       Worse than Abiram's.

Him the vindictive rod of angry justice
Sent quick and howling to the centre headlong;
I, fed with judgment, in a fleshly tomb, am
       Buried above ground.

MATTHEW ARNOLD

Dover Beach

The sea is calm to-night,
The tide is full, the moon lies fair
Upon the Straits; – on the French coast, the light
Gleams, and is gone; the cliffs of England stand,
Glimmering and vast, out in the tranquil bay.
Come to the window, sweet is the night air!

Only, from the long line of spray
Where the ebb meets the moon-blanch'd sand,
Listen! you hear the grating roar
Of pebbles which the waves suck back, and fling,
At their return, up the high strand,
Begin, and cease, and then again begin,
With tremulous cadence slow, and bring
The eternal note of sadness in.

Sophocles long ago
Heard it on the Aegaean, and it brought
Into his mind the turbid ebb and flow
Of human misery; we
Find also in the sound a thought,
Hearing it by this distant northern sea.

The sea of faith
Was once, too, at the full, and round earth's shore
Lay like the folds of a bright girdle furl'd;
But now I only hear
Its melancholy, long, withdrawing roar,
Retreating to the breath
Of the night-wind down the vast edges drear
And naked shingles of the world.

Ah, love, let us be true
To one another! for the world, which seems
To lie before us like a land of dreams,
So various, so beautiful, so new,
Hath really neither joy, nor love, nor light,
Nor certitude, nor peace, nor help for pain;
And we are here as on a darkling plain
Swept with confused alarms of struggle and flight,
Where ignorant armies clash by night.

ELIZABETH BARRETT BROWNING

from Sonnets from the Portuguese

XXIV

Let the world's sharpness, like a clasping knife,
Shut in upon itself and do no harm
In this close hand of Love, now soft and warm,
And let us hear no sound of human strife
After the click of the shutting. Life to life –
I lean upon thee, Dear, without alarm,
And feel as safe as guarded by a charm
Against the stab of worldlings, who if rife
Are weak to injure. Very whitely still
The lilies of our lives may reassure
Their blossoms from their roots, accessible
Alone to heavenly dews that drop not fewer,
Growing straight, out of man's reach, on the hill.
God only, who made us rich, can make us poor.

CHARLES SIMIC

Late Call

A message for you,
Piece of shit:

You double-crossed us.
You were supposed to get yourself
Crucified
For the sake of Truth . . .

Who, me?

A mere crumb, thankfully,
Overlooked on a dinner table,
Lacking in enthusiasm . . .
An average nobody.

Oh, the worries . . .

In the dark windowpane
My mouth gutted open.
Aghast.
The panel of judges all black-hooded.

It must be a joke.
A misunderstanding, fellows.
A wrong number, surely?
A slipup?
An erratum?

DANNIE ABSE

In the Theatre

(A true incident)
Only a local anaesthetic was given because of the blood pressure problem.
The patient, thus, was fully awake throughout the operation. But in those
days – in 1938, in Cardiff, when I was Lambert Rogers' dresser – they
could not locate a brain tumour with precision. Too much normal brain
tissue was destroyed as the surgeon crudely searched for it, before he felt
the resistance of it . . . all somewhat hit and miss. One operation I shall
never forget . . .
DR WILFRED ABSE

Sister saying – 'Soon you'll be back in the ward,'
sister thinking – 'Only two more on the list,'
the patient saying – 'Thank you, I feel fine';
small voices, small lies, nothing untoward,
though, soon, he would blink again and again
because of the fingers of Lambert Rogers,
rash as a blind man's, inside his soft brain.

If items of horror can make a man laugh
then laugh at this: one hour later, the growth
still undiscovered, ticking its own wild time;
more brain mashed because of the probe's braille path;
Lambert Rogers desperate, fingering still;
his dresser thinking, 'Christ! Two more on the list,
a cisternal puncture and a neural cyst.'

341

Then, suddenly, the cracked record in the brain,
a ventriloquist voice that cried, 'You sod,
leave my soul alone, leave my soul alone,' –
the patient's dummy lips moving to that refrain,
the patient's eyes too wide. And, shocked,
Lambert Rogers drawing out the probe
with nurses, students, sister, petrified.

'Leave my soul alone, leave my soul alone,'
that voice so arctic and that cry so odd
had nowhere else to go – till the antique
gramophone wound down and the words began
to blur and slow, '... leave ... my ... soul ... alone ...'
to cease at last when something other died.
And silence matched the silence under snow.

RICHARD CHURCH

South Pole

There's no reversal now,
Our shadows point the way,
Into the virgin snow,
Into the endless day.

Here at the Southern Pole
We bear the globe, and feel
The burden of the whole,
And know it is not real.

Ocean and continent,
The race of beast and man,
Have shrunk into a point
That turns on a glove-span.

We know that where we stand,
The equatorial wars
Still rage, but in our hand,
Small as the southern stars.

Atlas, who shouldered Earth,
Knew less than we know now;
He sponsored mankind's birth:
We are silent in the snow.

STEVIE SMITH

Scorpion

'This night shall thy soul be required of thee'
My soul is never required of *me*
It always has to be somebody else of course
Will my soul be required of me tonight perhaps?

(I often wonder what it will be like
To have one's soul required of one
But all I can think of is the Out-Patients' Department –
'Are you Mrs Briggs, dear?'
No, I am Scorpion.)

I should like my soul to be required of me, so as
To waft over grass till it comes to the blue sea
I am very fond of grass, I always have been, but there must
Be no cow, person or house to be seen.

Sea and *grass* must be quite empty
Other souls can find somewhere *else*.

O Lord God please come
And require the soul of thy Scorpion

Scorpion so wishes to be gone.

EDWARD THOMAS

Lights Out

I have come to the borders of sleep,
The unfathomable deep
Forest where all must lose
Their way, however straight,

Or winding, soon or late;
They cannot choose.

Many a road and track
That, since the dawn's first crack,
Up to the forest brink,
Deceived the travellers,
Suddenly now blurs,
And in they sink.

Here love ends,
Despair, ambition ends;
All pleasure and all trouble,
Although most sweet or bitter,
Here ends in sleep that is sweeter
Than tasks most noble.

There is not any book
Or face of dearest look
That I would not turn from now
To go into the unknown
I must enter, and leave, alone,
I know not how.

The tall forest towers;
Its cloudy foliage lowers
Ahead, shelf above shelf;
Its silence I hear and obey
That I may lose my way
And myself.

WILLIAM SHAKESPEARE

from Measure for Measure, Act III, Scene I

Claudio   Ay, but to die, and go we know not where,
            To lie in cold obstruction and to rot;
            This sensible warm motion to become
            A kneaded clod; and the delighted spirit

To bathe in fiery floods, or to reside
In thrilling region of thick-ribbed ice,
To be imprisoned in the viewless winds
And blown with restless violence round about
The pendent world; or to be worse than worst
Of those that lawless and incertain thoughts
Imagine howling; 'tis too horrible!
The weariest and most loathèd worldly life
That age, ache, penury, and imprisonment
Can lay on nature is a paradise
To what we fear of death.

FRANCES BELLERBY

A Clear Shell

Then fire burned my body to a clear shell.
Though whether the fanning tempest blew from hell
Or heaven I could not, cannot, tell –
Who have no sense
Left for so nice a difference.

But I learned the essential function of extreme pain –
Of liquid fire pouring again and again
And again through the horrified body: such pain
Makes wholly innocent.
Therefore am I impenitent

Today. Today ask no forgiveness,
Having nothing to be forgiven. And my soul, no less
House-proud than at the beginning, shows Death
Smilingly over the place,
Trusting this new face.

Dead man's song, dreamed by one who is alive

A poem said to be by the dead man Aijuk, dreamed by Paulinaoq.

I am filled with joy
When the day peacefully dawns
Up over the heavens,
   ayi, yai ya.

I am filled with joy
When the sun slowly rises
Up over the heavens,
   ayi, yai ya.

But else I choke with fear
At greedy maggot throngs;
They eat their way in
At the hollow of my collarbone
And in my eyes,
   ayi, yai ya.

Here I lie, recollecting
How stifled with fear I was
When they buried me
In a snow hut out on the lake,
   ayi, yai ya.

A block of snow was pushed to,
Incomprehensible it was
How my soul should make its way
And fly to the game land up there,
   ayi, yai ya.

That door-block worried me,
And ever greater grew my fear
When the fresh-water ice split in the cold,
And the frost-crack thunderously grew

Up over the heavens,
    ayi, yai ya.

Glorious was life
When dancing in the dance-house.
But did dancing in the dance-house bring me joy?
No! Ever was I so anxious,
That I could not recall
The song I was to sing.
Yes, I was ever anxious,
    ayi, yai ya.

Glorious was life . . .
Now I am filled with joy
For every time a dawn
Makes white the sky of night,
For every time the sun goes up
Over the heavens,
    ayi, yai ya.

Glorious was life
In winter.
But did winter bring me joy?
No! Ever was I so anxious
For sole-skins and skins for *kamiks*,
Would there be enough for us all?
Yes, I was ever anxious,
    ayi, yai ya.

Glorious was life
In summer.
But did summer bring me joy?
No! Ever was I so anxious
For skins and rugs for the platform,
Yes, I was ever anxious,
    ayi, yai ya.

Glorious was life
When standing at one's fishing hole
On the ice.
But did standing at the fishing hole bring me joy?
No! Ever was I so anxious
For my tiny little fish-hook
If it should not get a bite,
   ayi, yai ya.

    translated from the Inuit by K. Rasmussen

PENELOPE SHUTTLE

Kingdom of Tiny Shoes

We are all dead, Lucy, Cush, Kilroy and me,
but we have about five or six ghosts each.
Imagine our embarrassment, here in the next world
where everything blazes with a terrible glassy
casino glamour, where it's never dark;
because for us the great egg of time is broken.

Because we all have so many ghosts,
there's a lot of singing,
dancing, gambling, drinking, depressions,
fights, shitting and blaspheming;

one of my ghosts and one of Cush's
go in for honey-eating,
we love it, spooning, yumming, lip-licking greedily.

For a long time we all refused to accept it,
being here. Then suddenly Cush said –
Okay. Here we are. At least the drinks are free.

Even here there are winter fogs
and mists and pictures of Lenin and Jesus
on the walls. There are golf courses,
movies and divorces. More and more of us arrive.

Girls fall from the air, naked.
Old men burst up through the ground.
Proudly their shaven-head ghosts rush to meet them,
welcoming them, touring the wreckage with them.
Sometimes royal dead arrive in style, by boat.

One of my ghosts is always sad. Again K
puts his best-ghost's arms around this sad one of me
and says, 'There is no baby, you had no baby, sugar.'
'I am unwilling to believe you,' retorts this ghost,
'I am sure there is a baby,' and she goes on
looking for baby and baby's ghosts.
So far this ghost of me has found several packets
of disposable nappies and a pair of tiny knitted shoes
and this gives her hope . . .
The rest of my ghosts just look on, blinking and
    sniggering,
I'm afraid, and even Lucy taps her big fanged skull,
shrugging at such foolishness.

Space

Conspiracy of the Clouds

In the afternoon the clouds become transparent.
The satellite pictures and the computer data
had indicated a tropical depression
in the Gulf. The weathermen flew out
expecting to enter the eye of the hurricane
as it formed on the coast of Louisiana
but found themselves flying in a blue sky
with not even clear-air turbulence
to record on their sensitive machines.

What had happened to the atmosphere?

The jet stream entering the continent
in northern California and dropping down
across New Mexico and Texas before
flowing over Maryland ought to have been
creating an upper-air disturbance. With
a dense flow of humid air from the Yucatan
pushing all the way to North Dakota,
the conditions were right for tornadoes.

But still the whole of the U.S. was without a cloud.

Suddenly the meteorologists got excited seeing
confirmed reports of low pressure across Kansas;
the potential was building right in the heart
of the country for really violent weather.

But now the satellite pictures picked up nothing!

Nothing but blue sky everywhere.
Even the astronauts on a space shuttle
looked down on a cloudless America.

The next day heavy rain fell and took
the farmers of Nebraska by surprise –
it had certainly not been forecast; what's more,
there wasn't a cloud visible in the sky.
The question everyone asked: Where is this
rain coming from, why weren't we told about it?

BLAKE MORRISON

The Kiss

His Buick was too wide and didn't slow,
our wing-mirrors kissing in a Suffolk lane,
no sweat, not worth the exchange of addresses.

High from the rainchecking satellites
our island's like a gun set on a table,
still smoking, waiting to be loaded again.

RICHARD WILBUR

Praise in Summer

Obscurely yet most surely called to praise,
As sometimes summer calls us all, I said
The hills are heavens full of branching ways
Where star-nosed moles fly overhead the dead;
I said the trees are mines in air, I said
See how the sparrow burrows in the sky!
And then I wondered why this mad *instead*
Perverts our praise to uncreation, why
Such savor's in this wrenching things awry.
Does sense so stale that it must needs derange
The world to know it? To a praiseful eye
Should it not be enough of fresh and strange
That trees grow green, and moles can course in clay,
And sparrows sweep the ceiling of our day?

Zoom!

It begins as a house, an end terrace
in this case
   but it will not stop there. Soon it is
an avenue
   which cambers arrogantly past the Mechanics' Institute,
turns left
   at the main road without even looking
and quickly it is
   a town with all four major clearing banks,
a daily paper
   and a football team pushing for promotion.

On it goes, oblivious of the Planning Acts,
the green belts,
   and before we know it it is out of our hands:
city, nation,
   hemisphere, universe, hammering out in all directions
until suddenly,
   mercifully, it is drawn aside through the eye
of a black hole
   and bulleted into a neighbouring galaxy, emerging
smaller and smoother
   than a billiard ball but weighing more than Saturn.

People stop me in the street, badger me
in the check-out queue
   and ask 'What is this, this that is so small
and so very smooth
   but whose mass is greater than the ringed planet?'
It's just words
   I assure them. But they will not have it.

JOSEPH BLANCO WHITE

To Night

Mysterious Night! when our first parent knew
    Thee from report divine, and heard thy name,
    Did he not tremble for this lovely frame,
This glorious canopy of light and blue.
Yet 'neath a curtain of translucent dew,
    Bathed in the rays of the great setting flame,
    Hesperus with the host of heaven came,
And lo! creation widened in man's view.
Who could have thought such darkness lay concealed
    Within thy beams, O Sun! or who could find,
Whilst fly and leaf and insect stood revealed,
    That to such countless orbs thou mad'st us blind!
        Why do we then shun Death with anxious strife?
        If Light can thus deceive, wherefore not Life?

FLEUR ADCOCK

The Ex-Queen among the Astronomers

They serve revolving saucer eyes,
dishes of stars; they wait upon
huge lenses hung aloft to frame
the slow procession of the skies.

They calculate, adjust, record,
watch transits, measure distances.
They carry pocket telescopes
to spy through when they walk abroad.

Spectra possess their eyes; they face
upwards, alert for meteorites,
cherishing little glassy worlds:
receptacles for outer space.

But she, exile, expelled, ex-queen,
swishes among the men of science
waiting for cloudy skies, for nights
when constellations can't be seen.

She wears the rings he let her keep;
she walks as she was taught to walk
for his approval, years ago.
His bitter features taunt her sleep.

And so when these have laid aside
their telescopes, when lids are closed
between machine and sky, she seeks
terrestrial bodies to bestride.

She plucks this one or that among
the astronomers, and is become
his canopy, his occultation;
she sucks at earlobe, penis, tongue

mouthing the tubes of flesh; her hair
crackles, her eyes are comet-sparks.
She brings the distant briefly close
above his dreamy abstract stare.

FRED D'AGUIAR

Oracle Mama Dot

I am seated at her bare feet.
The rocking chair on floorboards
Of the verandah is the repeated break
Of bracken underfoot. *Where are we heading?*

Who dare speak in these moments before dark?
The firefly threads its infinite morse;
Crapauds and crickets are a mounting cacophony;
The laughter of daredevil bats.

Dust thickens into night.
She has rocked and rocked herself to sleep.
She may hold silence for another millennium.
I see the first stars among cloud.

WALT WHITMAN

When I Heard the Learn'd Astronomer

When I heard the learn'd astronomer,
When the proofs, the figures, were ranged in columns
    before me,
When I was shown the charts and diagrams, to add,
    divide, and measure them,
When I sitting heard the astronomer where he lectured
    with much applause in the lecture-room,
How soon unaccountable I became tired and sick,
Till rising and gliding out I wander'd off by myself,
In the mystical moist night-air, and from time to time,
Look'd up in perfect silence at the stars.

BERNARD O'DONOGHUE

Timmy Buckley Observes the Pleiades

It's January on a moonless, frosty night;
But they're not visible here, the ice-cluster
Sisters. They're hiding in North Cork
In '53, observed by Timmy Buckley
Who's waiting for the end of night milking
To fill his paper-stoppered whiskey bottle.

'The Seven Sisters, called the Pleiades,
Were the daughters of a famous king of Greece
Whose lands overflowed with milk and honey.
Electra was the fairest one of them.
There was this rich man in Kerry long ago
Who had a prize bull called Currens Atlas . . .'

Timmy had a name as a bit of a poet,
So we'd leave him to it. And once that's said,
Suddenly I see them here, low in the Bull
And realize they stood there all the time,
Waiting. I fix on them, knowing you're out as well
Watching, on whatever eminence.

Do you think that the eye's determined drawstring
That leads from me to them homes back to you,
As reliably as the mind's to Timmy Buckley? –
That such weightless communication
Influences the far receiving heart
To shrink the gap in space as well as time?

WILLIAM HABINGTON

'When I survey the bright'

When I survey the bright
    Celestial sphere;
So rich with jewels hung, that night
Doth like an Ethiop bride appear:

My soul her wings doth spread
    And heaven-ward flies,
The Almighty's mysteries to read
In the large volumes of the skies.

For the bright firmament
    Shoots forth no flame
So silent, but is eloquent
In speaking the creator's name.

No unregarded star
    Contracts its light
Into so small a character,
Removed far from our human sight,

But if we steadfast look
    We shall discern
In it, as in some holy book,
How man may heavenly knowledge learn.

It tells the conqueror,
    That far-stretch'd power,
Which his proud dangers traffic for,
Is but the triumph of an hour:

That from the farthest north,
    Some nation may,
Yet undiscover'd, issue forth,
And o'er his new-got conquest sway:

Some nation yet shut in
    With hills of ice
May be let out to scourge his sin,
Till they shall equal him in vice.

And then they likewise shall
    Their ruin have;
For as yourselves your empires fall,
And every kingdom hath a grave.

Thus those celestial fires,
    Though seeming mute,
The fallacy of our desires
And all the pride of life confute:—

For they have watch'd since first
    The world had birth:
And found sin in itself accurst,
And nothing permanent on Earth.

The Galaxy and the Snail

However fraught with perilous chasms, this world
looked at through the eyes of the dead
is nothing but a banquet
that has absolutely ended.

And yet I smell the starry sky
and my heart, as always, aches to lie down in lightning.
I crane my neck, longing to be struck
by an unprecedented bolt from the farthest edge of space.

A winch screeches for a snail
that is acquainted with the galaxy.
Today, as ever,
the bell clangs wildly, clangs in the sky.

The darkness brewing inside snails . . .
the darkness that brews inside as long as we live
grows bright, brighter,
and, outside, the wind that rises, rises in the sky.

translated from the Japanese by William I. Elliott

HUGH MACDIARMID

The Bonnie Broukit Bairn

For Peggy

Mars is braw in crammasy,
Venus in a green silk goun,
The auld mune shak's her gowden feathers,
Their starry talk's a wheen o' blethers,
Nane for thee a thochtie sparin',
Earth, thou bonnie broukit bairn!
— *But greet, an' in your tears ye'll droun*
The haill clanjamfrie!

SEAMUS HEANEY

from Singing School

EXPOSURE

It is December in Wicklow:
Alders dripping, birches
Inheriting the last light,
The ash tree cold to look at.

A comet that was lost
Should be visible at sunset,
Those million tons of light
Like a glimmer of haws and rose-hips,

And I sometimes see a falling star.
If I could come on meteorite!
Instead I walk through damp leaves,
Husks, the spent fluke of autumn,

Imagining a hero
On some muddy compound,
His gift like a slingstone
Whirled for the desperate.

How did I end up like this?
I often think of my friends'
Beautiful prismatic counselling
And the anvil brains of some who hate me

As I sit weighing and weighing
My responsible *tristia*.
For what? For the ear? For the people?
For what is said behind-backs?

Rain comes down through the alders,
Its low conducive voices
Mutter about let-downs and erosions
And yet each drop recalls

The diamond absolutes.
I am neither internee nor informer;
An inner émigré, grown long-haired
And thoughtful; a wood-kerne

Escaped from the massacre,
Taking protective colouring
From bole and dark, feeling
Every wind that blows;

Who, blowing up these sparks
For their meagre heat, have missed
The once-in-a-lifetime portent,
The comet's pulsing rose.

GERARD MANLEY HOPKINS

'I am Like a Slip of Comet ...'

   – I am like a slip of comet,
Scarce worth discovery, in some corner seen
Bridging the slender difference of two stars,
Come out of space, or suddenly engender'd
By heady elements, for no man knows;
But when she sights the sun she grows and sizes
And spins her skirts out, while her central star
Shakes its cocooning mists; and so she comes
To fields of light; millions of travelling rays
Pierce her; she hangs upon the flame-cased sun,
And sucks the light as full as Gideon's fleece:
But then her tether calls her; she falls off,
And as she dwindles shreds her smock of gold
Between the sistering planets, till she comes
To single Saturn, last and solitary;
And then she goes out into the cavernous dark.
So I go out: my little sweet is done:
I have drawn heat from this contagious sun:
To not ungentle death now forth I run.

SHEENAGH PUGH

The Comet-Watcher's Perspective

Granted, it was a streak of cobalt ice
a million miles across; it came from the edge
of creation, once in a thousand years,
but look as he might, it was just a blue smudge.

This is small, but that is far away:
there's a face, a silver stud in a pointed chin,
black hair, brown eyes, that he can no more hold
with his, than he could stare into the sun.

MICHAEL LONGLEY

Halley's Comet
Homage to Erik Satie

It was the seventeenth variation after all.
The original theme had fluttered out of my hands
And upside down on the linoleum suggested it.
An ink blot on the stave inspired the modulation,
Or was it a bloodstain, a teardrop's immortality
Perfectly pitched between parallels, horizontals,
The provisional shorelines, amphibian swamps?
I got drunk on a pint mug full of white feathers.
I couldn't sleep because inside my left nostril
A hair kept buzzing with signals from Halley's comet
As it swung its skirt of heavenly dust particles
On a parabola around the electric light bulb.
This won't recur for another seventy-six years.

Work-in-progress

1

They crawled out slowly
from their caves,
silver spiders.
The night held them
static in its net
of black jelly.
When the earth turned
        the sun
melted the night's blackness.
the stars fell over
the edge
   and we were freed
from our enslavement.

2

The stars came out
one night without
their faces.
They had no eyes
nor spoke to us
through their dark lips.
A crippled shadow
wept over the clouds
where the moon might have been.
They said in the village
that a woman lost her child.
When the sun came out
we discovered the unity

of faceless dreamers.

3
Nobody thought
that it could be so small, so ugly
When the star fell,
all eyes turned upwards.
Its silver signature
tore the darkness.
A visual scream
in the silence of night.
When they found the star
they could not believe it.

4
It was the black
star
in the white sky.
Shining in its brilliance.
It was the shadow of the sun
but at night
it became all space.
The night belonged
to the black star
but the silver stars

stood out smiling.
They did not know
how many had lost their way
in the laughter
of the black star.

GEORGE MEREDITH

Lucifer in Starlight

On a starred night Prince Lucifer uprose.
Tired of his dark dominion swung the fiend
Above the rolling ball in cloud part screened,
Where sinners hugged their spectre of repose.

Poor prey to his hot fit of pride were those.
And now upon his western wing he leaned,
Now his huge bulk o'er Afric's sands careened,
Now the black planet shadowed Arctic snows.
Soaring through wider zones that pricked his scars
With memory of the old revolt from Awe,
He reached a middle height, and at the stars,
Which are the brain of heaven, he looked, and sank.
Around the ancient track marched, rank on rank,
The army of unalterable law.

ROBERT GRAVES

Star-Talk

'Are you awake, Gemelli,
    This frosty night?'
'We'll be awake, till reveillé,
Which is Sunrise,' say the Gemelli,
'It's no good trying to go to sleep:
If there's wine to be got we'll drink it deep,
    But sleep is gone for to-night,
    But sleep is gone for to-night.'

'Are you cold too, poor Pleiads,
    This frosty night?'
'Yes, and so are the Hyads:
See us cuddle and hug,' say the Pleiads,
'All six in a ring: it keeps us warm:
We huddle together like birds in a storm:
    It's bitter weather to-night,
    It's bitter weather to-night.'

'What do you hunt, Orion,
    This starry night?'
'The Ram, the Bull and the Lion,
And the Great Bear,' says Orion,
'With my starry quiver and beautiful belt

I am trying to find a good thick pelt
   To warm my shoulders to-night,
   To warm my shoulders to-night.'

'Did you hear that, Great She-bear,
   This frosty night?'
'Yes, he's talking of stripping *me* bare
Of my own big fur,' says the She-bear,
'I'm afraid of the man and his terrible arrow:
The thought of it chills my bones to the marrow,
   And the frost so cruel to-night!
   And the frost so cruel to-night!'

'How is your trade, Aquarius,
   This frosty night?'
'Complaints is many and various
And my feet are cold,' says Aquarius,
'There's Venus objects to Dolphin-scales,
And Mars to Crab-spawn found in my pails,
   And the pump has frozen to-night,
   And the pump has frozen to-night.'

FREDA DOWNIE

Starlight

Three kings embark on a long journey
Under the dry acres of the moon,
Whose light is well disposed,
But of no special significance.
It is the nailhead light
Of one sparky planet
That draws them on –
Although at times,
One king thinks the star
Has the look of crayon
Drawn on dark paper;
While another thinks it

Looks no more than a sliver
Of silver pasted on indigo;
And the third king, observing
A certain unsteadiness,
Thinks the heavenly guide
Trembles on its cotton thread.

GEORGE HERBERT

The Star

Bright spark, shot from a brighter place,
  Where beams surround my Saviour's face,
    Canst thou be any where
      So well as there?

Yet, if thou wilt from thence depart,
  Take a bad lodging in my heart;
    For thou canst make a debter,
      And make it better.

First with thy fire-work burn to dust
  Folly, and worse than folly, lust:
    Then with thy light refine,
      And make it shine:

So disengaged from sin and sicknesse,
  Touch it with thy celestial quickness,
    That it may hang and move
      After thy love.

Then with our trinity of light,
  Motion, and heat, let's take our flight
    Unto the place where thou
      Before didst bow.

Get me a standing there, and place
  Among the beams, which crown the face
    Of him, who died to part
      Sin and my heart:

That so among the rest I may
　　Glitter, and curl, and wind as they:
　　　　That winding is their fashion
　　　　　　Of adoration.

Sure thou wilt joy, by gaining me
　　To fly home like a laden bee
　　　　Unto that hive of beams
　　　　　　And garland-streams.

BEN JONSON

Hymn to Diana

Queen and Huntress, chaste and fair,
　　Now the sun is laid to sleep,
Seated in thy silver chair
　　State in wonted manner keep:
　　　　Hesperus entreats thy light,
　　　　Goddess excellently bright.

Earth, let not thy envious shade
　　Dare itself to interpose;
Cynthia's shining orb was made
　　Heaven to clear when day did close:
　　　　Bless us then with wishéd sight,
　　　　Goddess excellently bright.

Lay thy bow of pearl apart
　　And thy crystal-shining quiver;
Give unto the flying hart
　　Space to breathe, how short soever:
　　　　Thou that mak'st a day of night,
　　　　Goddess excellently bright!

from The Merchant of Venice, Act V, Scene 1

Lorenzo   How sweet the moonlight sleeps upon this bank!
Here will we sit, and let the sounds of music
Creep in our ears: soft stillness and the night
Become the touches of sweet harmony.
Sit, Jessica. Look, how the floor of heaven
Is thick inlaid with patines of bright gold:
There's not the smallest orb which thou behold'st
But in his motion like an angel sings,
Still quiring to the young-eyed cherubins, –
Such harmony is in immortal souls;
But whilst this muddy vesture of decay
Doth grossly close it in, we cannot hear it.

SYLVIA PLATH

The Moon and the Yew Tree

This is the light of the mind, cold and planetary.
The trees of the mind are black. The light is blue.
The grasses unload their griefs on my feet as if I were God,
Prickling my ankles and murmuring of their humility.
Fumy, spiritous mists inhabit this place
Separated from my house by a row of headstones.
I simply cannot see where there is to get to.

The moon is no door. It is a face in its own right,
White as a knuckle and terribly upset.
It drags the sea after it like a dark crime; it is quiet
With the O-gape of complete despair. I live here.
Twice on Sunday, the bells startle the sky –
Eight great tongues affirming the Resurrection.
At the end, they soberly bong out their names.

The yew tree points up. It has a Gothic shape.
The eyes lift after it and find the moon.
The moon is my mother. She is not sweet like Mary.
Her blue garments unloose small bats and owls.
How I would like to believe in tenderness –
The face of the effigy, gentled by candles,
Bending, on me in particular, its mild eyes.

I have fallen a long way. Clouds are flowering
Blue and mystical over the face of the stars.
Inside the church, the saints will be all blue,
Floating on their delicate feet over the cold pews,
Their hands and faces stiff with holiness.
The moon sees nothing of this. She is bald and wild.
And the message of the yew tree is blackness – blackness
    and silence.

TED HUGHES

Full Moon and Little Frieda

A cool small evening shrunk to a dog bark and the clank of
    a bucket –
And you listening.
A spider's web, tense for the dew's touch.
A pail lifted, still and brimming – mirror
To tempt a first star to a tremor.

Cows are going home in the lane there, looping the hedges
    with their warm wreaths of breath –
A dark river of blood, many boulders,
Balancing unspilled milk.

'Moon!' you cry suddenly, 'Moon! Moon!'

The moon has stepped back like an artist gazing amazed at
    a work

That points at him amazed.

'With how sad steps . . .'

With how sad steps, O Moon! thou climb'st the skies!
    How silently, and with how wan a face!
    What! may it be that even in heavenly place
That busy archer his sharp arrows tries?
Sure, if that long-with-love-acquainted eyes
    Can judge of love, thou feel'st a lover's case.
    I read it in thy looks. Thy languisht grace
To me that feel the like, thy state descries.
    Then even of fellowship, O Moon, tell me
Is constant love deemed there but want of wit?
    Are beauties there as proud as here they be?
Do they above love to be loved, and yet
    Those lovers scorn whom that love doth possess?
    Do they call virtue there, ungratefulness?

Sad Steps

Groping back to bed after a piss
I part thick curtains, and am startled by
The rapid clouds, the moon's cleanliness.

Four o'clock: wedge-shadowed gardens lie
Under a cavernous, a wind-picked sky.
There's something laughable about this,

The way the moon dashes through clouds that blow
Loosely as cannon-smoke to stand apart
(Stone-coloured light sharpening the roofs below)

High and preposterous and separate –
Lozenge of love! Medallion of art!
O wolves of memory! Immensements! No,

One shivers slightly, looking up there.
The hardness and the brightness and the plain
Far-reaching singleness of that wide stare

Is a reminder of the strength and pain
Of being young; that it can't come again,
But is for others undiminished somewhere.

ALLEN CURNOW

With How Mad Steps

Nightwatchman in some crater of the moon –
No, not that lunatic
But the dumb satellite itself, my tune
The cold sphere's silence; and I stick

(Abiding, law-abiding) to that orbit
Fire once described, tossed into space to cool
From my earth's body; a gyrating habit.
What if she watches? She'll

Mask with the mirror of her tides those shores
Her flesh makes in the heavens, and even
While dawn destroys me her young foliage stirs;
Neither is mathematical space forgiven

My dear earth's distance, though her heart descry
With how mad steps, her moon, I climb the sky.

WENDY COPE

from Strugnell Lunaire

The silver moon pours down her light.
I drink it in with thirsty eyes.
I'd rather have another pint of lager
But all the pubs are closed.
The poet must drink deep of life
To find poetic ecstasy.

The silver moon pours down her light.
I drink it in with thirsty eyes.
Tonight I am intoxicated
And every night it is the same.
I wander down the beauteous High Street
And, if the weather isn't cloudy,
The silver moon pours down her light.

IAN HAMILTON

Familiars

If you were to look up now you would see
The moon, the bridge, the ambulance,
The road back into town.
        The river weeds
You crouch in seem a yard shorter,
A shade more featherishly purple
Than they were this time last year;
The caverns of 'your bridge'
Less brilliantly jet-black than I remember them.

Even from up here, though, I can tell
It's the same unfathomable prayer:
If you were to look up now would you see
Your moon-man swimming through the moonlit air?

FEDERICO GARCÍA LORCA

A Game of Moons

Moon is round.
Roundabout it is a treadmill
built with mirrors.
Roundabout it is a wheel
like a waterwheel.
Moon's become a gilt leaf
like a loaf of white gold.
Moon sheds its petals

375

like moons.
Swarms of fountains
float through the sky.
In each fountain's a moon
lying dead.
Moon
becomes a cane made of light
in bright torrents.
Moon
like a large stainedglass window
that breaks on the ocean.
Moon
through an infinite
screen.
And the Moon? And the Moon?

(Up above
nothing left but a ring
of small crystals.)

translated from the Spanish by Jerome Rothenberg

LAVINIA GREENLAW

For the First Dog in Space

You're being sent up in Sputnik 2,
a kind of octopus with rigor mortis.
Ground control have sworn allegiance
to gravity and the laws of motion;
they sleep without dreams,
safe in the knowledge
that a Russian mongrel bitch
can be blasted through the exosphere
at seven miles a second,
but can never stray far from home.
You will have no companion,
no buttons to press, just six days' air.

Laika, do not let yourself be fooled
by the absolute stillness
that comes only with now knowing
how fast you are going. As you fall
in orbit around the earth, remember
your language. Listen to star dust.
Trust your fear.

W. H. AUDEN

Moon Landing

It's natural the Boys should whoop it up for
so huge a phallic triumph, an adventure
 it would not have occurred to women
  to think worth while, made possible only

because we like huddling in gangs and knowing
the exact time: yes, our sex may in fairness
 hurrah the deed, although the motives
  that primed it were somewhat less than *menschlich*.

A grand gesture. But what does it period?
What does it osse? We were always adroiter
 with objects than lives, and more facile
  at courage than kindness: from the moment

the first flint was flaked this landing was merely
a matter of time. But our selves, like Adam's,
 still don't fit us exactly, modern
  only in this – our lack of decorum.

Homer's heroes were certainly no braver
than our Trio, but more fortunate: Hector
 was excused the insult of having
  his valor covered by television.

Worth *going* to see? I can well believe it.
Worth *seeing*? Mneh! I once rode through a desert
	and was not charmed: give me a watered
	lively garden, remote from blatherers

about the New, the von Brauns and their ilk, where
on August mornings I can count the morning
	glories, where to die has a meaning,
	and no engine can shift my perspective.

Unsmudged, thank God, my Moon still queens the
	Heavens
as She ebbs and fulls, a Presence to glop at,
	Her Old Man, made of grit not protein,
	still visits my Austrian several

with His old detachment, and the old warnings
still have power to scare me: Hybris comes to
	an ugly finish, Irreverence
	is a greater oaf than Superstition.

Our apparatniks will continue making
the usual squalid mess called History:
	all we can pray for is that artists,
	chefs and saints may still appear to blithe it.

ROBERT LOWELL

Moon-Landings

The moon on television never errs,
and shares the worker's fear of immigration,
a strange white goddess imprisoned in her ash,
entombed Etruscan, smiling though immortal.
We've clocked the moon; it goes from month to month
bleeding us dry, buying less and less –
chassis orbiting about the earth,
grin of heatwave, spasm of stainless steel,
gadabout with heart of chalk, unnamable

void and cold thing in the universe,
lunatic's pill with poisonous side-effects,
body whose essence is its excess baggage,
compressed like a Chinese dried caterpillar . . .
our hallucinator, the disenchantress.

GWYNETH LEWIS

from Zero Gravity

VIII

Thousands arrive when a bird's about to fly,
crowding the causeways. 'Houston. Weather is a go
and counting.' I pray for you as you lie
on your back facing upwards. A placard shows
local, Shuttle and universal time.
Numbers run out. Zero always comes.
'Main engines are gimballed' and I'm
not ready for this, but clouds of steam
billow out sideways and a sudden spark
lifts the rocket on a collective roar
that comes from inside us. With a sonic crack
the spaceship explodes to a flower of fire
on the scaffold's stamen. We sob and swear,
helpless, but we're lifting a sun
with our love's attention, we hear
the Shuttle's death rattle as it overcomes
its own weight with glory, setting car alarms
off in the Keys and then it's gone
out of this time zone, into the calm
of black and we've lost the lemon dawn
your vanishing made. At the viewing site
we pick oranges for your missing light.

IAIN MAC A'GHOBHAINN (IAIN CRICHTON SMITH)

The space-ship

I think of you and then I think of this
picture of an astronaut lacking air,
dying of lack of it in the depths of space,

his face kneading and working under glass,
lolling inside his helmet. Then I see
a foreign space-ship steadily from space

swimming implacably, a black helmet
rearing out of the limitless azure and
a sun exploding with tremendous light.

The black mediaeval helmet fits his face
and the glass breaks without a single sound
and becomes the crystals of unnumbered stars.

EDWIN MORGAN

The First Men on Mercury

– We come in peace from the third planet.
Would you take us to your leader?

– Bawr stretter! Bawr. Bawr. Stretterhawl?

– This is a little plastic model
of the solar system, with working parts.
You are here and we are there and we
are now here with you, is this clear?

– Gawl horrop. Bawr. Abawrhannahanna!

– Where we come from is blue and white
with brown, you see we call the brown
here 'land', the blue is 'sea', and the white
is 'clouds' over land and sea, we live
on the surface of the brown land

all round is sea and clouds. We are 'men'.
Men come –

– Glawp men! Gawrbenner menko. Menhawl?

– Men come in peace from the third planet
which we call 'earth'. We are earthmen.
Take us earthmen to your leader.

– Thmen? Thmen? Bawr. Bawrhossop.
Yuleeda tan hanna. Harrabost yuleeda.

– I am the yuleeda. You see my hands,
we carry no benner, we come in peace.
The spaceways are all stretterhawn.

– Glawn peacemen all horrabhanna tantko!
Tan come at'mstrossop. Glawp yuleeda!

– Atoms are peacegawl in our harraban.
Menbat worrabost from tan hannahanna.

– You men we know bawrhossoptant. Bawr.
We know yuleeda. Go strawg backspetter quick.

– We cantantabawr, tantingko backspetter now!

– Banghapper now! Yes, third planet back.
Yuleeda will go back blue, white, brown
nowhanna! There is no more talk.

– Gawl han fasthapper?

– No. You must go back to your planet.
Go back in peace, take what you have gained
but quickly.

– Stretterworra gawl, gawl . . .

– Of course, but nothing is ever the same,
now is it? You'll remember Mercury.

ARCHIBALD MACLEISH

The End of the World

Quite unexpectedly as Vasserot
The armless ambidextrian was lighting
A match between his great and second toe
And Ralph the lion was engaged in biting
The neck of Madame Sossman while the drum
Pointed, and Teeny was about to cough
In waltz-time swinging Jacko by the thumb –
Quite unexpectedly the top blew off:

And there, there overhead, there, there, hung over
Those thousands of white faces, those dazed eyes,
There in the starless dark the poise, the hover,
There with vast wings across the canceled skies,
There in the sudden blackness the black pall
Of nothing, nothing, nothing—nothing at all.

CRAIG RAINE

A Martian Sends a Postcard Home

Caxtons are mechanical birds with many wings
and some are treasured for their markings –

they cause the eyes to melt
or the body to shriek without pain.

I have never seen one fly, but
sometimes they perch on the hand.

Mist is when the sky is tired of flight
and rests its soft machine on ground:

then the world is dim and bookish
like engravings under tissue paper.

Rain is when the earth is television.
It has the property of making colours darker.

Model T is a room with the lock inside –
a key is turned to free the world

for movement, so quick there is a film
to watch for anything missed.

But time is tied to the wrist
or kept in a box, ticking with impatience.

In homes, a haunted apparatus sleeps,
that snores when you pick it up.

If the ghost cries, they carry it
to their lips and soothe it to sleep

with sounds. And yet, they wake it up
deliberately, by tickling with a finger.

Only the young are allowed to suffer
openly. Adults go to a punishment room

with water but nothing to eat.
They lock the door and suffer the noises

alone. No one is exempt
and everyone's pain has a different smell.

At night, when all the colours die,
they hide in pairs

and read about themselves –
in colour, with their eyelids shut.

HENRY VAUGHAN

The World

I saw Eternity the other night,
Like a great ring of pure and endless light,
   All calm, as it was bright;
And round beneath it, Time, in hours, days, years,
     Driven by the spheres,

Like a vast shadow moved; in which the world
    And all her train were hurl'd.
The doting Lover in his quaintest strain
    Did there complain;
Near him, his lute, his fancy, and his slights,
    Wit's sour delights;
With gloves and knots, the silly snares of pleasure;
    Yet his dear treasure
All scatter'd lay, while he his eyes did pour
    Upon a flower.

The darksome Statesman hung with weights and woe,
Like a thick midnight-fog, moved there so slow,
    He did not stay, nor go;
Condemning thoughts – like sad eclipses – scowl
    Upon his soul,
And clouds of crying witnesses without
    Pursued him with one shout;
Yet digg'd the mole, and lest his ways be found,
    Work'd under ground,
Where he did clutch his prey; but One did see
    That policy;
Churches and altars fed him; perjuries
    Were gnats and flies;
It rain'd about him blood and tears, but he
    Drank them as free.

The fearful Miser on a heap of rust
Sate pining all his life there; did scarce trust
    His own hands with the dust;
Yet would not place one piece above, but lives
    In fear of thieves:
Thousands there were as frantic as himself,
    And hugg'd each one his pelf.
The down-right Epicure placed heaven in sense,
    And scorn'd pretence;
While others, slipped into a wide excess,

Said little less;
The weaker sort, slight, trivial wares enslave,
  Who think them brave;
And poor, despisèd Truth sat counting by
  Their victory.

Yet some, who all this while did weep and sing,
And sing, and weep, soar'd up into the ring;
  But most would use no wing.
O fools – said I – thus to prefer dark night
  Before true light!
To live in grots, and caves, and hate the day
  Because it shews the way: –
The way, which from this dead and dark abode
  Leads up to God;
A way where you might tread the Sun, and be
  More bright than he!
But as I did their madness so discuss,
  One whisper'd thus, –
This ring the Bride-groom did for none provide
  But for His Bride.

Acknowledgements

I am grateful to Mary Enright and the staff of the Arts Council Poetry Library on the South Bank in London for their patience and help as I worked on this anthology. I am also indebted to my wife Jan Dalley, my friends Alan Hollinghurst and Jon Cook, and my editors at Faber – Paul Keegan and Jane Feaver. Anticipating that this book may find its way into the hands of young men and women who may not have read much poetry before, I would also like to thank the person who first opened my eyes to literature: my school English teacher, Peter Way.

A.M.

The editor and publishers gratefully acknowledge permission to reprint copyright material in this book as follows:

DANNIE ABSE: from *Selected Poems*, published by Hutchinson, 1989. FLEUR ADCOCK: from *Poems 1960–2000*, published by Bloodaxe Books, 2000. PATIENCE AGBABI: 'Northwestern' reprinted by kind permission of the author. MONIZA ALVI: from *Carrying My Wife*, published by Bloodaxe Books, 2000. YEHUDA AMICHAI: from *Selected Poetry*, published by Viking, 1987; reprinted by permission of Hana Amichai. SIMON ARMITAGE: from *Zoom!*, published by Bloodaxe Books, 1989; also from *Dead Sea Poems*, published by Faber and Faber Ltd, 1995. JOHN ASHBERY: from *Selected Poems*, published by Carcanet Press Ltd, 1985. MARGARET ATWOOD: from *Selected Poems*, published by Simon and Schuster, 1976. W. H. AUDEN: from *Collected Poems*, published by Faber and Faber Ltd, 1976. JAMES K. BAXTER: from *Selected Poems*, published by Oxford University Press, 1982. PATRICIA BEER: from *Collected Poems*, published by Carcanet Press Ltd. MARTIN BELL: from *Complete Poems*, published by Bloodaxe Books, 1998. FRANCES BELLERBY: from *Selected Poems*, published by Enitharmon Press, 1970. JAMES BERRY: from *Hot Earth Cold Earth*, published by Bloodaxe Books, 1995. JOHN BERRYMAN: from *The Dream Songs*, published by Faber and Faber Ltd. JOHN BETJEMAN: from *Collected Poems*, published by John Murray (Publishers) Ltd., 1998. ELIZABETH BISHOP: from *Complete Poems of Elizabeth Bishop*, published by Chatto & Windus,

1983; reprinted by permission of Farrar Straus & Giroux. EDWARD KAMAU BRATHWAITE: from *Third World Poets*, published by Longman, 1983. BERTOLT BRECHT: from *Poems 1913–1956*, published by Methuen Publishing Ltd, 1976. BASIL BUNTING: from *Complete Poems*, published by Bloodaxe Books, 2000. JOHN BURNSIDE: from *The Hoop*, published by Carcanet Press Ltd., 1988. NORMAN CAMERON: from *Collected Poems*, published by the Hogarth Press, reprinted by permission of Jane Aitken Hodge. CIARAN CARSON: from *The Irish for No*, published by The Gallery Press, 1987; reprinted by kind permission of the author and The Gallery Press, Loughcrew, Oldcastle, County Meath, Ireland. NINA CASSIAN: from *Life Sentence*, translated by Brenda Walker and Andrea Deletant and edited by William Jay Smith, published by Anvil Press, 1990. CHARLES CAUSLEY: from *Collected Poems 1951–2000*, published by Macmillan, 1992; reprinted by permission of David Higham Associates. C. P. CAVAFY: from *Collected Poems* translated by Edmund and Philip Sherrard, published by Chatto & Windus; reprinted by permission of the Random House Group Ltd. PAUL CELAN: from *Poems of Paul Celan*, translated by Michael Hamburger, published by Anvil Press Poetry, 1988. RENE CHAR: from *Selected Poems*, published by New Directions, 1992. AMY CLAMPITT: from *Collected Poems*, published by Faber and Faber Ltd, 1998. GILLIAN CLARKE: from *Letter from a Far Country*, published by Carcanet Press. WENDY COPE: from *Serious Concerns*, published by Faber and Faber Ltd. ROBERT CRAWFORD: from *A Scottish Assembly*, published by Chatto & Windus; reprinted by permission of the Random House Group Ltd. IAN CRICHTON SMITH: from *Love Poems and Elegies*, published by Gollancz, 1972. ALLEN CURNOW: from *Selected Poems*, published by Penguin, 1990. BIDDY CUSSROEE: from *Love Songs of Connaght*, published by Irish Academic Press, 1985. FRED D'AGUIAR: from *Mama Dot*, published by Chatto & Windus; reprinted by permission of the Random House Group Ltd. ELIZABETH DARYUSH: from *Collected Poems*, published by Carcanet Press Ltd, 1976. MICHAEL DONAGHY: from *Shibboleth*, published by Oxford University Press, 1988; reprinted by permission of Macmillan Ltd. ED DORN: from *Collected Poems*, reprinted by kind permission of Jennifer Dorn. KEITH DOUGLAS: from *Complete Poems*, published by Oxford University Press, 1978, 1985. RITA DOVE: from *Thomas and Beulah*, copyright © 1986 by Rita Dove; reprinted by kind permission of the author. FREDA

DOWNIE: from *Plainsong*, published by Secker and Warburg; reprinted by permission of the Random House Group Ltd. CAROL ANN DUFFY: from *Selling Manhattan*, published by Anvil Press Poetry, 1987; also from *Mean Time*, published by Anvil Press Poetry, 1993. HELEN DUNMORE: from *Out of the Blue: New and Selected Poems*, published by Bloodaxe Books, 2001. DOUGLAS DUNN: from *Terry Street*, published by Faber and Faber Ltd, 1969, and *Elegies*, published by Faber and Faber Ltd, 1985. BOB DYLAN: from *Lyrics 1962–1985*, published by Harper Collins, 1994. RICHARD EBERHART: from *Collected Poems*, published by Oxford University Press, 1988. T. S. ELIOT: from *Collected Poems 1909–1962*, published by Faber and Faber Ltd, 1963. WILLIAM EMPSON: from *Collected Poems*, published by Chatto & Windus; reprinted by permission of the Random House Group Ltd. HANS MAGNUS ENZENSBERGER: from *Selected Poems*, published by Penguin, 1968. U. A. FANTHORPE: from *Standing To*, published by Peterloo Poets, 1987; reproduced by permission of Peterloo Poets. VICKI FEAVER: from *The Handless Maiden*, published by Jonathan Cape; reprinted by permission of the Random House Group Ltd. ELAINE FEINSTEIN: from *Selected Poems*, published by Carcanet Press Ltd, 1994. JAMES FENTON: from *Out of Danger*, published by Penguin, 1993; also from *The Memory of War*, published by Penguin 1983. IAN HAMILTON FINLAY: from *The Dancers Inherit the Part*, published by Polygon Press, 1996. ROY FISHER: from *The Low Dow Drop: New and Selected Poems*, published by Bloodaxe Books, 1996. ROBERT FROST: from *The Poetry of Robert Frost*, edited by Edward Connery Lathem, published by Jonathan Cape; reprinted by permission of the Random House Group Ltd. JOHN FULLER: from *Stones and Fires*, published by Chatto & Windus; reprinted by permission of the Random House Group Ltd. ZULFIKAR GHOSE: from *Selected Poems*, published by Oxford University Press, 1966. ALAN GINSBERG: from *Selected Poems 1947–1997*, published by Penguin, 1997. W. S. GRAHAM: 'The Night City' and 'The Stepping Stones' reprinted by permission of Michael and Margaret Snow, literary executors for the literary estate of W. S. Graham. ROBERT GRAVES: from *Complete Poems*, published by Cassell, 1975; reprinted by permission of Carcanet Press. LAVINIA GREENLAW: from *A World Where News Travelled Slowly*, published by Faber and Faber Ltd, 1997, and *Night Photograph*, published by Faber and Faber Ltd, 1993. THOM GUNN: from *Collected Poems*, published by Faber and Faber Ltd,

1993. IVOR GURNEY: 'To His Love' reprinted by permission of
Carcanet Press Ltd. MARILYN HACKER: from *Love, Death and the
Changing of the Seasons*, published by Onlywomen Press, 1987.
SOPHIE HANNAH: from *Hotels like Houses*, published by Carcanet
Press, 1996. TONY HARRISON: from *Selected Poems*, published by
Penguin, 1986. SEAMUS HEANEY: from *Seeing Things*, published
by Faber and Faber Ltd, 1991; *Field Work*, published by Faber and
Faber Ltd, 1979; *North*, published by Faber and Faber Ltd, 1975;
and *The Spirit Level*, published by Faber and Faber Ltd., 1996.
ANTONY HECHT: from *Collected Earlier Poems*, published by
Oxford University Press, 1991. GEOFFREY HILL: from *Collected
Poems*, published by Penguin, 1985. SELIMA HILL: from
Trembling Hearts in the Bodies of Dogs: New and Selected Poems,
published by Bloodaxe Books, 1994. MICHAEL HOFMANN: from
Acrimony, published by Faber and Faber Ltd, 1995. MOLLY
HOLDEN: 'Seaman, 1941' copyright © Alan Holden, 2001,
reprinted by kind permission of Alan Holden; and from *Selected
Poems*, published by Carcanet Press Ltd, 1981. TED HUGHES: from
Moortown Diary, published by Faber and Faber Ltd, 1979;
Birthday Letters, published by Faber and Faber Ltd, 1998; *Wodwo*,
published by Faber and Faber Ltd, 1967. MICK IMLAH: from
Birthmarks, published by Chatto & Windus; reprinted by
permission of the Random House Group Ltd. PHILIPPE
JACCOTTET: from *Selected Poems*, translated by Derek Mahon,
published by Penguin, 1988. KATHLEEN JAMIE: from *Jizzen*,
published by Picador, 1999. RANDALL JARRELL: from *Complete
Poems*, published by Farrar Straus & Giroux, 1975. ELIZABETH
JENNINGS: from *Collected Poems*, published by Macmillan;
reprinted by permission of David Higham Associates Ltd. JUAN
RAMON JIMINEZ: from *Light and Shadows*, translated by Robert
Bly, copyright © 1984 by White Pine Press, Buffalo. DAVID
JONES: from *In Parenthesis*, published by Faber and Faber Ltd,
1937. JACKIE KAY: from *Off Colour*, published by Bloodaxe Books,
1998. WELDON KEES: from *Collected Poems*, published by Faber
and Faber Ltd., 1993. AUGUST KLEINZAHLER: from *Red Sauce,
Whiskey, and Snow*, published by Faber and Faber Ltd, 1995.
LINTON KWESI JOHNSON: from *Tings and Times*, published by
Bloodaxe Books. PHILIP LARKIN: from *The Less Deceived*,
published by The Marvell Press, England and Australia; also from
Collected Poems, published by Faber and Faber Ltd, 1988.
GEOFFREY LEHMANN: from *Spring Forest*, published by Faber and

Faber Ltd, 1994. GWYNETH LEWIS: from *Zero Gravity*, published by Bloodaxe Books, 1998. D. H. LAWRENCE: from *Complete Poems*, published by Penguin, 1977. DENISE LEVERTOV: from *Selected Poems*, published by New Directions Publishing Corporation, reprinted by permission of Laurence Pollinger Ltd. CHRISTOPHER LOGUE: from *Selected Poems*, published by Faber and Faber Ltd, 1997. MICHAEL LONGLEY: from *Selected Poems*, published by Jonathan Cape. Reprinted by permission of the Random House Group Ltd. FREDERICO GARCIA LORCA: from *Selected Poems*, published by Penguin, 1997. ROBERT LOWELL: from *Selected Poems*, published by Faber and Faber Ltd, 1976, and *History*, published by Faber and Faber Ltd, 1973. SORLEY MACLEAN: from *From Wood to Ridge*, published by Carcanet Press Ltd. ARCHIBALD MACLEISH: from *Collected Poems 1917–1982*, copyright © 1985 by The Estate of Archibald MacLeish; reprinted by permission of Houghton Mifflin Company, all rights reserved. LOUIS MACNEICE: from *Collected Poems*, published by Faber and Faber Ltd, 1966; reprinted by permission of David Higham Associates. HUGH MACDIARMID: from *Complete Poems*, published by Penguin, 1995. MEDBH MCGUCKIAN: from *Selected Poems*, published by The Gallery Press, 1997; reprinted by kind permission of the author and The Gallery Press, Loughcrew, Oldcastle, County Meath, Ireland. DEREK MAHON: from *Collected Poems*, published by The Gallery Press, 1999; reprinted by kind permission of the author and The Gallery Press, Loughcrew, Oldcastle, County Meath, Ireland. OSIP MANDELSTAM: from *Selected Poems*, published by Penguin, 1977. CHARLOTTE MEW: from *Collected Poems and Selected Prose*, published by Carcanet Press Ltd. CZESLAW MILOSZ: from *Collected Poems*, published by Penguin, 1988. ROBERT MINHINNICK: from *Selected Poems*, published by Carcanet Press Ltd, 1999. ELMA MITCHELL: from *People Etcetera*, copyright © Harry Chambers, 1987; reproduced by permission of Peterloo Poets. MARIANNE MOORE: from *Selected Poems*, published by Faber and Faber Ltd, 1969. DOM MORAES: from *Collected Poems*, published by Penguin. EDWIN MORGAN: from *Collected Poems*, published by Carcanet Press Ltd, 1990. BLAKE MORRISON: from *Selected Poems*, published by Granta, 1999; reprinted by permission of Peters, Fraser and Dunlop Ltd on behalf of Blake Morrison. PAUL MULDOON: from *New Selected Poems*, published by Faber and Faber Ltd, 1976. LES MURRAY: from 'The Sydney Highrise Variations', reprinted by permission of Carcanet Press Ltd. GRACE NICHOLS: from *I Is A Long Memoried Woman*, published by Caribbean Cultures International, 1983. SEAN O'BRIEN: from *The Indoor Park*, published by Bloodaxe Books, 1983. BERNARD O'DONOGHUE: from *Here Not There*, published by Chatto & Windus, reprinted by permission of the Random House Group Ltd. OODGEROO, of the tribe Noonuccal: from *My People Jacaranda*, published by John Wiley & Sons, 1981; reprinted by permission of John Wiley & Sons, Australia. RUTH PADEL: from *Summer Snow*, published by Hutchinson; reprinted by permission of the Random House Group Ltd. DAN PAGIS: from *Selected Poetry of Dan Pagis*, edited by Stephen Mitchell, copyright © 1996 The Regents of the University of California. DON PATERSON: from *God's Gift to Women*, published by Faber and Faber Ltd, 1997. TOM PAULIN: from *Selected Poems*, published by Faber and Faber Ltd, 1993. FERNANDO PESSOA: from *Selected Poems*, published by Penguin, 1974. SYLVIA PLATH: from *Collected Poems*, published by Faber and Faber, 1981. KATRINA PORTEOUS: from *The Lost Music*, published by Bloodaxe Books, 1996. EZRA POUND: from *Selected Poems*, published by Faber and Faber Ltd, 1928. SHEENAGH PUGH: from *Stonelight*, published by Seren, 1999; reprinted by permission of Seren Books. JOHN CROWE RANSOM: from *Selected Poems*, 3rd edition, revised and enlarged, copyright © 1924 by Alfred A. Knopf Inc and renewed 1952 by John Crowe Ransom; used by permission of Alfred A. Knopf, a division of Random House, Inc. PETER READING: from *Collected Poems, Vol I: Poems 1970-1984*, published by Bloodaxe Books, 1995. CHRISTOPHER REID: from *Expanded Universes*, published by Faber and Faber Ltd, 1996. EDGELL RICKWORD: from *Collected Poems*, published by Bodley Head; reprinted by the permission of the Random House Group Limited. PETER REDGROVE: from *Selected Poems*, published by Jonathan Cape; reprinted by permission of David Higham Associates. HENRY REED: from *Collected Poems*, edited by John Stallworthy, published by Oxford University Press, 1991; reprinted by permission of Oxford University Press. ADRIENNE RICH: from *Selected Poems*, published by W. W. Norton & Co. DENISE RILEY: from *Dry Air*, published by Virago, 1985. TADEUSZ RÓŻEWICZ: from *They Came to See a Poet*, translated by Adam Czerniawski, published by Anvil Press Poetry, 1991. MURIEL RUKEYSER: from *Collected Poems*, published by McGraw Hill, 1978, copyright © Muriel Rukeyser, 1978; reprinted by

permission of International Creative Management Inc. CAROL
RUMENS: from *Thinking of Skins: New and Selected Poems*,
published by Bloodaxe Books, 1993. CARL SANDBURG: from
Chicago Poems, copyright © 1916 by Holt Rinehart and Winston
and renewed 1944 by Carl Sandburg; reprinted by permission of
Harcourt, Inc. MARIN SORESCU: from *Selected Poems*, translated
by Michael Hamburger, published by Bloodaxe Books, 1983.
SIEGFRIED SASSOON: from *Collected Poems*, published by Faber
and Faber Ltd, 1961; reprinted by kind permission of George
Sassoon. C. H. SISSON: from *Collected Poems*, published by the
Carcanet Press Ltd. JO SHAPCOTT: from *Her Book*, published by
Faber and Faber Ltd, 2000. PENELOPE SHUTTLE: from *Selected
Poems 1980–1996*, published by Oxford University Press, 1998;
reprinted by permission of Carcanet Press. CHARLES SIMIC: from
Looking for Trouble, published by Faber and Faber Ltd, 1997.
STEVIE SMITH: from *Collected Poems*, published by Penguin,
1975; reprinted by permission of the Estate of James MacGibbon.
BERNARD SPENCER: from *Collected Poems*, edited by Roger
Bowen, published by Oxford University Press, 1981, copyright ©
Mrs Anne Humphreys, 1981; reprinted by permission of Oxford
University Press. STEPHEN SPENDER: from *Collected Poems*,
published by Faber and Faber Ltd, 1935. MATTHEW SWEENEY:
from *The Bridal Suite*, published by Jonathan Cape, reprinted by
permission of the Random House Group Ltd. WISLAWA
SZYMBORSKA: from *The Burning Forest*, published by Bloodaxe
Books, 1989. GEORGE SZIRTES: from *The Budapest File*, published
by Bloodaxe Books, 2000. GRETE TARTLER: from *Orient Express*,
published by Oxford University Press, 1989. EDWARD THOMAS:
from *Collected Poems*, published by Oxford University Press,
1978; reprinted by kind permission of Myfanwy Thomas.
ANTHONY THWAITE: from *Poems 1953–1983*, published by
Secker & Warburg, 1984. R. S. THOMAS: from *Collected Poems*,
published by J. M. Dent, 1993. ROSEMARY TONKS: from *Head of
Broken Sentences*, published by Bodley Head, 1967, copyright ©
Rosemary Tonks, 1967. TOMAS TRANSTROMER: from *New
Selected Poems*, translated by Robin Fulton, published by
Bloodaxe Books, 1997. DEREK WALCOTT: from *Collected Poems*,
published by Faber and Faber Ltd, 1986. SYLVIA TOWNSEND
WARNER: from *Selected Poems*, published by Carcanet Press Ltd.
ANNA WICKHAM: from *The Writings of Anna Wickham*, published
by Virago; reprinted by kind permission of George W. Hepburn

and Margaret Hepburn. SUSAN WICKS: from *Singing Underwater*, published by Faber and Faber Ltd, 1992. RICHARD WILBUR: from *Poems 1943–1956*, published by Faber and Faber Ltd, 1957. C. K. WILLIAMS: from *New and Selected Poems*, published by Bloodaxe Books, 1995. HUGO WILLIAMS: from *Dock Leaves*, published by Faber and Faber Ltd, 1994. JUDITH WRIGHT: from *The Human Pattern*, published by Carcanet Press Ltd, 1992. W. B. YEATS: from *Collected Poems*, published by Macmillan; reprinted by permission of A. P. Watt Ltd. on behalf of Michael B. Yeats. BENJAMIN ZEPHANIAH: from *Schools Out: Poems Not For School*, published by A. K. Press, 1997.

Index of Poets